"G" is for Growing

Thirty Years of Research
on Children and *Sesame Street*

LEA's COMMUNICATION SERIES
Jennings Bryant/Dolf Zillmann, General Editors

Selected titles include:

Dennis/Wartella • American Communication Research:
The Remembered History

Greene • Message Production: Advances in Communication
Theory

Harris • A Cognitive Psychology of Mass Communication,
Second Edition

Jensen • Ethical Issues in the Communication Process

Salwen/Stacks • An Integrated Approach to Communication
Theory and Research

Van Evra • Television and Children, Second Edition

For a complete list of other titles in LEA's Communication
Series, please contact Lawrence Erlbaum Associates, Publishers.

"G" is for Growing

Thirty Years of Research
on Children and *Sesame Street*

Edited by

Shalom M. Fisch
Rosemarie T. Truglio
Children's Television Workshop

LAWRENCE ERLBAUM ASSOCIATES, PUBLISHERS
2001   Mahwah, New Jersey   London

Lawrence Erlbaum Associates, Inc., Publishers
10 Industrial Avenue
Mahwah, NJ 07430

Cover design by Kathryn Houghtaling Lacey

Front cover photo by Charles Baum.
Back cover photo by Richard Termine.
Photos © 2000, by Children's Television Workshop. *Sesame Street* Muppets
© 2000, by the Jim Henson Company. All rights reserved.

Library of Congress Cataloging-in-Publication Data

"G" is for growing:Thirty years of research on children and *Sesame Street*/
Shalom M. Fisch & Rosemarie T. Truglio (eds.).
    p.   cm.
    Includes bibliographical references and index.
    ISBN 0-8058-3394-3 — 0-8058-3395-1 (pbk.).
      1. Televison in preschool education—United States.
    2. Sesame Street (Televison program). I. Fisch, Shalom
    M. II. Truglio, Rosemarie T.

LC6579.S47 G58 2001
791.45'72—dc21
                                  00-027980

*This book is dedicated to Ed Palmer
and Gerry Lesser, who started it all,
and to the generations of children
who have made it possible*

Contents

PART II: IMPACT OF *SESAME STREET*

PART III: EXTENDING *SESAME STREET*:
OTHER SETTINGS, OTHER MEDIA

Foreword

Without research, there would be no *Sesame Street*.

For all its obviousness now, the notion of combining research with television production was positively heretical in 1967 when we first began making plans for the Children's Television Workshop (CTW) and what would eventually become in fact, the most researched television show in history.

Our goal was simple: to use television to help children learn, particularly children in low-income families. We knew that young children watched a great deal of television in the years before they went to school (and quite a bit after they started too). We also knew that they liked cartoons, game shows, and situation comedies, that they responded to slapstick humor, music with a beat, and above all, fast-paced, oft-repeated commercials.

We believed that if we created an educational show that capitalized on some of commercial television's most engaging traits—its high production value, its sophisticated writing, its quality film and animation—we could attract a sizeable audience. The wasteland of children's television was too vast and the yearning for something better too great: *Sesame Street* became an instant hit.

From the beginning, we—the planners of the project—conceived and carried out the series as an experiment in which educational advisors, researchers, and television producers acted as equal partners—equal partners united by a shared vision. Unique in its purpose and in its plan, *Sesame Street*'s creative, educational, and research components functioned as inseparable parts of the whole—indeed, it was an "arranged marriage" that has endured and delighted now for 30 years.

Don't think for a minute that we didn't meet with enormous resistance and worse, ridicule. "Researchers helping producers design a show? You must be kidding!" came the reaction of practically everyone in TV willing to give an honest opinion. Producers believed exclusively in intuition and experience as the means to a successful show—with luck, always luck, as the sine qua non of any big hit.

What we were proposing was something altogether different—that material, as it was produced, be tested on the target audience for both appeal and comprehension, that researchers report back to producers, and that producers modify or discard material based on almost continuous reports from the field. In other words, we were suggesting a kind of informed luck, or at the very least, that luck's role be lessened by something more akin to science.

Looking back, perhaps it wasn't the theory of marrying research to production that raised so many doubts as much as it was the thought of the reality—temperamental, creative people working with outside advisors and inside researchers to determine and then accomplish specific educational goals—social scientists telling TV producers what was "good" or "bad" based on the reactions of a small sample, long before the show went on the air where a mass audience would judge it.

To the amazement and near disbelief of outside (and some inside) observers, the arranged marriage went smoothly, if not always lovingly, and the union produced the most famous street in America in its first television season.

This book reflects all the aspects of research that went into and continues to inform *Sesame Street*—a book truly 30 years in the making—and I couldn't be more pleased.

It's been my privilege to have worked with a number of contributors to this collection and when asked why this marriage of research and production has worked so well, my reply has always been, "Personalities."

There can be no question that the personalities, patience, and know-how of two of the original architects of CTW research, Edward Palmer and Gerald Lesser, were critical to winning the hand of the production department. (Although in all fairness and with great warmth, the receptivity of our producers to research input, their very gameness in agreeing to try a new model for producing shows, remains one of the cornerstones of the house that CTW built.)

As our first Director of Research, Ed's responsibility was to design and execute the formative research for the series and work with the Educational Testing Service to do the same for the summative. This was trail-blazing of the highest order, and his collegial manner and collaborate nature were instrumental to our success. Gerry was CTW's first Chairman of the Board of Advisors. Without his energy, intellect, and humor, and quite frankly, without his skepticism toward my emotional conviction that television could educate, that only a good scientist could bring to an amateur's passion, *Sesame Street* never would have educated as it entertained, never would have lasted as long, or have quite the impact it still does today.

I'm delighted, as well, that this collection includes a section on the research we inspire in addition to the research we conduct. I understand that there are now over 1,000 studies on record about *Sesame Street*—its efficacy, its impact, and its contribution to our culture. Three of the most rigorous and most powerful are included here as evidence that the right kind of television—educational television—makes a positive, lasting, *measurable* contribution to learning.

With *Sesame Street* the product of a workshop and all that implies, it's only fitting that the final section of this collection examine the role of *Sesame Street* research in the hands of a new generation—a new generation carrying messages into new markets through new media.

When we began, none of us had any idea that *Sesame Street* and CTW would grow into the international institutions they are today, that *Sesame Street*, winner of more Emmys than any other single show, would also become the longest street in the world, benefiting more children in more countries than any programming in history. None of us had any idea that the characters we were creating—wonderful, zany, vulnerable Muppets to teach children letters, numbers, and concepts—would become so much a part of our culture, or that we were creating a family that every child watching would feel part of.

We only knew that we wanted to make a difference in the lives of children and families. And in the late 1960s in which we were first working, this seemed immanently possible, a time when many of us believed we had both the responsibility and the power to try to make the world a better place.

Research was our compass in this mission. I'm delighted to have the story told in one collection here, now and for generations to come.

—Joan Ganz Cooney
Children's Television Workshop

Introduction

Rosemarie T. Truglio
Shalom M. Fisch
Children's Television Workshop

Numerous research studies have provided empirical evidence of the power of *Sesame Street* as an educational tool. However, the true impact of *Sesame Street* may best be grasped through the dozens of personal anecdotes that reach the offices of the Children's Television Workshop (CTW), the producers of the series, on an almost daily basis. As an example, consider two personal anecdotes from the editors that occurred while working on this volume:

> One of us (SF) has a son who was 3 years old in 1998, when Senator John Glenn returned to space. On the day of the launch, the boy's mother explained that many years before, Glenn was the first American to travel in space and although he was much older now, he was finally going back. However, when she suggested that they watch the launch together, the boy replied, "I already saw it." Puzzled, she asked what he meant. He explained that he had already seen Oscar's pet worm, Slimey, travel to the moon on *Sesame Street*.

> The other of us (RT) recently brought her 17-year-old niece to visit the *Sesame Street* set and see how the program is made. This was a special event for the niece because she had been a daily viewer of *Sesame Street* as a preschooler. While there, the young woman had the opportunity to talk with the actor who plays Gordon, one of the human cast members on the show. She told him how important *Sesame Street* had been to her as a young child; she didn't have many neighborhood friends at that age, and had seen the people on *Sesame Street* as her friends. When she finished, the actor smiled. He said, "The people on *Sesame Street* are still your friends."

These two brief anecdotes are only small indications of the magnitude of *Sesame Street*'s impact on children over the past 30 years. Many people conceive of *Sesame Street* as a television series about letters and numbers, and indeed, exposure to *Sesame Street* has been found to result in significant effects in these areas. However, *Sesame Street* also reaches far beyond letters and numbers. Over the years, it has introduced literally millions of young children to a broad range of ideas, information, and experiences, on topics ranging from nutrition, to space, to the way crayons are made. At the same time, it has provided a fun, inviting context in which to nurture preschool children's social development in areas such as cooperation and diversity. For many children, the first place they see a ballet may be on *Sesame Street*. Moreover, it may be the only place they see a ballet performed by a girl in a wheelchair.

November 1999 marked the 30th anniversary of the broadcast premiere of *Sesame Street* on American television. When the creators of *Sesame Street* first embarked on producing the series, no one expected that it would last for more than 1 or 2 years. Yet, what began as an attempt to help inner-city preschool children become ready for school has grown into a cultural icon. *Sesame Street* has won more Emmy awards than any other series in the history of television (a total of 76 to date). It has been viewed in more than 140 countries around the world. Indeed, within the United States, a 1996 survey suggested that 95% of American preschoolers have watched *Sesame Street* at some point by the time they are 3 years old (Tessier, 1996).

Sesame Street has also spawned a broad variety of educational materials in other media, including 11 award-winning CD-ROMs and a magazine with a circulation of more than 1,000,000 copies per month. The *Sesame Street* Preschool Education Program, an ongoing outreach program that applies the power of *Sesame Street* in child care settings, has trained nearly 55,000 child care providers. For 30 years, *Sesame Street* has entertained and enlightened children across the United States and around the world.

It is difficult to recognize today what a revolutionary departure *Sesame Street* represented from the existing state of children's television in the late 1960s. Although some television series had conveyed positive messages to children, none had attempted to address specific educational curricula or goals with preschool children. Moreover, *Sesame Street* was the first series to employ empirical research as an integral part of its production; formative research was—and continues to be—used on an ongoing basis to inform production decisions, whereas summative research has been used to assess *Sesame Street*'s educational impact on its target audience. This unique, ongoing integration of curriculum development, formative research, and summative research into the process of production has come to be known as the *CTW Model* (e.g., Mielke, 1990), and after the pioneering efforts of *Sesame Street*, it has become essential to the success of other, subsequent educational television series, such as *The Electric Company, 3-2-1 Contact*, and (outside CTW) *Blue's Clues*. Under the CTW Model, producers, researchers, and educational content specialists collaborate closely throughout the life of a project, from its initial inception through the completion of the final product (Fig. I.1). Each group brings its unique perspective to the table to ensure that the results will be entertaining, educationally sound, and both appealing and comprehensible to the target audience.

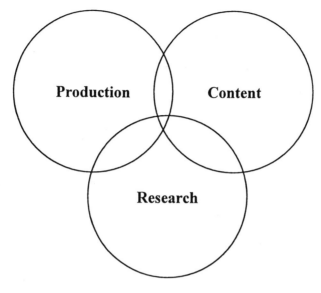

FIG. I.1. The CTW Model.

Today, *Sesame Street* is the most heavily researched series in the history of television. More than 1,000 studies have examined *Sesame Street* and its power in areas such as literacy, number skills, and promoting prosocial behavior, as well as formal features pertaining to issues such as children's attention. This body of literature has not only contributed to our understanding of children's interaction with *Sesame Street* itself, but also constitutes a significant portion of the literature on the educational impact of television in general. It is safe to say that, if not for *Sesame Street*, the research literature on children and television would be very different than it is today, as would the shape of educational television itself.

And yet, despite the significance of this extensive body of research on *Sesame Street*, it often has been difficult for researchers interested in children and television to make full use of the data. Although the origins of *Sesame Street* have been chronicled several times, most notably by Gerald Lesser (1974), and a few review papers on the educational impact of *Sesame Street* have seen print (e.g., Fisch, Truglio, & Cole, 1999), no single source has ever drawn together the entire body of research on *Sesame Street* across media. Empirical and theoretical papers have been scattered across a spate of books, scholarly journals, theses, and dissertations, making it difficult for individual researchers to assemble a comprehensive view of children's interaction with *Sesame Street*. Indeed, much of the research—particularly formative research conducted within CTW—has remained unpublished and, thus, largely inaccessible to researchers outside the Workshop.

To correct this state of affairs and contribute to the efforts of our colleagues in the research, education, and media production communities, this volume collects and synthesizes, for the first time, key aspects of research on *Sesame Street* during the past 30 years. It describes the process by which educational content and research are integrated into production, reviews major studies on the impact of *Sesame Street* on children, and examines the extension of *Sesame Street* into both other cultures (via international coproductions such as the Mexican *Plaza Sesamo*, the Russian *Ulitsa Sesam*, or the joint Israeli-Palestinian *Rechov Sumsum/Sha'ara Simsim*) and other media (e.g., hands-on child-care materials, print, interactive material for CD-ROMs and online). In the course of this discussion, the volume also draws on data and experiences regarding *Sesame Street* to explore broader topics such as methodological issues in conducting media-based research with young children, the longitudinal impact of preschoolers' viewing of educational versus noneducational television (with effects extending into the early grades and even high school), and cross-cultural differences in the treatment of educational content, among many others.

These discussions simultaneously serve to broaden our understanding of children's interactions with educational media and to illustrate the spirit of constant experimentation that has been integral to *Sesame Street*'s continued success as an educational tool. Since the late 1960s, *Sesame Street* has been built on a firm confidence in young children's potential to succeed, ongoing research into the most effective ways to meet their changing needs, and a constant striving to bring children the best that educational media have to offer. In this way, *Sesame Street* attempts to encourage children of all backgrounds to reach for a bigger, richer, and better world. The present volume lends insight into the knowledge and process that underlies these efforts, as well as data that gauge the degree of their success. We hope that it will serve, not only as a chronicle of the work that has been done to date, but as a springboard to future study and further efforts that follow *Sesame Street* in using media to help children achieve their highest potential.

OVERVIEW OF CONTENTS

The present volume is divided into three broad parts. Part I focuses on curriculum development, formative research, and the ways in which these have been integrated into production. The first Director of Research for *Sesame Street*, Edward Palmer, describes the challenges inherent in integrating educational content and formative research into television production in the late 1960s and early 1970s (at a time when neither had been attempted on this scale before). Gerald Lesser and Joel Schneider then discuss the evolution of the *Sesame Street* curriculum, including its initial conceptualization and the process by which it has grown to encompass areas ranging from science to race relations. Next, Shalom Fisch and Lewis Bernstein explore a variety of broad methodological and process issues in conducting formative research for educational television (e.g., the validity and usefulness of competing measures of appeal, the strengths of behavioral vs. verbal data, considerations in working with producers to implement formative research effectively), with insights drawn from experiences in the production of *Sesame Street*. The section closes with a paper by Rosemarie Truglio, Valeria Lovelace, Ivelisse Seguí, and Susan Scheiner, which presents specific case studies of formative research on *Sesame Street* that span a variety of subject areas and illustrate the diverse nature of formative research: to assess children's needs and prior knowledge, to measure appeal, to identify ways in which to maximize viewers' comprehension, and so on.

Part II of the book examines the educational impact of *Sesame Street*. The section begins with a review of research on the impact of *Sesame Street* on children's school readiness and social behavior, written by Keith Mielke. This review is followed by several chapters, each focusing on an individual assessment of the impact of *Sesame Street* in the 1990s. The first, by John Wright, Aletha Huston, Ronda Scantlin, and Jennifer Kotler, describes a 3-year longitudinal study that examined the educational benefits of *Sesame Street*, both immediately and when children subsequently entered first and second grade. The second, by Nicholas Zill, deals with a national survey of 10,000 children that used data collected for the U.S. Department of Education's 1993 National Household Education Survey to examine correlations between *Sesame Street* viewership and emerging literacy in the preschool years and early elementary grades. The third, by Aletha Huston, Daniel Anderson, John Wright, Deborah Linebarger, and Kelly Schmitt, provides the longest-ranging evidence for the impact of *Sesame Street*; in this study, *Sesame Street* viewers and nonviewers were contacted approximately 10 years later, to see whether measurable differences between the two groups could be found in school performance and attitudes toward academic pursuits in the high school years.

The third section turns to the extension of *Sesame Street* into other cultures and other media. Charlotte Cole, Beth Richman, and Susan McCann Brown discuss the development of international coproductions of *Sesame Street* (including the processes by which formats, characters, and even curricula are tailored to the needs and lifestyles of particular countries) and data on their impact. William Yotive and Shalom Fisch move beyond television in a chapter on the creation and use of hands-on, *Sesame Street*-based outreach materials for use in child-care settings; included in the chapter is a consideration of the ways in which such materials are designed to be responsive to the needs of different types of settings (e.g., day care centers vs. home-based family child care) and the diverse populations of children they serve. Renée Cherow-O'Leary describes the adaptation of *Sesame Street* to print form via *Sesame Street* books and the monthly *Sesame Street Magazine*, with data on children's use of the magazine and its potential educational benefits, plus the subsequent creation of an accompanying magazine for parents. Glenda Revelle, Lisa Medoff, and Erik Strommen then explore the role of research in the production of interactive *Sesame Street* software and products, and the ways in which CTW's approach has changed with the meteoric evolution of the medium—from software for 64K PCs in the early 1980s through CD-ROMs in the 1990s and, most recently, activities available for hand-held video games or through the World Wide Web.

Finally, the concluding chapter, by Shalom Fisch and Rosemarie Truglio, synthesizes the aforementioned chapters in a discussion of characteristics of *Sesame Street* that contribute to its educational impact.

ACKNOWLEDGMENTS

A book of this scope cannot come into being without a tremendous amount of help. First and foremost, we are grateful to our friends, coworkers, and families for their undying support and patience throughout the long days, nights, and weekends spent writing and editing.

We are also greatly indebted to all of the authors who contributed their time and expertise to this volume. Whatever value exists within these pages comes from them.

In addition, we owe a tremendous debt of gratitude to series editor Jennings Bryant, and Lawrence Erlbaum Associates editor Linda Bathgate. It was Jennings who first suggested the idea of this book and who directed our proposal to the appropriate parties at LEA. To a pair of novice editors such as ourselves, Jennings and Linda have been unflagging sources of advice and wisdom on topics ranging from style to page length to the best way to approach an index (i.e., hire someone else to compile it).

Within the walls of CTW, we thank Vice President for Education and Research Joel Schneider and Executive Vice President for Marketing, Communications, and Research Sherrie Rollins Westin for the ongoing support that helped to make this book a reality. Many of the members of the Education and Research staff (and many of the interns) cheerfully tracked down vital information and source material. In addition, several of our colleagues outside the Education and Research Department provided information, reviewed drafts of chapters, and made sure that our feet stayed outside of our mouths. In particular, thanks are due to Gail David, who reviewed the text of the entire volume and provided contributions that enhanced its quality greatly. Perhaps most importantly, Maria Betances and Evangelean Pope did a masterful job of coordinating all of the time-consuming and often difficult logistical details on which a work such as this relies.

Finally, we must credit the fine work of all of our colleagues who have contributed to the production of *Sesame Street* and all of its varied ancillary products and activities over the past 30 years. This group encompasses a veritable army of producers (in many media), editors, curriculum specialists, researchers, business people, and many others. Without their efforts, there would be nothing to write about.

REFERENCES

Fisch, S. M., Truglio, R. T., & Cole, C. F. (1999). The impact of *Sesame Street* on preschool children: A review and synthesis of 30 years' research. *Media Psychology, 1,* 165–190.

Lesser, G. S. (1974). *Children and television: Lessons from* Sesame Street. New York: Vintage Books/Random House.

Mielke, K. W. (1990). Research and development at the Children's Television Workshop. *Educational Technology Research and Development, 38*(4), 7–16.

Tessier, B. (1996). Sesame Street *brand survey results, 1995–1996* (unpublished research report). New York: Children's Television Workshop.

I Integrating Research and Educational Content Into Production

1 The Beginnings of *Sesame Street* Research*

Edward L. Palmer
World Media Partners
with
Shalom M. Fisch
Children's Television Workshop

The Children's Television Workshop (CTW) was established in March 1968, with Joan Ganz Cooney as Director. Cooney had worked under the umbrella of the Carnegie Corporation and in collaboration with its vice president, Lloyd Morrisett, to craft the original *Sesame Street* proposal, generate essential grant support, plan, and launch CTW. With major grant funding in hand, and a nascent organization that existed mainly on paper, Cooney launched immediately into conducting five *Sesame Street* curriculum planning seminars (under the able leadership of Harvard University professor Gerald S. Lesser) and recruiting the key members of the CTW professional staff. The proposed television series, according to the organizational plan, was to be created through a collaboration among two independently headed, in-house departments—one consisting of experts in television production, and the other of experts in empirical research, child development, and learning—and a cadre of outside curriculum advisors. The first author of this chapter joined the

---

*Editors' note: Edward Palmer, the first Director of Research for *Sesame Street*, passed away in August 1999. Palmer had intended to contribute a chapter to this volume, focusing on the origins of *Sesame Street* research and the challenges inherent in integrating educational content and empirical research into television production at a time when such efforts had never before been attempted. Unfortunately, poor health prevented him from completing his chapter as planned. Because we wanted this volume to represent Palmer's pioneering contribution to both *Sesame Street* and the larger field of television research as a whole, Shalom Fisch (with Palmer's approval and review) used Palmer's outline, several of his past publications (Gibbon, Palmer, & Fowles, 1975; Palmer, 1972, 1988; Palmer, Chen, & Lesser, 1976), and a set of unpublished interviews (Palmer, 1976, 1991, 1999) to complete the remainder of the chapter. All of the ideas presented in this chapter have come from Edward Palmer, and use of first person refers to him. Any inadvertent misstatements or errors are our own.

CTW staff, after some prior participation in curriculum planning, in July 1968 as the Workshop's first Director of Research (and subsequently as a corporate officer and Vice President for Research), and in this capacity became, as Joan Cooney in later years often introduced him, "a founder of CTW and founder of its research function."

Backed by an extraordinarily generous $8 million in grant funds for a 2-year project, CTW's sole initial mandate was to create, broadcast, promote, and evaluate an experimental educational television series of 130 hour-long programs that would seek to advance the school readiness of 3- to 5-year-old children, with special emphasis on the needs of youngsters from low-income and minority backgrounds.

All who contributed in key roles to the creation of *Sesame Street* shared an appreciation for its timeliness, speaking of it often and unabashedly as "the right idea at the right time." Clearly, the series' educational focus and rationale were directly rooted in the broad social-political forces and specific educational priorities of the era. This timeliness, combined with *Sesame Street's* lavish scale of initial funding support and high national visibility, generated a heady but sobering sense among the staff that we were privileged participants in an activity of some moment. First, we knew that we held in our hands a once-in-a-lifetime opportunity to contribute significantly to an urgent and otherwise unmet, national educational need—that, in specific and palpably human terms, we might measurably enhance the life chances of millions of educationally deprived youngsters. Second, we knew that a nationally broadcast television series that featured popular television forms would be highly visible. Third, we knew that we had the luxury of working under close-to-ideal conditions: nearly 18 months for planning, experimental production, and child testing of program approaches before putting the television series on the air; the resources to enlist not only the most expensive of television's popular entertainment forms, but also the services of a major promotional and public relations firm; and the involvement of a nationally prominent, third-party evaluator to assess the series' educational effectiveness. Our extent of success or failure, we knew, would figure prominently in shaping educational television policies and practices for many years to come.

BACKGROUND OF HISTORICAL EVENTS
AND EDUCATIONAL POLICIES

The historical events and educational policies of the late 1960s that shaped *Sesame Street's* educational goals and audience priorities also directly framed the activities and policy positions of the in-house research team. One major historical force of the time was the Civil Rights movement; among its many accomplishments, the movement focused unprecedented national attention on the crucial role education would have to play if children from low-income circumstances, including disproportionately large numbers of minority-group members, were to escape the cycle of poverty. Head Start and *Sesame Street* were two outgrowths of broad education policies that recognized that special efforts to stimulate the educational progress of children from low-income backgrounds should include an emphasis on school-readiness skills starting at a very early (preschool) age. A research study of the era, published by Benjamin Bloom (1964) at the University of Chicago and quoted in the original *Sesame Street* proposal, had concluded that more than one half of a child's lifetime intellectual capacity is formed by 5 years of age. A spate of studies, such as those published by Carl Bereiter (Bereiter & Engelman, 1966) and Martin Deutch (1965), found that low-income, minority children, on arriving at first grade, not only tested substantially lower on average that their white, middle-class counterparts in school-related skills, but also, over the course of their early school years, logged a cumulative education deficit. Head Start therefore set out to provide not only early but also "compensatory" education (i.e., education geared preferentially to children of poverty).

Sesame Street operated outside this compensatory model, because of its ubiquity as a television program. Already, at the time of the series' premiere in 1968, 97% of all U.S. households possessed a television set (A. C. Nielsen Company, 1967), thus making the series equally accessible to children of all socio-economic and ethnic backgrounds. Some confusion occurred due to a statement in the initial *Sesame Street* proposal that suggested that the television series might help to narrow the academic achievement gap between the middle-class children and those from low-income, minority backgrounds—a goal consistent with a compensatory education model, but that I considered unrealistic for the reason mentioned previously. Instead, CTW adopted an alternative policy that eliminated this unrealistic goal from all subsequent *Sesame Street* funding proposals, starting with the second-season funding proposal written in early 1970, and from CTW publicity releases. I also encouraged the company that conducted the third-party evaluations of *Sesame Street* during its first two broadcast seasons, the Educational Testing Service (ETS), to forego conducting analysis that focused on the narrowing of the achievement gap. ETS elected not to comply, which was its prerogative as independent evaluator. One team of academic researchers published a book-length report much later arguing that *Sesame Street* should be held accountable to bring about compensatory, "narrow the gap" results (Cook et al., 1975). CTW's policy position on the subject, forged early in the 1970s, was expressed many times in CTW policy pronouncements to the effect that there is a basic level of literacy whose achievement opens up greatly expanded opportunities for employment and many other privileges. While *Sesame Street* could not determine which group of children would cross that line first, it could—and did—aim to ensure that the maximum number possible would do so.

A second historical factor, closely associated with the first, was President Lyndon Johnson's push to create the Great Society. His policies, along with his widely noted powers of persuasion over Congress, gave rise to high levels of government leadership and funding involvement in education.

Still a third historical phenomenon was the rapid growth of public broadcasting. The Ford Foundation alone channeled $300 million into public broadcasting over the 20-year period that ended in 1971. One propitious result of this investment, viewed from the CTW perspective, was the creation of the first nationwide public television network in 1969, just in time for *Sesame Street*'s premiere broadcast. This network harnessed the combined signal capacity of the (then) 300 independent public television stations, and so afforded public television a signal coverage area that reached an estimated 65% to 70% of all U.S. television households. This coverage would soon grow to exceed 95%. To CTW, at the time of *Sesame Street*'s inauguration in 1969, the ability to reach two thirds of the country's 12 million 3- to 5-year-olds meant that a given episode of the series potentially could be seen by as many as 8 million members of the intended viewing-learning audience. To funders of public television programs, nationwide networking afforded them desired access to large national audiences, and, in the process, allowed them to achieve highly favorable cost-effectiveness by driving down the cost per viewer reached.

In 1969, the service we now call public television included 130 local stations with a combined signal coverage that reached about two thirds of all U.S. households, mostly on hard-to-tune UHF channels. One might have thought that the "big eight"—the largest and strongest of public television's urban production centers—somehow would have divided the turf, with one or two specializing in the news, another one or two specializing in culture and the arts, and somewhere along the line, one taking the lead in the field of children's programming, but this is not the way the system shook out. No large station chose to be the preeminent supplier of quality children's programs to the entire system.

BACKGROUND OF CHILDREN'S
AND EDUCATIONAL TELEVISION

Prior to *Sesame Street* and public television networking, many public television stations carried their own locally produced children's programs. More often than not, these programs represented the vision and agenda, as well as the script and studio direction, of a single individual. True to the insight of then-popular media guru, Marshall McLuhan, the children's television pioneers of the 1950s and 1960s simply imitated prior media forms. Many, for example, created "storybook television," filled with shots of book covers and static, illustrated pages. Others created a type of "proscenium television," in which child viewers were treated to a camera's-eye view of a classroom, railroad station, or other fantasy location filled with children. The hosts of these programs were often insufferably condescending. In a fictitious but fairly typical example, a local host might try to enhance the illusion of audience participation by looking directly into camera and pretending to be able to see and interact with the viewing children: "Oh, my, aren't we all having just so much fun here today! Are you having fun, too? Miss Patty is so happy to see that all of you out there in television land are having fun today!" *Sesame Street* was a sharp contrast, with its educational mandate and accountability, its dedication to exploring what might be accomplished in education through the unique language of television, its hip, popular style, and its frequent "winks" to the adult viewers. *Sesame Street* was not the first children's television series in the United States to combine education and entertainment. The *Captain Kangaroo* series, for example, which had been a staple of American children's television since 1955, touched on many educational themes, and couched these in popular entertainment forms. What distinguished *Sesame Street* (and, to a lesser degree, the contemporaneous *Mister Rogers' Neighborhood*) was the combination of narrowly focused and expertly planned educational curriculum, its attempt to forge the most effective possible methods of televised teaching, and its accountability to bring about rigorously measured educational results. *Captain Kangaroo*, for all its merits, offered "education" only in the broadest sense of the term: lessons invented by scriptwriters who possessed no training in education or child development, made no use of expert consultants or advisors, and answered to no education stakeholders.

THE ORIGINS AND SCOPE
OF *SESAME STREET* RESEARCH

The story of *Sesame Street* research must begin with an understanding of the conditions at the time. Without the proper conditions, CTW could not have been established as the world's first, largest, and most enduring center for children's out-of-school educational programs, nor could its work have been grounded so firmly in curriculum, formative research, and accountability for bringing about measured learning results. In the 1980s, a comparative study of children's television organizations in the United States and selected industrial countries identified factors in their respective histories and incentive structures that caused them to serve children either better or less well. The study found that Britain and Japan both supported their public broadcasting organizations by levying television and radio taxes adequate to support comprehensive program offerings (i.e., program offerings that strived to provide equitable amount of schedule time and level of program quality to every major audience category, including children). By contrast, funding for U.S. public television was woefully inadequate to support a similarly comprehensive program offering (Palmer, 1988).

The existence of great program gaps in the U.S. public television schedule in turn opened the way for enterprising, independent organizations to step in and establish themselves as program suppliers. It was this circumstance that allowed CTW to become a major supplier of children's out-of-school educational television programs. The Workshop's educational programming purview soon expanded to include a new kind of hybrid, home-and-school television series (as exemplified by *The Electric Company*, a reading series for children of early elementary school age; *3-2-1 Contact*, a science series for 8- to 12-year-olds; *Square One Television*, a series about mathematics for 8- to 12-year-olds; and *Ghostwriter*, a writing and reading series

also geared to elementary school-age children), along with several adult educational series. The emphasis on curriculum, formative research and outcome evaluation in connection with its programs is the direct result of
CTW's need to seek funding for these programs on an ad hoc basis, series by
series and year by year. Clearly, the grant-giving organizations that funded
Sesame Street and these additional educational television series would not
have invested as they did to support the creation of programs that were only
broadly educational. What they were attracted to, instead, was the opportunity to invest in a succession of large-scale educational television productions, each addressed to a national education need or deficiency that was
major, clearly recognized, and otherwise unmet. In this manner, *Sesame
Street* responded to the need for early childhood education, *The Electric Company* to a poor national "report card" on reading, and *3-2-1 Contact* to studies
showing that too few children were preparing in high school to pursue further study and, eventually, careers in science and technology. CTW further
enticed prospective program funders by outlining for each new educational
series a model curriculum planning and production approach, complete
with provisions for summative evaluation.

    Sesame Street's three chief initial architects—Cooney, Morrisett, and
Lesser—recognized that its extensive use of innovative television techniques
meant that it would be highly experimental in nature. Morrisett and Lesser
had known each other as students at Yale University, where both received de-
grees in psychology. They shared a commitment to the use of empirical methods of research and evaluation in education. They saw in such methods not
only the means to measure the series' educational effectiveness, but also the
means by which to submit innovative pilot production approaches to field
testing, both to reduce the risks and to enhance the chances of bringing about
significant educational gains. Accordingly, the initial *Sesame Street* funding
proposal included, not only a substantial emphasis on the evaluation of educational outcomes, but also a provision to establish an in-house research department that would work hand-in-hand with the television producers in the
actual design and development of the television series. The logic behind the
creation of this in-house research function was also dictated in part by
Cooney's insistence on recruiting the series' creative scriptwriters and direc-
tors, not from education backgrounds, but from among the ranks of successful commercial television producers. For these noneducators to create a
television series that merged education and entertainment, they would need
to team up with in-house educators.

    As a perspective on the scope and intensity of this collaboration, consider
that fact that *Sesame Street* contains about 40 program segments (skits) in
each of its 130 hour-long episodes. Allowing for segment repetition, the
in-house research group thus would need to contribute to the creation of approximately 2,400 distinct program segments, each addressed to a preas-
signed educational goal. To accomplish this marathon task, the researchers
met frequently with members of the production team on preliminary scripts
and animation planning, reviewed and commented on each draft script's edu-

cational approach, and screened each script at the draft stage for mistakes such as stereotypic portrayals and inappropriate use of language.

CTW's commitment to incorporating a strong in-house research function was bolstered by a letter that Cooney and Morrisett received around the time of CTW's launching from Sam Messick and Scarvia Anderson of ETS. They couched their letter in terms of the methodological distinction that was suggested just 1 year previously by Michael Scriven of Berkeley (1967). Specifically, Scriven drew a distinction between *formative research* (which uses empirical data to guide improvements in educational materials and procedures while they are in development) and *summative* evaluation (which is done to measure the educational effectiveness of completed educational materials and procedures). Messick and Anderson's key recommendation—that CTW should conduct a balance of formative research and summative evaluation, if possible—was qualified by a rather startling suggestion, considering that it came from a major national player in the business of summative evaluation: They felt that if, for any reason, CTW were forced to choose between formative and summative research, it should opt for the formative. The strong ETS endorsement of formative research greatly bolstered Cooney's commitment to establishing a strong in-house research function at CTW.

Over time, the research function for *Sesame Street* took on several important roles. Three of these pertained directly to the production of the television series: working with producers to find effective ways to integrate educational curriculum into *Sesame Street*, conducting formative research to inform production, and contracting with independent outside researchers to evaluate the impact of the series through summative research. Other facets centered on contributions to CTW's communication, as an organization, with the outside world through interactions with the academic research community, the public, and the governmental agencies and private foundations that provided financial support for *Sesame Street*. Each of these roles will be considered in turn.

INTEGRATING CURRICULUM INTO TELEVISION PRODUCTION

Lesser and Schneider (chap. 2, this volume; cf. Lesser, 1974) discuss the series of curriculum seminars and the process that shaped the initial curriculum for *Sesame Street*. Even after the curriculum was written, however, there remained the tremendous challenge of finding concrete ways to actualize that curriculum in an engaging and entertaining television series.

Much of this challenge stemmed from the fact that, prior to *Sesame Street*, no other television series had attempted to address a curriculum that was as detailed or stated in terms of measurable outcomes. Advisors at the seminars had often spoken in broad terms, but the curriculum document itself eliminated any ambiguity by expressing each goal using terms such as "The child will...."

This approach was received well by the producers, but not everyone understood its intent immediately. One member of the CTW staff became terribly agitated when he first saw the curriculum statement. His concern was that if this document, with all its educational jargon, set the tone for the series, *Sesame Street* would be terribly dull instead of light and lively. However, head writer Jon Stone spoke for all of the key producers in his response to the concern; he said, first, that the curriculum document did not set the tone for the entertainment content of the program, and second, that in sitting down to write a script, he would far rather start with a curriculum goal at the top of the page than with a totally empty page. What Stone understood was that stating a curriculum goal did not limit creativity, because there were still an infinite number of ways in which to express it on the screen.

Establishing Priorities Among Goals.   Because of the large number of goals in the *Sesame Street* curriculum, it was clear that not all of them could be addressed equally within the first season of the series. Attempting to do so would have resulted in none of the goals receiving sufficient treatment to have a significant impact on the target audience. Thus, with a draft of the curriculum completed, one of the next steps was to identify a subset of the goals to receive the greatest emphasis in the first season of *Sesame Street* and to serve as the focus for the summative evaluation of the series.[1]

Producers and researchers reviewed the curriculum together, placing asterisks next to the goals to be emphasized (in a process that executive producer David Connell termed, "You Bet Your Asterisk"). Apart from explicitly educational criteria, these decisions were also based on considerations of what might be suitable for television presentation. Other considerations included parental expectations for an educational program and the contribution that mastery of the curriculum might make to the self-image of the child. The expectation was that if most parents felt that the goals were important for their children (e.g., letter naming and counting), they would be more likely to reinforce their children's viewing and the lessons learned.

The overarching principle for narrowing down the goals to the few for which we would be accountable was this: If *Sesame Street* promised 100 things and accomplished 25 successfully, it would look terrible. If it promised 10 and accomplished 25, *Sesame Street* would look wonderful.

The Writer's Notebook.   As the producers and writers began to develop scripts, animations, and films addressed to particular behaviorally stated goals, it became apparent that there was a need for an annotated document that would assist writers and producers in translating the goals into material for television. After having been given several successive assignments in the same goal area, they began to express the need for extended and enriched definitions that would provide creative stimulation. Gradually,

---

[1]Indeed, this process has carried through to the present, with a subset of the goals selected as a specific "curriculum focus" in each subsequent season (Lesser & Schneider, chap. 2, this volume).

through trial and error, a format for a Writer's Notebook was developed that the producers and writers themselves found useful.

Suggestions for the Notebook were developed according to a number of criteria: (a) to emphasize the psychological processes involved in a particular form of behavior, (b) to exploit and extend a child's own experiential referents for such behavior, (c) to prompt the creation of various similar approaches by the producers and writers themselves by presenting them with highly divergent examples, and (d) to provide suggestions free of any reference to particular characters or contexts from the television program so that the ways in which the suggestions could be implemented would be left as open and flexible as possible. For example, within the area of Symbolic Representation, the word-matching objective was stated as follows: "Given a printed word, the child can select an identical printed word from a set of printed words." To implement this objective, the Notebook encouraged producers: to use words with different numbers of letters; to vary the location within the word of the letter or letters that fail to "match;" and to present various matching strategies, such as comparing two given words letter by letter, moving initially separated words into superimposition, or spelling out each of the two given words and comparing to see if one has made the same sound both times.

Involving advisors and consultants in the creation of these suggestions provided one more opportunity for making use of expert input. In addition, the Notebook provided a place and a format for collecting the ideas of the in-house research staff and a channel for helping to ensure that these ideas would be seen and used.

Merging Education and Entertainment.   The clever use of Muppets and animation helped to bring the educational curriculum to life, but coordinating the two required careful thought. For example, consider one early segment that was intended to address the issues of imagination and children's fear of the dark. In this segment, Bert is sleeping but Ernie can't sleep because he imagines that there might be monsters outside. As Ernie's imagination gets the best of him, the viewers sees monsters who are transparent (to signal the fact that they are imaginary) first overrunning Sesame Street and then invading Bert and Ernie's bedroom as Ernie desperately sings, "Go away, bad things, go away!" Ernie makes so much noise that he wakes Bert, at which point Bert suggests that he try imagining good things instead of scary things. Bert then sings a beautiful, slow-paced song called "Here in the Middle of Imagination" and a colorful rain of transparent balloons falls on Sesame Street.

Although this segment contained a wonderful message and high production values, researchers were concerned that it might frighten viewers more than it reassured them. In fact, data from an extensive program of formative research confirmed this concern. Attention data showed that children were highly attentive during the frightening part of the segment, but that their attention waned during the slow ballad that Bert sang in bed. As a result, the message of the segment was not well comprehended.

This sort of fine-grained analysis of children's attention made the *Sesame Street* team aware that while watching television, children make a continual series of judgments as to whether to attend to the screen. These judgments are made on a moment-to-moment basis and are highly responsive to the qualities of the program at the moment. In this instance, the dramatic tension, visual action, and loudness of the first part of the segment drew viewers' attention to the screen. However, their attention was lost by a slow, quiet song that was not accompanied by visual action. Data on this segment, and others like it, convinced both producers and researchers of the importance of considering, not only the attractiveness of the material and not only what children could comprehend, but also the *interaction* between attraction and comprehension. When humor, dramatic tension, or other attractive features were made to coincide with the heart of the educational message, this interaction could be used to enhance the effectiveness of the educational content. Yet, when the two did not coincide, children would recall the attractive material and not the educational message.[2]

Emphasis, Repetition, and Sequencing.   Whereas the above example speaks to the role of curriculum in the creation of individual segments, equally important issues pertained to the combination of segments and the more global structuring of the series as a whole.

One set of considerations centered on the distribution of educational content across the first 26-week season of *Sesame Street*. For example, in approaching the alphabet, decisions had to be made regarding the number of episodes that would feature each letter. On discussion, rather than simply attempting to divide the total number of episodes evenly across the letters of the alphabet, the decision was made to regard the alphabet as a set of 36 letters: 21 consonants, five vowels, and the same five vowels repeated twice more. Thus, vowels received triple the exposure given to consonants, allowing for treatment of (for example) both "short" and "long" vowel sounds. Three letters were introduced each week, so that the entire set could be represented over a 12-week period. This 12-week schedule was repeated once over the course of the first season, leaving 2 weeks open for experimentation with a different schedule of presentation or different ways of presenting the letters.

A second set of considerations centered on the use of repetition and reinforcement, which were easily accommodated by the segmented format of *Sesame Street*. As an instructional strategy, repetition on *Sesame Street* involved, not only exact repetition of intact program segments, but also repetition of program segments with variation. Varying the content while keeping the format constant promoted familiarity with format conventions. One of

---

[2]As a postscript to this anecdote: This particular Bert and Ernie segment was "retired" (i.e., no longer aired) on the basis of these research data. Subsequently, however, a revised version of the segment, which eliminated the difficulties of the original, was produced. The revised version does not show the imaginary monsters; instead, it begins with Ernie merely saying that he had a bad dream, which leads immediately into Bert's explanation and song about imagining good things. The revised version of the segment continues to appear in *Sesame Street* to this day.

the main instructional advantages was that it had the potential to entice the viewing child to attend to what was new in each succeeding application of the format by making it "stand out" against the familiar background more than if the entire presentation were novel. As a result, there was the potential for learning and concept formation to be enhanced. Indeed, summative research on *Sesame Street* subsequently showed that the greatest learning gains were associated with goal areas that had received the greatest emphasis in the series (see Mielke, chap. 5, this volume). In addition, the viewers appeared often to derive special pleasure from their familiarity with a repeatedly used format, from a sense of mastery of its special conventions, from the gamelike challenge of making guesses from format cues and then confirming their accuracy, and from a program's frequent use of comic twists, especially when these were parodies of familiar formats.

Finally, the problem of instructional sequence concerned the designers of *Sesame Street* from the very outset. Traditional instructional practice required that the teaching of any complex skill be carefully sequenced from the elementary to the elaborate. For *Sesame Street*, this posed serious problems because factors associated with the open broadcast circumstances made conventional sequencing patterns inappropriate. No matter how effective the information campaign might have been prior to going on the air, the audience was bound to start relatively small and grow during the course of the series. Furthermore, it was certain that no matter how entertaining the show proved to be, a sizable percentage of the audience would view irregularly. Then, too, members of this heterogeneous young audience would differ widely in age, background, prior experience, and learning style.

For all of these reasons, the decision was made that no single episode could require that the viewer have seen any other, and every program segment had to be designed with a wide range of individual learning needs in mind. Each episode would therefore include instruction in each major goal area. The schedule would include as much review as possible for the sake of the irregular viewer.[3]

Studio Production. Initially, there was a great deal of discussion about whether researchers should be present in the studio during production. Some producers felt that the intense demands of studio production made it impractical; studio production presents hundreds of details to which producers must attend simultaneously, and they felt that it would prove burdensome to have to haggle with researchers as well.

In the end, however, it was decided that there should be a research presence in the studio, and the reality of having researchers right in the studio turned out not to be as forbidding as the prospect. The fact of the matter is

---

[3]Ironically, the conviction that complex skills should be decomposed and set in a given sequence is no longer taken for granted in current educational theory. The decision not to be wedded to a strict sequence in *Sesame Street*, although made for practical reasons, may have been best in the long term, although it ran counter to the prevailing wisdom at the time.

that in producing a television show, there are many brief periods of 5 or 10 minutes when not much is happening, and these presented opportunities for discussing issues if and when they arose. Still, the researchers had to find a sufficient degree of sensitivity to the considerable pressures under which the producers were working. If the producers said, "I can't listen right now," that was it.

As the process of studio production unfolded, it became clear that there was actually great value in the researchers' presence. Many of the shots were taken more than once, and just as researchers could make a difference reviewing a draft of a script or storyboard, they could also make a difference right there in the studio.

Informing Production Through Formative Research

As novel as the use of a substantive educational curriculum was, *Sesame Street's* use of formative research was equally revolutionary. To be successful, CTW had to capture its intended audience with an educational television show whose highly attractive competition was only a flick of the dial away. Unlike the classroom teacher, *Sesame Street* had to earn the privilege of addressing its audience, and it had to continue to deserve its attention from moment to moment and from day to day. At stake was a variation in daily attendance that could run into millions. Measuring the preferences of the target audience for existing television and film materials was therefore crucial in the design of the new series.

Establishing the Use and Methods of Research. At the time,

there was little precedent for incorporating research into television production or, indeed, into any educational design. It was not unheard of for a producer to produce a rough cut and run it for a test audience, but no one had attempted to develop and assess a set of research methods, and use the best ones to identify the attributes of a program that would contribute to its effectiveness. Indeed, as noted above, even the term *formative research* itself had been coined only a short time earlier (Scriven, 1967).

Given this lack of precedent, the first challenge was to convince the producers of *Sesame Street* that such research would be of value. One issue lay in helping the producers understand that formative research was not intended to usurp their decision-making ability; it was simply one more source of information among many, including their own past experiences with children, input from expert advisers and consultants, and intuitive impressions. It was always understood on both sides that the producers had to make the final production decisions, based on the information available to them, from whatever source.

A second issue lay in developing research methods that would address the producers' information needs and yield data that they found convincing. Prior to coming to CTW, I had developed a research method called the *distractor technique*. One of my academic colleagues had received a grant from the Office of Education to research the question of what holds children's attention to television, and when he was unable to carry out the research for health reasons, I took over the grant. His idea was to pit two children's television programs against each other, running them at the same time, and see which one held a child's attention. However, I thought that would not provide a fair test of either program; the child would get caught up in one program or the other, depending on which one was closer or had the louder piece of music, and he or she would simply persist in viewing, rather than making a choice moment-to-moment. I felt that a more valid indicator would be to use just one program and see whether a distractor would be able to pull a child's attention away from it. At first, toys were considered as distractors, but that would have presented the same problem: The child would get caught up in an imaginative game with a toy and simply not attend to the television. Instead, the distractors became competing audiovisual stimuli—first, a projection of images taken through a kaleidoscope and subsequently, slides projected on a second, rear-projection screen—and these worked well. At 7.5-second intervals, a researcher would record whether the child was watching the television screen or looking away. When analyzed, the data represented a composite of all of the children who had been tested individually, via the percentage of children who attended to the television program at each point.

When the method was suggested to the *Sesame Street* producers, however, some doubted whether the data would be generalizable to home viewing, in which children could choose among multiple programs simultaneously. I had to work hard to convince them that there was some validity to laboratory-oriented research—that a program that would hold children's attention on a moment-to-moment basis was also likely to beat out the competition. To assess the validity of the method, we tested several Saturday morning cartoon shows and episodes of *Captain Kangaroo*, a television series on which all of the key producers had worked.

When the producers saw the data, they were convinced. David Connell had specifically chosen an episode of *Captain Kangaroo* that he knew 4-year-old children would not understand; it involved the Captain explaining to Mr. Greenjeans how government worked, including bicameral legislatures and reporting bills out of committee. As expected, the distractor data showed that as soon as the characters started talking about the Constitution, children's attention dropped dramatically, and as soon as Captain Kangaroo said, "And now a word from Mattel," attention jumped back up. At that point, Connell became a believer. Indeed, when Langbourne Rust (1987) later compared the distractor scores for a sample of children's television programs to their home viewing, he found a strong correspondence between the two.

Much of the value in the distractor technique came from the level of detail that the distractor graph provided. Each graph was approximately 10 feet long, with a data point every 7.5 seconds, so that it looked like a stock market graph going up and down. As the graph climbed, the producers could say, "This means the show is getting more interesting to the kids." As the graph dropped, they could infer reasons for the decline (e.g., "they left that animal on too long").

Over time, the research team also developed other methods for testing appeal, such as presenting programs to children in groups of three to five (rather than individually) and structured interviews that assessed the salient and lasting appeal of various program features, as opposed to their immediate appeal. Appeal research was used to bear on a wide range of program design decisions, including: the effects of various forms and applications of music; the most and least popular forms of live-action films, animations, puppets, and live performers; the attention-holding power of various types of individual or interpersonal activities, such as showing one person guiding another through a difficult task in a supportive versus demeaning manner; the effects of incongruity, surprisingness, or fantasy, as compared with straightforwardness, predictability, and realism; the most and least effective uses of dialogue, monologue, and the voice-over technique; and the relative effectiveness of ordinary or caricaturized voices. It also helped to indicate for various conditions: the amount of time over which attention could be maintained; the optimum amount of variety and the optimum pacing of events; the ability of a segment to bear up under exact repetition; the most and least salient (memorable) characters; and the effectiveness of special techniques such as pixilation, fast and slow motion, and unusual camera angles.

Research techniques were also developed to test comprehension of the material as it was produced. One useful approach was to present a program to an audience of one or more children, stop the presentation at predetermined points so as to "freeze the frame," and ask viewers about events leading up to or likely to follow from the pictured situation. A related method was to play a program or segment once or twice, then present it again without the sound (or, occasionally, with the sound but without the picture) and ask the viewer to give a running account of the events on screen or to respond to specific questions. Other methods useful for evaluating comprehensibility included: observing the spontaneous responses of children in viewing groups, testing for achievement gains following their exposure to a program or a segment, retelling stories, recreating scenes via doll play, and probing children in depth to tell everything they could about the segment they had viewed. The staff was very inventive in devising testing methods and very careful about their validity. We had to be careful not to read things in, not to misunderstand when individual children were unable to give a response because of their limited articulation, and to recognize when children gave responses that were intended simply to please the researcher.

Comprehension testing, although useful in evaluating viewers' understanding of the dramatic action, was undertaken primarily to identify and set down specific principles for program design to maximize the comprehensibility of the material being produced. Among these were: production approaches that could help to clarify the relationship between an event occurring on the screen and the theme, plot line, or logical progression of the dramatic component; the close juxtaposition of events to establish a metaphoric or analogic relationship between them; the use of fantasy conventions (e.g., presenting puppets and cartoon characters who move and talk like humans) and "magical" effects, such as making an object instantly appear or disappear from a scene, or grow smaller or larger; and the use of television conventions such as flashbacks, special lighting effects, various camera perspectives, fast or slow motion, and the matched dissolve between objects. Still other facets of comprehensibility related to timing, sequencing, and use of redundancy, as in repeating an event exactly or with an illuminating variation, restating a point from alternative perspectives, and making use of introductions or reviews. The list could go on indefinitely, a fact that itself suggests the significance of this attribute in educational television research.

Impact of the Research on Production. Unlike academic research, which is undertaken in the context of scientific validation, the only pervasive criterion for formative research is that it appears likely to contribute to the effectiveness of the product or procedure being developed. Formative research quickly came to play a critical role in countless production decisions throughout the production of *Sesame Street* (and, indeed, continues to do so today). For example, the first animated segment produced for *Sesame Street* was a segment about the letter *J* that told a story in which a character named Joe danced a jig with a June bug in a jar, went before a judge, and so on. In that animation, however, the letter *J* was static in the upper part of the screen while Joe was dancing his jig with a June bug in the lower part of screen. As a result, the research data showed that children were watching the action down below, and the connection to the letter was never made. Based on those data, the researchers concluded that the educational point needed to be better integrated into the action. One of the advisors suggested that the key was to treat the featured letter as a character in the show, and put the dramatic focus right on the letter. To this end, the production team then revised the segment, animating the *J* so that it moved as well, and this succeeded in drawing children's attention to the letter.

The producers came back later with two new pieces. One featured Kermit the Frog and the letter *W*, and in it the letter *W* was chopped into an *N*, and then into a *V*; Kermit kept looking back in surprise to see that it had changed. The letter was sitting right in the heart of the action, in the middle of the screen, with everything building around it; Kermit would stop and look at the letter and the viewer's eye would go to it. Similarly, in the other segment, Kermit sat still while the letter *W* wiggled and wobbled, right in the middle of the screen, so that all of the attention was focused on the letter. Both segments were right on target.

Another example concerns the use of music. There was always an interest in the role music could play, beginning with an initial interest in children's affinity for commercial jingles, which Joan Cooney had discussed in the initial proposal for *Sesame Street* (Cooney, 1966). The researchers began working early with composer Joe Raposo, because he came to us; we loved working with him, and he loved working with the researchers. At one point, early in production, Raposo had written a song to address a curriculum goal about rhyming (as part of reading readiness and language awareness). The problem with the piece was that, although it was intended to call children's attention to rhyming couplets, the rhyming word was obscured by a clatter of drums and cymbals. As a result, the data showed that children couldn't hear the word and were not grasping the rhyme. Some time later, Raposo came back with a new rhyming song, but this time, he had syncopated the last beat, so that there wasn't any music right where the rhyme word came. We applauded both the result and the spirit of creative cooperation between producers and researchers.

Measuring Impact: Summative Research

From the very beginning, there was a recognition among the CTW staff that, for *Sesame Street* to be considered a success, it would have to produce measurable outcomes in achieving its educational goals. Thus, in addition to formative research, the inclusion of a summative evaluation of the educational impact of *Sesame Street* was assumed even before the final curriculum document was written. Indeed, part of the reason for stating *Sesame Street* curriculum goals in terms of behavioral outcomes (e.g., "The child will ... ") was to provide clear guidance for subsequent evaluation. Summative research was intended both as a means of providing accountability to the financial backers who had provided funding for *Sesame Street* and, from the standpoint of the in-house producers and researchers, as a means of gauging its success for ourselves.

The summative research (Ball & Bogatz, 1970; Bogatz & Ball, 1971) was contracted out to ETS, so as to ensure an independent evaluation of impact. To avoid the appearance of any bias in the data, our interaction with the ETS researchers had to be utterly transparent to the profession, and we were successful in that respect. When the data showed significant effects of children's exposure to *Sesame Street*—and even when Cook and his colleagues (1975) performed their re-analysis of the data—no one ever accused CTW of trying to distort or influence the results of the study. (For information on the results of the ETS studies and the re-analysis by Cook et al., see Mielke, chap. 5, this volume.)

Communication Outside CTW

Relations With the Academic Community.   As in the case of more traditional academic research, the *Sesame Street* research staff was very active in producing academic publications and conference presentations regarding research methods and results. Over time, we built a substantial list of publications, considering that the *Sesame Street* researchers were not working in academia.

There were three motivations for establishing close relations with the academic research community. One was to share the innovative research methods being developed to investigate issues related to children and television. Because so little research in this area had been conducted up to that point, few others were publishing methodological papers. A second was to promote support for the educational aims and accomplishments of the series, by publicizing research results that demonstrated the educational potential of *Sesame Street*.

Finally, there was a practical value to establishing professional relationships with academic researchers. The pressures of production meant that in-house *Sesame Street* formative studies needed to address the information needs of the product designers and not primarily the individualistic or special theoretical interests of the researchers. As a result, many issues that potentially held implications for *Sesame Street* but were of less immediate priority had to remain unanswered. By stimulating interest in children and television among academics who had begun to pursue research in this area, we hoped for a "Tom Sawyer effect": enticing other researchers to continue to investigate these topics as well. CTW obtained grants to bring academic researchers such as Jennings Bryant, Keith Mielke, and Langbourne Rust to come to the Workshop for several months to work on research methods. Relationships were established with researchers such as John Murray, John Wright, and Aletha Huston as they were beginning to conduct research on issues related to television. Small seed grants to researchers such as Daniel Anderson resulted in key studies (e.g., Anderson, Lorch, Smith, Bradford, & Levin, 1981; Lorch, Anderson, & Levin, 1979) that informed CTW's efforts (e.g., by investigating the effect of toys or peer presence on children's attention to television) while simultaneously initiating programs of research that also made tremendous contributions to basic research. Some of these relationships were so successful that they eventually resulted in researchers such as Mielke and Rust joining the CTW research staff full-time.

Public Relations.   Apart from the traditional venues of scholarly journals and conferences, research also played an important role in the broader public relations efforts that surrounded *Sesame Street*. Under the direction of CTW Vice President for Information Robert Hatch and with the assistance of the Carl Byoir advertising agency, public relations was critical in building awareness and viewership of *Sesame Street*. The public television system did not cover the entire United States, and the public television stations in many areas—particularly areas serving the poor and minority children who were at the center of *Sesame Street*'s target audience—were broadcast on UHF, which had the potential to lead to low awareness and poor reception of *Sesame Street* broadcasts in those areas. Along with community-based outreach efforts (see chap. 10, this volume), public relations helped to build awareness of the series among the potential viewing audience. In addition, because *Sesame Street* was the first children's television series to employ a serious educational curriculum and formative research in service of production, public relations also helped to build public awareness of *Sesame Street* as an educational tool. What was being publicized was the use of this scientific technology.

It was the first time that research had been used systematically in promoting a television series. Indeed, research was the story for a long time, beginning with data from formative research that provided the earliest indications of learning, and continuing with data from the ETS evaluations after those studies had been run. I was constantly being interviewed on television programs, in newspapers, and in magazines, to discuss the research and children's learning from *Sesame Street*. It was fun, but also awkward; I wasn't accustomed to doing this because I was trained to be an academic, and I became very self-conscious trying to say things in ways that would be interesting to the media. We were terribly cautious not to say anything invalid or misleading, and Robert Hatch was extremely helpful in finding ways to present data and create charts that could be understood easily by a nontechnical audience.

Funding for Sesame Street.   Approximately one half of the $8 million budget for the first season of *Sesame Street* was covered by the U.S. Department of Health, Education, and Welfare (including the Office of Education and Office of Economic Opportunity, among others), with the remainder supplied by the newly-created Corporation for Public Broadcasting and private foundations such as the Carnegie Corporation, the Ford Foundation, and others. With such heavy reliance on outside funding, the research staff quickly came to play a integral role in all aspects of funder relations. This included everything from writing funding proposals to participating in quarterly reports, going to organization meetings, answering queries, testifying before Congress (on behalf of not only *Sesame Street*, but also public television and the Office of Education), and going on the road to speak to people in public television around the country.

Among the key pieces of evidence that helped to secure ongoing funding for *Sesame Street* over the next several years were the two summative studies conducted by ETS, which found *Sesame Street* to have a significant educational impact on its young viewers (Ball & Bogatz, 1970; Bogatz & Ball, 1971; cf. Mielke, chap. 5, this volume). However, it was clear that the data from even the first evaluation would not be available until significantly after the first 6-month broadcast season. The ETS posttest was scheduled after the broadcast season, and it would take time for the ETS staff to analyze the results and assemble a report. This meant that the data would not be available by the time funding was being sought for a second season.

Fortunately, we had wanted to track our progress sooner for our own purposes. Because we knew that some of the later shows would not be taped until after some of the earliest had already aired, we conducted research that we called *progress testing* to inform the later shows (Reeves, 1970). The progress tests employed a number of the ETS test items with a sample of approximately 200 children from Maine, New York, and Tennessee. A pretest was conducted with all of the children before the series went on the air. Six weeks later, we retested one third. After 3 months, we retested those children plus a new one third, and so on.

The results of this progress testing turned out to be the only real data that were available when the foundations and the federal government were considering the refunding of the series. An all-day conference was held with *Sesame Street*'s funders at a hotel in New York City, in which we reviewed the data from the in-house progress testing. The data were presented test-item-by-item, and many of them showed a clear increment of gain over the course of testing (foreshadowing the later ETS data). The funders accepted the results as valid and unbiased, both because Ray Norris of the Office of Education had overseen data collection at one of the three test sites (and his staff had conducted the computer data processing for all three sites), and because the Office of Education brought several independent experts to this meeting. On examining the data, they concluded that, indeed, the results suggested an effect of viewing. Everyone left the meeting with the feeling that *Sesame Street* was accomplishing something. I believe it had a significant effect on CTW's receiving funding for a second season.

Conclusion

When the research function was first integrated into the production of *Sesame Street*, there was some trepidation on all sides. No one knew how well the relationship would function. I accepted the position of Research Director on the basis that we would have to see if the research was going to work. There would be no contract, just a good faith agreement that if the experiment was not working on either side, we would give ample notice and take care of things properly. I took a 2-year leave of absence from my university position, and never expected to remain at CTW for the next 19 years.

Joan Ganz Cooney once wryly described the collaboration of researchers and producers as "a marriage worth keeping intact—for the sake of the children." The research function for *Sesame Street* blossomed into a multifaceted role that encompassed, not only the curriculum and research tasks directly related to the production of the series, but also ancillary activities that made valuable contributions to both *Sesame Street* and the broader field of research on children and television as a whole.

No one could have predicted the extent to which *Sesame Street* would become a national and worldwide institution. Yet, even at the time, we knew we were engaged in something important. The first season of *Sesame Street* was the world's biggest $8 million experiment in children's television. We were going to leave a footprint in the sands of time, and we knew that. The unique collaboration between production and research helped to ensure that the experiment of *Sesame Street* was a success, and to continue its success for 30 years.

ACKNOWLEDGMENTS

We gratefully acknowledge the input of: Leona Schauble, who reviewed the text of this chapter and made a number of very useful suggestions; Keith

Mielke, who supplied some of the unpublished interviews on which the chapter is based; and Maria Betances and Barbara Stewart, who located and provided several of Palmer's published papers for use in completing the chapter.

REFERENCES

A. C. Nielsen Company. (1967). Nielsen Television Index.

Anderson, D. R., Lorch, E. P., Smith, R. , Bradford, R., & Levin, S. R. (1981). Effects of peer presence on preschool children's television viewing. *Developmental Psychology, 17,* 446–453.

Ball, S., & Bogatz, G. (1970). *The first year of Sesame Street: An evaluation.* Princeton, NJ: Educational Testing Service.

Bereiter, C., & Engelman, S. I. (1966). *Teaching disadvantaged children in preschool.* Englewood Cliffs, NJ: Prentice-Hall.

Bloom, B. S. (1964). *Stability and change in human characteristics.* New York: Wiley.

Bogatz, G., & Ball, S. (1971). *The second year of Sesame Street: A continuing evaluation.* Princeton, NJ: Educational Testing Service.

Cook, T. D., Appleton, H., Conner, R. F., Shaffer, A., Tamkin, G., & Weber, S. (1975). *Sesame Street revisited.* New York: Russell Sage Foundation.

Cooney, J. G. (1966). *The potential uses of television in preschool education: A report to the Carnegie Corporation of New York.* New York: Carnegie Corporation.

Deutsch, M. (1965). Race and social class as separate factors related to social environment. *American Journal of Sociology, 70,* 474.

Gibbon, S. Y., Palmer, E. L., & Fowles, B. R. (1975). *Sesame Street, The Electric Company,* and reading. In J. Carroll & J. Chall (Eds.), *Toward a literate society* (pp. 215–256). New York: McGraw Hill.

Lesser, G. S. (1974). *Children and television: Lessons from Sesame Street.* New York: Vintage Books/Random House.

Lorch, E. P., Anderson, D. R., & Levin, S. R. (1979). The relationship of visual attention to children's comprehension of television. *Child Development, 50,* 722–727.

Palmer, E. L. (1972). Formative research in educational television production: The experience of the Children's Television Workshop. In W. Schramm (Ed.), *Quality in instructional television* (pp. 165–187). Honolulu: The University Press of Hawaii.

Palmer, E. L. (1988). *Television and America's children: A crisis of neglect.* New York: Oxford University Press.

Palmer, E. L. (1976). Unpublished interview.

Palmer, E. L. (1991). Unpublished interview.

Palmer, E. L. (1999). Unpublished interview.

Palmer, E. L., Chen, M., & Lesser, G. S. (1976). *Sesame Street*: Patterns of international adaptation. *Journal of Communication, 26,* 109–123.

Reeves, B. F. (1970). *The first year of Sesame Street: The formative research.* New York: Children's Television Workshop.

Rust, L. (1987). Using attention and intention to predict at-home program choice. *Journal of Advertising Research, 27*(2), 25–30.

Scriven, M. (1967). The methodology of evaluation. In R. Tyler, R. Gagné, & M. Scriven (Eds.), *Perspectives of curriculum evaluation* (pp. 39–83). Chicago: Rand McNally.

2 Creation and Evolution of the *Sesame Street* Curriculum

Gerald S. Lesser
Harvard University
Joel Schneider
Children's Television Workshop

Even after 30 years, production of *Sesame Street* adheres to its original conception as the product of a workshop, that is, subject to continual modification and refinement in response to experience and to changing needs. Three principal processes drive this continuing experiment: changes in knowledge and understanding of children's growth, development, and learning; changes in society; and our own collective staff experience. This massive long-term creative effort resides in a library of more than 30,000 televised segments. What are they about? How does one think about them in terms of education? What were and what are the guides and tests for the writers and producers in creating programs to meet their educational challenges? The answer to each of these and many other questions is found in *Sesame Street*'s curriculum. In this chapter we describe the context and origin of the curriculum. We continue with a discussion of its evolution and its role in the work of CTW.

ORIGINS OF THE *SESAME STREET* CURRICULUM

Thirty Years Ago: The Needs at the Time

Most of us who lived through the late 1960s in the United States remember it as a time of pain and disruption. The Vietnam War, assassinations, political and social upheaval all contributed to that sense of chaos and confusion. There was, however, one extraordinary exception: the "War on Poverty," a government-initiated program of great promise. Its intention was humane and visionary. Designed to lift the poor to a better standard of living, its pivotal purpose was to improve the quality of our schools, especially for children from poor, inner-city families.

25

Not only did the schools need to be improved, but also young children needed to be better prepared to do well in school. If poor children start school less successfully than their middle-class counterparts, it is likely that they will fall further and further behind as they progress through the grades (cf., Bereriter & Engelman, 1966; Bloom, 1964; Deutsch, 1965). In the late 1960s, however, poor children had few available resources. Nursery schools and other opportunities for formal early educational experiences were in short supply. Those that did exist were available only to those families that could afford them. Could other resources be enlisted to help? Television, for example, might provide a way to reach many, if not most, of the children who were in need of such help. Perhaps television's apparent natural appeal to young children could be turned to constructive educational use, especially for young children in the inner cities where television sets were quickly becoming almost ubiquitous. Television programming was clearly a powerful means to persuade and to inform. Advertising in particular depended on television's efficiency in delivering memorable messages. This supported the idea that the messages could be educational as well as entertaining and persuasive. Joan Ganz Cooney had developed the original vision of what later became *Sesame Street* in her 1966 report to the Carnegie Corporation, called "Television for Preschool Education" (Cooney, 1966). In 1968 Cooney proposed a variant of the report's recommendations to the Carnegie Corporation of New York, the Ford Foundation, and the U.S. Office of Education (later reconstituted as the U.S. Department of Education). With their funding assured, Cooney formally launched planning for *Sesame Street*.

Having decided that preparation for school was to be our primary purpose, we faced the task of determining which skills would help most to achieve this. Cooney had already discussed this question extensively with educators, psychologists, school practitioners, pediatricians, television and film producers, and others in preparing her Carnegie report. She gathered their many suggestions for school-preparation skills and combined them with relevant empirical studies on early education (e.g., Bereiter & Engelman, 1966; Bloom, 1964; Deutsch, 1965). Still another body of opinion fed into the selection of goals: what inner-city parents said they wanted for their children. They wanted what most other parents want—reading, writing, arithmetic, reasoning, and any other basic skills that would equip their children for school and later life. Their utilitarian view of education stressed the fundamental intellectual skills that have broad currency in our society.

Thus, several forces converged to influence the selection of the goals to be emphasized: the recommendations of Cooney's consultants, combined with data from empirical studies of school preparation, which, in turn, connected with the educational priorities emphasized by the parents of inner-city children. The result was that we identified five clusters of skills for further exploration:

1. Social, Moral, and Affective Development
2. Language and Reading
3. Mathematical and Numerical Skills

4. Reasoning and Problem-Solving
5. Perception

The Seminars

By the spring of 1968, we had reached the point of defining five broad areas of school-preparation skills. Of course we also needed a far more specific list of detailed instructional objectives to support the goals under each general area. To construct these lists, we conducted five seminars, each lasting for 3 days, to identify the specific skills in each area that we would try to foster in our young viewers.

We decided that, at each seminar, we would have as many different points of view as possible and as many different ideas for potential educational content as our seminar participants could generate. Seminar sessions were broad in scope, open-ended, and freewheeling.

To identify this wide range of prospective objectives, we invited professionals with diverse backgrounds and interests: preschool teachers, developmental psychologists, television producers and filmmakers, child psychiatrists, artists, musicians, children's book writers, performers, sociologists, puppeteers, and creative advertising designers. We anticipated that the great variety among the participants might create some difficulties in communication. Even so, we wanted to be sure to have the widest variety in thinking about the content that we should try to convey in our broadcast series. Misunderstandings, however, were few and we resolved them with good nature. Did a coherent variety of ideas emerge from professionals with such different backgrounds and experiences with children? As it turned out, combining people with such diverse backgrounds was widely successful. There was little defensiveness or friction among the teachers, the academics, the creative staff, and the other professionals, or those from different backgrounds and with different perspectives about children. Instead, everyone seemed to be stimulated by the variety of opinion and expertise. The seminars succeeded in producing long and detailed lists of specific instructional objectives that were candidates for inclusion in the *Sesame Street* curriculum.

There were several reasons for the great value of the seminars in generating useful sets of potential objectives for the school-preparation of inner-city children. Perhaps the most important reason was that seminar members knew that we were not asking them simply to review and ratify a product created by others. They recognized that we wanted their substantive contributions to the content, design, and implementation of the broadcast series. They were also correctly convinced that the project would depend on their detailed recommendations and that their ideas for objectives would be used as essential guides to the program's educational substance, characters, and style.

The Curriculum

With the success of the seminars, we had prepared the ground for proceeding. We had stated our educational objectives and our reasons for selecting them.

An enormous amount of creative work lay ahead to combine education with entertainment, but we now had considerable clarity about where we were headed in helping inner-city preschoolers to be better prepared to begin school successfully.

The success of the seminars resulted in an embarrassment of riches. After we had completed and recorded the five seminars, we faced far more educational objectives than we could realistically achieve, even in a broadcast season of 130 one-hour programs. In response, the creative and educational staffs devised a system to define priorities. Setting priorities involved several criteria, but two issues became pivotal: (a) which educational objectives seemed to be most salient in preparing young inner-city children for school, and (b) which types of educational content might be conveyed most effectively through the television medium. Using these criteria, we reconceived the categories and made a judicious choice of objectives within each category. The main categories now emerged as:

- Symbolic Representation
- Cognitive Processes
- The Physical Environment
- The Social Environment

In particular, "Symbolic Representation" combined two of the original categories having to do with language, reading, and mathematics. "Cognitive Processes" combined the two original categories having to do with thinking: "Reasoning and Problem Solving" and "Perception." We renamed "Social, Moral, and Affective Development" as "The Social Environment," comprising both social units and social interactions. "The Physical Environment" was new, suggestions for related objectives having come up in several contexts in the course of the seminars; we decided that we ought to help children to know about the world that they were growing up in, both the natural world and the human-made world. Table 2.1 lists the next level of detail under the new categories.

To guide the writers and producers, the curriculum document also illustrated each goal with many specific behavioral objectives that we hoped viewers would achieve after viewing for an extended period. For example, the section on "Letters" under "Symbolic Representation" listed several specific aspects of knowing and using letters (Table 2.2). The inclusion of behavioral objectives served both to make the curriculum goals more concrete for writers and producers, and to guide the subsequent design of summative research to gauge the educational effectiveness of *Sesame Street* (see Mielke, chap. 5, this volume).

Because of the large number of behavioral objectives included in the *Sesame Street* curriculum, the complete curriculum document is too lengthy to be included here. Readers interested in this level of detail can find the complete Season 1 (1969–1970) curriculum in Lesser, 1974.

TABLE 2.1
Goals for the First Season of *Sesame Street*

I. *Symbolic Representation*. The child can recognize such basic symbols as letters, numbers, and geometric forms, and can perform rudimentary operations with these symbols:

    A. Letters.
    B. Numbers.
    C. Geometric Forms.

II. *Cognitive Processes*. The child can deal with objects and events in terms of certain concepts of order, classification, and relationships, can apply certain reasoning skills, and possesses certain attitudes conducive to effective inquiry and problem solving:

    A. Perceptual Discrimination.
    B. Relational Concepts.
    C. Classification.
    D. Ordering.
    E. Reasoning and Problem Solving.

III. *The Physical Environment*. The child's conception of the physical world should include general information about natural phenomena, both near and distant; about certain processes that occur in nature; about certain interdependencies that relate various natural phenomena, and about the ways in which man explores and interacts with the natural world:

    A. The Natural Environment.
    B. The Man-made Environment.

IV. *The Social Environment*. The child can identify himself and other familiar individuals and role-defining characteristics. The child is familiar with forms and functions of institutions that he or she may encounter. The child can see situations from more than one point of view and begin to see the necessity for certain social rules, particularly those insuring justice and fair play:

    A. Social Units.
        1. Self.
        2. Social Roles.
        3. Social Groups and Institutions.

    B. Social Interactions.
        1. Differences in Perspectives.
        2. Cooperation.
        3. Rules for Justice and Fair Play.

TABLE 2.2
Objectives Supporting the Goal: "Symbolic Representation: Letters"

I. Symbolic Representation. The child can recognize such basic symbols as letters, numbers, and geometric forms, and can perform rudimentary operations with these symbols:

C. Letters

1. Given a set of symbols, either all letters or all numbers, the child knows whether those symbols are used in reading or in counting.

2. Given a printed letter, the child can select the identical letter from a set of printed letters.

3. Given a printed letter, the child can select its other-case version from a set of printed letters.

4. Given a verbal label for a letter, the child can select the appropriate letter from a set of printed letters.

5. Given a printed letter, the child can provide its verbal label.

6. Given a series of words presented orally, all beginning with the same letter, the child can make up another word or produce another word starting with the same letter.

7. Given a spoken letter, the child can select a set of pictures or objects beginning with that letter.

8. The child can recite the alphabet.

EVOLUTION OF THE CURRICULUM

No one in 1969 was thinking about a long term for *Sesame Street*. No one anticipated continuing to produce the show for more than 30 years. After completing the original curriculum, our problem was to produce 130 hours of appealing television programming that would also be educationally effective. Every new television series has significant problems to solve, such as defining and developing characters and formats and developing a structure to carry them. Our additional requirement of meeting educational objectives was a significant extra load on the producers. The series had to be attractive to an audience in order to have any chance of meeting educational objectives. Therefore, entertainment imperatives had more force than educational imperatives in resolving natural creative tensions.

The immediate success, however, contributed to our growing confidence in our abilities to deliver on our goals and created an opportunity and a demand for more. With that opportunity came the chance to expand the curriculum to include objectives originally held out of our scheme. In some cases, this has entailed adding new subject areas to the continuing *Sesame Street* curriculum, revising our approach to existing subject areas, or adopting specific areas as the primary focus for one or more seasons. In others, it has meant concentrating on narrower "special topics," on a more limited basis in a small number of episodes (or even one episode) within a single season.

Expansion and Revision of the Curriculum

In the course of the first several seasons of *Sesame Street*, we added topics to the curricular mix. In some cases, we went more deeply into a topic (e.g., by treating simple sight words in addition to letter-related objectives and by expanding the set of counting numbers from 10 to 20). We also added new objectives (e.g., verbal blends and classification by more than one attribute). We also began to add objectives that were less skill oriented, such as clusters of objectives having to do with emotions and with Latino-American culture. Table 2.3 lists the new topics and objectives that appeared in each season.

Our changes to the curriculum followed a process consistent with and parallel to the development of the original curriculum. As in the original development process, our staff consulted with experts representing pertinent disciplines. We usually chose one discipline per season, and consultation took place in individual or small group meetings or in full-blown seminars, as freewheeling as the five seminars that guided the development of the original curriculum.

TABLE 2.3
Original, Additional, and Special Topics in the *Sesame Street* Curriculum

Season 1 (1969–1970)	Original topics: letters; alphabet; counting numbers 10; simple geometric shapes; ordering; classification; reasoning; problem solving; relational concepts; perceptual discrimination; self; roles; differing perspectives; cooperation; fair play; the human-made environment.
Season 2 (1970–1971)	Curriculum focus/additional topics: sight words; counting numbers to 20; simple addition and subtraction; multiple classification; regrouping; property identification; emotions; the mind and its uses; conflict resolution.
Season 3 (1971–1972)	Curriculum focus/additional topics: rhyming; verbal blending; ecology; Latino-American culture.
Season 4 (1972–1973)	Curriculum focus/additional topics: measurement; sorting by activity; Spanish sight words.
Season 5 (1973–1974)	Curriculum focus/additional topics: complex geometric shapes; coping with failure; self-esteem; entering social groups.
Season 6 (1974–1975)	Curriculum focus/additional topics: creativity; divergent thinking; career awareness.

(Continues)

TABLE 2.3 (Continued)

Season 7 (1975–1976)	Curriculum focus/additional topics: diversity—children with special needs; the Taos Pueblo Indians. Special topic: the nation's bicentennial celebration.
Season 8 (1976–1977)	Special topics: roles of women and countering gender-based stereotypes.
Season 9 (1977–1978)	Special topic: the multicultural, ocean-oriented society of Hawaii.
Season 10 (1978–1979)	Curriculum focus/additional topics: deafness; sign language; nutrition; dental care; exercise; and science—"What's alive?" and "What's inside?" Special topic: ethnic diversity in New York City.
Season 11 (1979–1980)	Additional topic: literacy goals related to school workbook activities (e.g., draw a line; follow the arrow; cross out; circle and underline). Special topic: fire safety.
Season 12 (1980–1981)	Special topic: general safety (e.g., crossing the street and where to play).
Season 13 (1981–1982)	Curriculum focus/additional topics: sound pattern recognition—order, number, rhythm, dynamics, pitch, and tempo. Special topics: getting along in school (e.g., structure of the day, role of the teacher, social rituals, listening, and paying attention).
Season 14 (1982–1983)	Curriculum focus/additional topics: reading in a context; reading as useful and enjoyable; literary forms (e.g., stories, poems, letters, and newspapers).
Season 15 (1983–1984)	Special topics: computers—parts and uses; the death of Mr. Hooper.
Season 16 (1984–1985)	Curriculum focus/additional topics: writing as enjoyable and useful; language appreciation and the value of a rich vocabulary. Special topics: broken bones; hospital procedures.
Season 17 (1985–1986)	Curriculum focus/additional topic: simple songs in preparation for school music. Special topics: adoption; the physical development of infants.
Season 18 (1986–1987)	Curriculum focus/additional topics: addition and subtraction involving numbers between 10 and 15; counting numbers to 40; the concept of zero; recognizing numerical patterns.

TABLE 2.3 (Continued)

Season 19 (1987–1988)	Curriculum focus/additional topics: storybook reading; consonant blends and digraphs. Special topics: love and marriage.
Season 20 (1988–1989)	Curriculum focus/additional topics: science appreciation and physical science—air. Special topics: pregnancy, prenatal care, fetal development, and birth.
Season 21 (1989–1990)	Curriculum focus/additional topics: water and energy conservation; littering and recycling. Special topic: geography—land and water; maps; the seven continents and the United States.
Season 22 (1990–1991)	Curriculum focus/additional topics: beginning a four-season treatment of race relations among White Americans, African Americans, American Indians, Latino Americans, and Asian Americans; exploring physical and cultural differences; modeling positive responses to differences (friendship, mutual cultural appreciation, and inclusion). Initial emphasis on African Americans.
Season 23 (1991–1992)	Curriculum focus/additional topics: treatment of race relations continues, emphasis on American Indians, featuring the Cherokee, Crow, Iroquois, and Navajo.
Season 24 (1992–1993)	Curriculum focus/additional topics: treatment of race relations continues, emphasis on Latinos, featuring Puerto Ricans, Cuban Americans, and Mexican Americans.
Season 25 (1993–1994)	Curriculum focus/additional topics: treatment of race relations continues, emphasis on Asian Americans, featuring Asian-Indian Americans, Chinese Americans, Filipino Americans, Japanese Americans, and Korean Americans; strategies for dealing with rejection and name calling (especially as applied to exclusionary behavior based on physical or cultural differences in the context of the continuing race relations curriculum).
Season 26 (1994–1995)	Curriculum focus/additional topics: beginning a three-season exploration of emergent literacy, building on the introduction of reading storybooks in Season 19; reading for information; expanded list of sight words; phonemes. The production couples with a multiple-media literacy campaign, "Let's Read & Write."
Season 27 (1995–1996)	Curriculum focus/additional topics: exploration of emergent literacy continues.

(Continues)

TABLE 2.3 (Continued)	
Season 28 (1996–1997)	Curriculum focus/additional topics: exploration of emergent literacy continues.
Season 29 (1997–1998)	Curriculum focus/additional topics: science—strengthening the relationship between children and their world by encouraging integrating reasoning and critical thinking in science contexts such as "What's Alive" and "Body Parts/Senses."
Season 30 (1998–1999)	Curriculum focus/additional topics: social and emotional development, drawing on the existing curricular topics having to do with the neighborhood, school, and people and their jobs; pride and self-esteem related to abilities and accomplishments; friendship, sharing, and turn taking; motivation (i.e., practice, persistence, and coping with failure).

There is, however, one extra dimension to the discussion and debate in these seminars, namely, criticism of the existing *Sesame Street* product. Although the original curriculum seminars could not use existing *Sesame Street* segments as a reference point (because none existed), more recent seminars have been able to incorporate reviews of past segments relevant to the topic at hand. This type of review can be extremely helpful in helping outside advisors (who generally have little prior experience in television production) understand what is possible within the medium, while simultaneously providing a means by which the advisors' suggestions can be made more concrete for the production team. In addition, a close review of existing material can help point to subtle issues that otherwise might be missed. For example, an advisor in one literacy seminar showed the production team that the *Sesame Street* characters often did not point to printed words as they read them. She suggested that, by simply running a finger beneath the words as they read, the characters could subtly convey the idea that English text is read from left to right. The change was easy to make, and we did so in the following season's production.

Apart from the formal setting of regularly scheduled curriculum seminars, CTW has also set up its own robust internal review and critique that serves as a continuing corrective and guide for future production. Continuing review of *Sesame Street* material by in-house research and production staff complements a continuing cycle of formative research into viewers' comprehension of the educational content of selected segments as they emerge from production (Fisch & Bernstein, chap. 3, this volume; Palmer & Fisch, chap. 1, this volume; Truglio, Lovelace, Segui, & Scheiner, chap. 4, this volume). Data from these studies tell us what is most useful and interesting to children and what works in our method. They inform, not only the production of new material, but also directions for the curriculum as a whole. Children's misconceptions, as reflected in their responses in formative research, help to clarify the subjects we deal with and to refine our approach to them.

Sources of Change. The impetus for change in the *Sesame Street* curriculum stems from several sources. One source is the changing (and increasingly diverse) makeup of the U.S. population and accompanying societal concerns. For example, diversity had always been a major concern for *Sesame Street*. We began to include segments having to do with Latino-American culture as early as Season 3 (1971–1972). We also presented Pueblo Indian culture in Season 7 (1975–1976) and Hawaiian culture in Season 9 (1977–1978). However, the growing societal focus on multiculturalism, coupled with racial tensions in the late 1980s and early 1990s, led to the addition to the curriculum of a set of objectives that grew out of a 4-year curricular focus on race relations in Seasons 22–25 (1990–1994). Segments responding to these objectives explored and modeled positive responses to physical and cultural differences among White Americans, African Americans, American Indians, Latino Americans, and Asian Americans. (For more detail on research efforts under the race relations curriculum, see Truglio et al., chap. 4, this volume.)

The curriculum has also evolved in response to changes in professional understanding of children's growth, development, and learning. For example, educational theory and practice in literacy had come to rely more heavily on the use of meaningful contexts in teaching children to read and write. In response, *Sesame Street* began to treat reading-in-context in Season 14 (1982–1983), pleasure in writing, and the value of vocabulary in Season 16 (1984–1985), and storybooks in Season 19 (1987–1988). We also revised the related parts of the overall curriculum during a 3-season focus on emergent literacy in Seasons 26–28 (1994–1997). Similarly, as science educators have moved toward an orientation that emphasized the processes of discovery itself as much as the information that results, we mirrored that point of view in our treatment of science beginning in Season 29 (1997–1998).

A third source of change in the curriculum is change in the society around us. The original *Sesame Street* curriculum emphasized academic skills to help inner-city children become ready for school, because both parents and experts in education identified that as the area of greatest need. More recently, experts have recognized that children's success in school is also a function of various aspects of their social behavior, such as their ability to communicate with others and act cooperatively (Szanton et al., 1992). Moreover, parents today do not rank cognitive learning over social and emotional learning in preparation for school (Tessier, 1996). In part, this attitude derives from the increasing number of young children in child care where they have more access to educational devices and influences than did their counterparts in 1969. Although *Sesame Street* began to expand its focus on social behavior as early as Season 3 (1971–1972), we responded to these shifts by renewing the series' commitment to social behavior in recent years. In Season 25 (1993–1994), we began to offer strategies for dealing with rejection and name-calling. And in Season 30 (1998–1999), we added objectives focused on motivation as well as a special topic cluster on social and emotional development, including for example, friendship, sharing, and turn-taking.

Curriculum Focus.   As discussed earlier, an essential component of the process of curriculum development in Season 1 (1969–1970) was to identify priorities among the various curriculum objectives. Attempting to address all of the objectives simultaneously would have resulted in none of them being treated in sufficient depth to be effective. In many ways, then, the gradual expansion of the *Sesame Street* curriculum over subsequent years held the potential to result in the same situation: a proliferation of educational objectives too numerous to address effectively.

To avoid this situation, we designate a *curriculum focus* for each season of production. That is, we identify a small set of related objectives to which we give special emphasis in that season. In some seasons, the focus has been on areas that are new to the curriculum, such as the focus that gave rise to the race relations objectives in Seasons 22–25 (1990–1994). In other seasons, the focus has been on existing areas to which we made a substantial reexamination, as with the focus on emergent literacy in Seasons 26–28 (1994–1997).

Each curriculum focus serves to guide the efforts of both the production and the research team for that season. We produce more segments to address the subject of the curriculum focus, and the scripts treat the topic in greater depth. Moreover, we organize additional resources to support the production team. For example, during each of the 4 seasons that focused on race relations, we organized a series of lectures by prominent representatives of the culture in focus (e.g., chiefs of several Native American nations). We also assembled a detailed resource guide with information about customs, history, holidays, cuisine, and children's books from that culture.

Because we emphasize different topics in different seasons, the curriculum focus ensures that each receives the attention it requires over one or more seasons of *Sesame Street*. In this way, the cumulative curriculum has covered a wide variety of subjects without sacrificing the depth needed to achieve its goals.

Special Topics

As well as deepening and broadening its treatment of the original goals, *Sesame Street* has also presented a series of special topics, meant to appear in the curriculum for a short time only. Some of these special topics were opportunistic—for example, contributing to the celebration of the nation's bicentennial in 1976 and, when one of the actors (Emilio Delgado) broke his arm during production of Season 16 (1984–1985), including a series on broken bones and emergency room procedures. Perhaps the most poignant special topic was the treatment of death following the death of Mr. Hooper (Will Lee) in 1983. A happier example was Maria's (Sonia Manzano) pregnancy during Season 20 (1988–1989). For the most part, special topics have complemented the main curriculum, rather than becoming part of the ongoing curriculum themselves.

As in the case of each season's curriculum focus, we pay extra attention to special topics in both production and research. Because of their narrower application, we do not usually mount full-scale curriculum seminars, but we consult with appropriate experts to understand the educational issues that pertain to the topic and to identify the educational messages.

THE CURRICULUM IN THE FUTURE

As the preceding discussion shows, *Sesame Street* has always been responsive to the educational needs of its young audience as gauged by several methods. The guiding curriculum has evolved over time in response to changing circumstances, to reassessments of needs, and to opportunity. We have already noted that CTW relies on the curriculum not only in producing the television series, but also in producing materials and services for other venues and media such as child-care facilities and computer-based media. These also include books, magazines, records, audiotapes, and videotapes.

Our efforts to evolve and to apply the curriculum will continue as the experiment moves into its fourth decade. Several influences are already apparent. The role of computers in our lives can only be expected to grow. We anticipate addressing this issue as a special topic as early as Season 31. In doing so, we expect to go much further than the simple nuts-and-bolts approach that we used when in first addressing computers in Season 15 (1983–1984), when the treatment centered largely on labeling the parts of the computer.

Another influence on the curriculum is the fact that large numbers of younger children, even as young as 18 months, watch *Sesame Street*. We have already begun to investigate the educational needs of this young audience and how they differ from those of the traditional 3-to-5-year-old *Sesame Street* target audience. Such considerations informed the introduction in Season 30 of "Elmo's World," a recurring segment within *Sesame Street*, which targets younger children (see Fisch & Bernstein, chap. 3, this volume). During the next several seasons, we may make further changes to accommodate the needs of this younger audience in the broader *Sesame Street* curriculum as well.

In fact, at the time of this writing, we have embarked on a thorough evaluation of the entire curriculum. For more than 30 seasons the mode was additive, and sometimes subtractive. We have examined every objective in light of what we know about the needs of our audience today and what we can anticipate about the needs of tomorrow's audience.

Conclusion

No other television program for children matches the comprehensive curriculum of *Sesame Street*. Other chapters in this volume describe ways in which the *Sesame Street* curriculum informs development of educational products in other media, and how it influences informal education around the world (Cherow-O'Leary, chap. 11, this volume; Cole, Richman, & McCann Brown, chap. 9, this volume; Revelle, Medoff, & Strommen, chap. 12, this volume; Yotive & Fisch, chap. 10, this volume). No other television program for children matches the variety, experience, and expertise that reside in the *Sesame Street* television library. Even so, designing and producing a new season each year remains a continuing challenge as the producers aim to keep *Sesame Street* fresh, appealing, and responsive to the educational needs of their young viewers. A robust curriculum guided the first production of *Sesame Street*. Continual evolution allows it to continue to be an effective guide.

REFERENCES

Bereiter, C., & Engelmann, S. I. (1966). *Teaching disadvantaged children in preschool*. Englewood Cliffs, NJ: Prentice-Hall.

Bloom, B. S. (1964). *Stability and change in human characteristics*. New York: Wiley.

Cooney, J. G. (1966). *The potential uses of television in preschool education: A report to the Carnegie Corporation*. New York: Children's Television Workshop.

Deutsch, M. (1965). Race and social class as separate factors related to social environment. *American Journal of Sociology, 70*, 474.

Lesser, G. S. (1974). *Children and television: Lessons from Sesame Street*. New York: Vintage Books/Random House.

Szanton, E. S., Szanton, P. L., Pawl, J. H., Barnard, K. E., Greenspan, S. I., Lally, J. R., & Weissbourd, B. (1992). *Heart Start: The emotional foundations of school readiness*. Arlington, VA: Zero to Three, National Center for Clinical Infant Programs.

Tessier, B. (1996). *Sesame Street brand survey results, 1995–1996* (unpublished research report). New York: Children's Television Workshop.

3 Formative Research Revealed: Methodological and Process Issues in Formative Research

Shalom M. Fisch
Lewis Bernstein
Children's Television Workshop

Early in the production of the first season of *Sesame Street*, the production team created a set of five 1-hour test shows. These shows resembled *Sesame Street* as it would later appear on the air, but they were not intended for broadcast. Instead, the shows had been assembled for research purposes, to test the degree to which preschool children found them comprehensible and appealing. If the results had proven negative, the staff was fully prepared to scrap all 5 hours, despite the $230,000 investment that had been required to produce them. However, the results of the test were generally very positive; children showed evidence of learning from the shows, and their appeal was as high as any other television programs that had been tested. These results spurred the team on to create the remainder of the first season of *Sesame Street*.

Still, not everything within the test shows was equally appealing. In particular, children tended to enjoy the animation and Muppet insert segments more than the live-action segments set on the "Street" set. The lower appeal of these "first-draft" Street segments was largely due to the fact that, because advisors had recommended against blending reality and fantasy, Muppets appeared in their own segments but not alongside the humans in the Street segments. The appeal of the human characters on the Street by themselves was simply not as high as the appeal of the Muppets or animation. To boost the appeal of the Street segments, the *Sesame Street* team decided to include Muppets on the Street after all, and to create two new Muppets expressly for that purpose (or, in the words of the producers, "Put the 8-foot canary on the

Street!"). In this way, research findings from the test shows led directly to the creation of two of *Sesame Street*'s most enduring Muppets: Oscar the Grouch and Big Bird (Fisch, 1998; Lesser, 1974).

This anecdote illustrates the power of *formative research*—that is, research conducted to inform the process of production. Despite its impact, the field of formative research is still relatively young. It has been less than 40 years since Cronbach (1963) first argued for the use of empirical research in revising course curricula, and just over 30 years since Scriven (1967) first coined the term *formative evaluation*. Yet, in the years since, formative research has been instrumental in helping to improve the quality of school programs, as well as educational print materials, television series, and interactive software products (e.g., Dow, 1991; Druin, 1999; Flagg, 1990; Higgins & Sullivan, 1990). As prior chapters in this volume show, formative research has also played a key role in the production of *Sesame Street* (Palmer & Fisch, chap. 1, this volume; Truglio, Lovelace, Segui, & Scheiner, chap. 4, this volume).

This chapter focuses on methodological and process issues that are crucial in conducting formative research that is both valid and useful. These issues reach beyond *Sesame Street* to apply to any situation in which formative research is used. Nevertheless, our discussion draws on experiences in *Sesame Street* research, to help lend insight into some of the underlying issues involved.

FORMATIVE VERSUS BASIC RESEARCH

Before proceeding to a discussion of issues, it may be helpful to begin by outlining some of the features that distinguish formative research from basic, academic research. Many of these distinguishing factors were summarized well by Keith Mielke (1983), former Vice President for Research at CTW:

> The major criterion by which in-house formative research is to be judged ... is its actual utility in reaching informed decisions in the design and production of television materials. This utility is indeed affected by methodological factors; issues of internal and external validity are relevant to all data-based research. Perhaps even more important to actual utility, however, are such factors as addressing research questions that feed real production decisions, feeding data and interpretation back in time to actually affect the decision, putting results in a nonjargonized form that is easily comprehended by nonresearchers, and skill in going beyond the data to extract message design implications in discussion with the production staff. (p. 248)

Several important distinctions are embedded within this brief quote. Perhaps the most fundamental distinction lies in the respective purposes of the two types of research. Where the ultimate purpose of basic social science research is typically to expand our understanding of mental or physical processes, the ultimate purpose of formative research is to inform the creation or revision of a product. Thus, for example, although children's interaction with television has been the subject of both basic and formative research, these two types of research have pursued different goals. The ultimate purpose of basic research in this area generally has been to inform our understanding of children's processing of, interactions with, and reactions to television (see Huston & Wright, 1997 for a review). Although such concerns are also important in formative research, they are not the end goal of the research. Rather, the ultimate purpose in this case is to use that information to inform the design of television programs that will be comprehensible, appealing, and age-appropriate for their target audience. In other words, the implications of basic research focus on children; the implications of formative research focus on the television program.

As such, the success of basic research is judged by the degree to which the data inform our understanding of children. The success of formative research, on the other hand, is judged by the degree to which the data inform the production of effective educational materials. Stemming from this fundamental distinction come several further points discussed in the following paragraphs.

Formative Research Is Oriented Toward Practical Purposes or Questions.

Formative research is rarely, if ever, done simply out of the researcher's own interest or curiosity on a particular topic. Rather, formative research speaks to concrete questions that are essential to informing specific production decisions (what Stufflebeam & Webster [1980], among others, termed *decision-oriented research*). These questions include such diverse issues as: Is a particular segment comprehensible and appealing to its target audience? Where on the screen should text be placed to catch viewers' attention and encourage reading as they watch? Which of several potential character designs (i.e., alternate approaches to the visual appearance of a proposed character) will be most appealing to children? What do children already know about a particular topic and where do their misconceptions lie, so that subsequent scripts can address these misconceptions directly?

Formative Research Must Be Done Quickly.

Because the purpose of formative research is to inform production decisions, the data must be available by the time those decisions are made, or they will be useless. As a result, the schedule for conducting formative research must fit into the larger production schedule. Unlike basic research, in which a single study may be conducted over a period of months, formative researchers typically have a turnaround time of no more than 1 or 2 weeks for a study, from the posing of the initial question to the reporting of the data. Indeed, in our experience, it is unusual but not unprecedented to have to meet a turnaround time of only 24 hours when a last-minute question arises unexpectedly.

Formative Research Must Be Generalizable.

Because of the speed with which it is typically conducted, formative research occasionally has been called *quick and dirty* research (although the term is only sometimes intended to be disparaging). However, this term is actually a misnomer; formative research may be "quick," but it cannot be "dirty" if it is to be useful. Formative data must be clean enough to be generalizable beyond the sample tested to the larger target audience. Otherwise, the data are likely to mislead producers into decisions that will hurt, rather than help, the material being developed. Indeed, data collected for other CTW television series have shown that formative data, when collected and analyzed with appropriate care and controls, can be highly consistent across geographically and demographically different samples, and over a gap of as much as 3 years between studies (*Big Bag*, New Mexico Research, 1995; Fisch, McCann, Body, & Cohen, 1993).

In addition to being generalizable across children, formative data must also be generalizable beyond the material tested to help inform decisions about other, untested material. For example, formative research on early *Sesame Street* segments identified features that helped to draw children's attention to these segments, such as the use of children's voices or physical humor (as opposed to puns). Clearly, such findings were helpful, not only in providing a greater understanding of the particular segments that had been tested, but also in developing guidelines for judging the likely appeal of future segments—and in identifying appealing elements that could be built into these future segments.

Generalizability to other material is achieved, not only through care in methodology and analysis, but also through a careful selection of material to test. We return to this point in the "What and When to Test" section on the next page.

Formative Research Is Conducted for an Audience of Nonresearchers.

Where basic research is generally conducted for an audience of other researchers, via journals, books, and conferences, the primary audience for formative research data consists of nonresearchers: producers, writers, animators, puppeteers, and others with little or no technical background in research. Moreover, this audience must find the research to be credible and convincing if it is to inform their decisions (particularly if the data conflict with the producers' own instincts). Thus, formative research must be seen as relevant, reported clearly for a lay audience, and presented in a way that is persuasive and carries concrete implications for production. In many ways, this is one of the most difficult aspects of formative research to master. It is discussed in greater detail in the "Process Issues" section later in this chapter.

Taken together, the features that characterize formative research—its focus on practical issues, the need for clean, generalizable data in a timely fashion, and the nature of the audience for the research—raise two broad classes of issues. One class is *methodological issues* that pertain to the conduct of the research itself. The second is *process issues* that pertain to the effective use of data in informing and influencing production decisions. We consider each class of issues in turn.

METHODOLOGICAL ISSUES

There is no one "best" method for conducting formative research. Rather, the best methods for any given study depend on the purpose of the study. Clearly, the kinds of methods appropriate for testing comprehension of a segment are different from the methods that are best suited to testing appeal of visual designs for a new character, and the best methods for assessing children's prior knowledge of a topic are different from methods for testing participation during viewing.

Nevertheless, numerous broad methodological issues are relevant across these various types of methods. This discussion focuses on several such issues: decisions about what and when to test (and when to allocate resources elsewhere), the use of behavioral versus verbal measures in conducting formative research with young children, and the use of individual versus group data.

What and When to Test

Particularly when dealing with a magazine-format television series like *Sesame Street*, where every episode consists of several dozen segments, it is impossible (barring unlimited resources) to conduct a study to test every aspect of every segment, or to collect empirical data to answer every question that arises throughout production. Fortunately, however, it is not necessary to do so, either. As noted above, the results of one study can—and typically do—hold implications beyond the specific material being tested, and those implications can be helpful in approaching other material that is produced subsequently. As Tina Peel, former Vice President of Production Research at CTW, once said, "the ultimate purpose of formative research is to inform our own instincts," (personal communication) so that the lessons learned from testing one set of materials can also inform recommendations made about others in the future.

One of the most basic questions in conducting formative research, then, is how to allocate resources: when to conduct studies in the first place, and which material to test. Cronbach and his colleagues (1983) have suggested that such choices depend on four factors: (a) prior uncertainty about a question, (b) anticipated information yield, (c) leverage of the information on subsequent thinking and action, and (d) costs of information (cf. the standards proposed by the Joint Committee on Standards for Educational Evaluation, 1981). These considerations can be operationalized as several basic questions:

- Are the relevant answers obvious from existing data on past material?
- How prominent will the material be within the series?
- Does the material pertain to a primary educational goal?
- Is there likely to be disagreement?
- Is change possible?
- Is it practical?

We consider each of these questions in turn.

Are the Relevant Answers Obvious From Existing Data on Past Material?

If the researchers' experience has already provided them with a basis for providing the necessary answers or recommendations (and if those answers are likely not to be controversial), there is no need to conduct a study that will merely rediscover the same answers. For example, a major formative study was conducted in 1995 to assess the appeal of most of the major *Sesame Street* Muppets (*Sesame Street* Research, 1995). These data were used, not only immediately, but also over the course of the next few years; because extensive information about the characters' appeal was already available, there was no need to conduct further studies that would simply replicate the earlier data.

However, that situation changed in 1998, when researchers decided to test character appeal once again (*Sesame Street* Research, 1998a). The *Sesame Street* team could no longer simply rely on the earlier data, because questions had arisen as to the appeal of Muppet and human characters who were not covered in the earlier study. Because the issues of interest had not been investigated in earlier research, a new study was justified—and, indeed, essential.

How Prominent Will the Material Be Within the Series?

If a new character will appear throughout the series, then it may be important to conduct research to inform the development of that character. For example, when producers planned the creation of Zoe, the first primary female monster character on *Sesame Street*, researchers tested drawings of proposed designs for the character, with a focus on issues ranging from the best color for her fur to physical characteristics that would help children recognize Zoe as a girl (e.g., barrettes, a necklace; *Sesame Street* Research, 1990). Such research is rarely used for a character who will appear sporadically or only in a single segment.

Similarly, it is more important to test segments if they are part of a series that will appear throughout the season; indeed, it may be necessary to test several of these segments with the same children to ensure that appeal holds over repeated viewing. Consider, for example, the role of formative research in a major reformatting of *Sesame Street* for its 30th season. During the preproduction phase of Season 30, the *Sesame Street* team revisited the structure and content of *Sesame Street* on a broader scale than had ever been attempted before. The production team came together for an intensive, 2-week series of all-day meetings, with researchers serving an integral role in the process. Together, the group dissected virtually every aspect of *Sesame Street*, considered children's viewing habits and program preferences, and reviewed research data on children's and parents' reactions to *Sesame Street*.

One of the most prominent changes in the series stemmed from a consideration of three factors. The first was data from research with children and parents that indicated that, although the original target age group for *Sesame Street* had been 3- to 5-year-old children, children at home actually begin viewing the series when they are much younger (Tessier, 1996). The second was the shifting pattern of children's television viewing. Although the magazine format of *Sesame Street* originally grew out of children's attraction to commercials and fast-paced magazine format television series such as *Laugh-In* (Lesser, 1974), the widespread use of videocassette recorders in recent years has led to young children's becoming accustomed to watching longer narrative-based material on television—indeed, even 90-minute movies in some cases. A third factor was a recurring finding in recent formative research: Preschoolers' attention to *Sesame Street* tended to decline somewhat between 40 and 45 minutes into the hour-long program. In response to these considerations, it was decided that the target age for *Sesame Street* would shift from 4 to 3 years old, and that a portion of each episode would be targeted specifically to the developmental level of the younger children in the audience. Like the rest of *Sesame Street*, this portion of the show would feature a variety of elements (animation, Muppets, music, live-action film), but it would sustain a more uninterrupted narrative thread than the rest of the show.

And so was created "Elmo's World," a recurring segment, hosted by Elmo, that now occupies approximately 15 minutes at the end of every episode of *Sesame Street*. Each segment focuses on a child-centered topic (e.g., balls, shoes, dancing) from the point of view of a 3-year-old child, and is designed to foster exploration, imagination, and curiosity.

Because it was intended to occupy a significant portion of every episode of *Sesame Street*, considerable resources were committed to conducting formative research in support of "Elmo's World." Apart from several studies conducted to inform the meetings that led to the creation of "Elmo's World," all 10 episodes of "Elmo's World" were tested for appeal and comprehensibility among preschoolers. The first of these studies assessed reactions to the first "Elmo's World" segment that was produced at a stage when the bulk of the segments had been scripted but not yet produced (*Sesame Street* Research, 1998b). Indeed, the shooting schedule was specifically tailored to allow time for data on the first segment to be collected before the majority of segments were shot, so that changes in the remaining segments could still be made if necessary. Subsequent studies examined children's reactions to additional "Elmo's World" segments (*Sesame Street* Research, 1998c, 1998d) and the degree to which appeal was sustained over repeated viewing by the same children (*Sesame Street* Research, 1998e, 1999).

Together, the data from these studies pointed to the high appeal of "Elmo's World" across sex, age, and socioeconomic status, and its continuing appeal over repeated viewing. Attention was high throughout the segments, and many children participated while viewing (e.g., by clapping, moving to music, or counting along with characters); this participation increased with repeated viewing. The appeal of "Elmo's World" was sufficiently strong, in fact, that the production team decided to continue the format in Season 31.

If "Elmo's World" had been intended to appear only once, or only occasionally within the series, the effort and resources required to conduct this program of research would not have been called for. Given the major change this represented in the series as a whole, however, the research was not only called for but necessary.

Does the Material Pertain to a Primary Educational Goal?   As Lesser and Schneider (chap. 2, this volume) have discussed, each season of *Sesame Street* centers around a specific curriculum focus. Because of the additional attention devoted to material that addresses this focus, it is often important to devote research resources to such material as well. For example, because the curriculum focus in Season 29 was "The Science of Discovery," formative research was used before production to assess children's prior knowledge about topics within science and after production to assess the appeal and comprehensibility of material that had been produced (as discussed in greater detail by Truglio et al., chap. 4, this volume).

Is There Likely to be Disagreement?   Even if past research has been sufficiently definitive to allow researchers to feel absolutely certain about recommendations for a new piece of material, that does not guarantee that those recommendations will be taken. If producers and researchers are in agreement, then there may not be the need for an additional study. However, if producers are likely to disagree from a creative perspective, then empirical data from a new study may be more convincing than the researchers' opinions, no matter how well-grounded those opinions might be.

Is Change Possible?   Conversely, if there is little likelihood of change—either because there is no room for change in the production schedule, or because producers feel so strongly about a particular decision that they are unlikely to be swayed by data—then research resources are probably better allocated elsewhere (cf. Flagg, 1990, p. 139).

Is It Practical?   Finally, formative researchers must consider the demands of a study that would provide empirical answers to the issues at hand: What will the study cost in terms of time, effort, and money? Is that the best use of resources, or are there other, more pressing issues that need to be addressed instead? It is common for the research plan for a season of a television series to change dramatically over the course of the season, as production concerns give rise to unexpected questions that overshadow some of the issues that were originally planned to be addressed.

In the end, the choice of what and when to test is always one of prioritization. Almost every issue that arises during production can be addressed through formative research. However, it is rare for formative researchers to have the resources available to test every one—and, in fact, it is not necessary. The central question, then, is not whether a given question *can* be answered through formative research, but whether it *should*.

Behavioral Versus Verbal Data

A key methodological issue, not only in formative research but in any developmental research is the choice between behavioral (e.g., observations, hands-on tasks) and verbal (e.g., interview) measures. To some degree, of course, the choice among methods depends on the issues being investigated; some types of issues naturally lend themselves to particular kinds of measures. In many cases, however, there are both behavioral and verbal measures that might be appropriate. In these cases, researchers must consider the relative strengths and weaknesses of the various methodological choices, as they relate to both the validity of the data and their usefulness in informing production decisions.

Strengths of Behavioral Data. Some of the strengths of behavioral measures over verbal measures are the following:

- Assuming a well-crafted coding scheme, behavioral measures provide data that can be coded more easily and objectively than qualitative verbal data. Such data can be compared easily across studies, and are reliable across samples of children. In fact, this reliability may also extend across demographically different samples of children as well; the lack of reliance on verbal responses also means that behavioral measures may be less susceptible to the kinds of unintended cultural biases that have long been concerns for educational assessment in general (e.g., Eells, 1953).
- When conducting research with young children, behavioral measures are less likely than verbal measures to be affected by shyness or poor articulation, a notion akin to the *competence-performance distinction* discussed in literature on language development (e.g., Dale, 1976; deVilliers & deVilliers, 1978)—that is, the idea that children may be capable of more than they are able to articulate. For shy children dealing with an unfamiliar adult researcher, or for children whose language skills are poor, verbal measures may not accurately reflect their comprehension or opinions. In such cases, observations of naturalistic behavior during viewing or physical tasks that allow children to demonstrate their comprehension or reactions (e.g., pointing to a photo of the character they like best) may reflect their true feelings or abilities better than verbal measures would.
- Behavioral observations during viewing provide for on-line measurement of appeal and viewer participation as the children watch material on television. By contrast, verbal measures typically must be employed after viewing, so verbal measures of children's reactions to a particular segment may be subject to confusion with other segments viewed.

Strengths of Verbal Measures.   Conversely, verbal measures provide a different set of strengths:

- Perhaps most important, whereas behavioral measures provide determinations of *how* appealing some given material might be, verbal measures allow children to express the reasons *why*. These reasons are often invaluable in suggesting direction for improvement of materials, and for the creation of other materials in the future.
- In many ways, verbal measures can be more flexible than behavioral measures, allowing researchers to probe responses via alternate or follow-up questions until they feel they understand those responses sufficiently. This type of flexibility is less available in behavioral data (unless, of course, a behavioral measure is followed by verbal probes).
- Often, verbal measures also lend themselves more directly to assessments of comprehension. For example, an elaborate sorting task might be necessary to assess comprehension of a particular segment, where a small number of verbal questions might yield an equally valid assessment.

In general, it is probably self-evident that the best choice is not either behavioral or verbal measures, but rather, a combination of the two. When used together, the respective strengths of these different methods can complement each other and yield a richer picture of children's knowledge, reactions, and responses than either can alone.

When formative research for *Sesame Street* began, behaviorism was a very prominent movement within psychology (e.g., Skinner, 1971). In light of behaviorism's emphasis on observable behavior over intangible mental processes, it is not surprising that the methods used in early research were primarily behavioral. The most prominent of these methods was the *distractor method*, developed by Edward Palmer (Palmer & Fisch, chap. 1, this volume; cf. Lesser, 1974), in which children were seated before one screen that showed material from *Sesame Street* and a second screen that simultaneously showed unrelated slides, as researchers continuously noted the screen to which children attended.

As time went on, and dominant philosophies—as well as production needs—shifted, verbal measures began to be introduced alongside behavioral measures. At the same time, the behavioral measures themselves were continually refined. Even the distractor method itself was later modified; for example, under the research team headed by Valeria Lovelace, the technique evolved into an *eyes-on-screen* method that allowed data to be collected from entire groups of children simultaneously and replaced distractor slides with the distractions that were provided naturally by the other children viewing. In this method, groups of 15 children sat in three rows in front of a television; researchers observed the children at 5-second intervals (cued by beeps through a headset) to note their visual attention to the television, as well as any relevant behaviors or verbal comments. More recently, the method has evolved into an *engagement measure* that takes into account, not only visual attention but also other behaviors that indicate engagement by individual children (e.g., laughing, moving in time to music). Each successive method was built on the knowledge gained from experience with its predecessor, and each new approach helped the methods respond to the needs of the time.

Individual Versus Group Data

Concurrent with the choice between behavioral and verbal measures is the choice of collecting data from children either individually or in groups. Within formative research for television, this choice often holds implications for two aspects of data collection: whether to have children view material alone or in groups (particularly if observational data are being collected to assess children's reactions during viewing), and whether to administer subsequent postviewing measures to children individually or in small groups (typically groups of no more than two or three children apiece). As in the preceding discussion about behavioral and verbal data, the choice between individual and group data necessarily involves weighing the relative strengths and weaknesses of each.

Strengths of Individual Data. Probably the greatest strengths of individual data lie in the reduction of noise in the data:

- Within the realm of research on children's use of television, one might assume individual data to hold greater *ecological external validity* than group data (cf. Smith & Glass, 1987). In other words, because home viewing typically is not characterized by large groups of same-age peers watching together, data from children watching television individually (even if not in their homes) might represent home viewing better than group viewing would. (In fact, however, research has shown this assumption to be reasonable but not completely true, as will be discussed below.)
- Researchers can be certain that reactions observed among children who view individually are purely their own, and not influenced by other children who are viewing at the same time. By contrast, in group viewing, one child's participation while viewing (e.g., spontaneously singing along with a televised song) may encourage others to join in, and one child's distraction may lead others to pay less attention to the screen as well.
- Similarly, in measures administered after viewing, researchers can be certain that responses obtained from children individually reflect their own ideas, and have not been influenced by other children who may have responded first.

Strengths of Group Data. On the other hand, the strengths of group data pertain more to the potential richness of the data set and practical considerations:

- Being in a small group with other children (particularly friends) can make children feel more comfortable. Because young children who are confronted with an unfamiliar adult researcher can grow shy and be reluctant to answer questions, the presence of other children can sometimes increase comfort and help children to produce more elaborate responses.
- On a practical level, group data (both during viewing and in subsequent measures) can be collected far more quickly than individual data. As a result, data collection for a given sample size can be completed in less time and/or with fewer researchers if group data are used. Given the time constraints under which formative research operates and the limited resources that are typically available, this can be an important consideration.
- Although group data are often noisier than individual data, various procedural techniques can help to minimize this additional noise; for example, children can be discouraged from mimicking neighbors' answers by starting with a different child in the group for every question or asking children to state responses in their own words. Most important, it is generally not very difficult for an experienced researcher, after sitting with the group, to have a sense of which responses are genuine and which are not. Such considerations are taken into account during data collection (e.g., in shaping interview probes), weighing individual responses in data analysis, and in interpreting the data and drawing conclusions.

For *Sesame Street*, the choice between individual and group data has shifted more than once through the years, depending on the needs of the time, the personal philosophies of the researchers involved, and the cumulative experience that was built up at each point (cf. Bernstein, 1977). At first, data were almost always collected individually, for the reasons described previously. Through the years, however, the practical constraints under which researchers worked led them to experiment with group viewing of *Sesame Street*. The concern, of course, was that the additional noise in the data would distort the trends and provide inaccurate results. However, this proved not to be the case; a study commissioned from Daniel Anderson and his colleagues, comparing data collected from children who viewed *Sesame Street* individually and in groups, showed great consistency between the two conditions (Anderson, Lorch, Smith, Bradford, & Levin, 1981). As a result, group viewing became the norm. In fact, our own experience suggests that group viewing produces comparable but more pronounced—and thus, more easily detectable—trends than individual viewing. Because one child's engagement can encourage others', successful material can emerge as *very* successful. Conversely, because distractions can also be contagious, unsuccessful material can seem *very* unsuccessful.

By contrast, postviewing measures for *Sesame Street* have almost always been administered to children individually, to minimize noise in the data. In recent years, then, the trend in *Sesame Street* research has been toward group viewing and individual postviewing interviews.

PROCESS ISSUES

As noted at the beginning of this chapter, the ultimate standard by which formative research is judged lies, not in the actual testing itself, but in the degree to which the data are useful and effective in informing production (e.g., Mielke, 1983). Thus, although methodological issues are important, they are only half the story. The other—and in many ways, more challenging—half lies in the relationship between researchers and production staff and in the ways in which researchers use formative research to influence production decisions. These interpersonal communication issues are critical if formative research is to succeed. However, as other researchers have observed, scholarly works on formative research tend to focus almost entirely on methods and neglect the process by which findings are communicated and revisions are made (Briggs & Wager, 1981; Weston, McAlpine, & Bordonaro, 1995).

The present discussion focuses on four aspects of the relationship between formative research and production: the multifaceted role played by formative researchers; the importance of producers' personal investment in any research that is conducted; the necessity of clear communication and interpretation of data when dealing with an audience of nonresearchers; and the need for all parties to approach the relationship with tact and mutual respect.

To frame this discussion, it should be made clear that our focus is on in-house formative researchers, as opposed to outside research consultants who might be hired to evaluate draft or final materials without prior (or subsequent) involvement in the production process. In fact, whereas some researchers, such as Cronbach (1963; Cronbach et al., 1980), have argued for the value of ongoing involvement by in-house researchers, others, such as Scriven (e.g., 1967, 1993), have argued that, for the sake of objectivity, researchers should be as removed from the project as possible—to the degree of not even knowing its goals. Yet, as Stufflebeam (1983) observed, this apparent debate is not a true disagreement at all, because Cronbach's and Scriven's positions were actually formulated in relation to two different types of research; Cronbach's points referred to the types of production-oriented formative research discussed in this paper, but Scriven focused on educational policy research (which we consider to be closer to summative research than the kind of formative research used to inform the production of *Sesame Street*).[1] Thus, although a vast range of possible relationships might exist among producers and researchers—from the extreme of researchers' and producers' having virtually no contact with each other to the opposite extreme of producers' and researchers' actually being the same people—the present discussion focuses

---

[1]We are indebted to Ed Palmer for first bringing this point to our attention.

on the relationship described by the CTW Model, where producers and researchers work hand-in-hand at all stages of production (Mielke, 1990; Truglio & Fisch, Introduction, this volume).

Role of Formative Researchers

In some ways, the relationship between producers and researchers seems almost primed to be adversarial. Even David Connell, the first Executive Producer for *Sesame Street*, recalled his own initial fears at the beginning of the series:

> My background was in commercial television, where we felt we had developed a pretty good sense of instincts about what kind of show would appeal to children at any given age. I frankly was skeptical about the idea of researching every moment of a television show, and certainly of being told how to design it. There was the risk of intellectualizing the material to death and ending up with a program most notable for its monumental boredom. It would be like trying to analyze the elements of a joke, only to find that when we had isolated all the pieces, there was nothing learned and nothing to laugh about. ... I kept thinking of the biologists who cross-bred a crocodile with an abalone in hopes of getting an abadile. Only something went wrong and they ended up with a [crock a' b'loney]. (Connell & Palmer, 1971, p. 67)

Additionally, creative people naturally have a certain personal interest in material that springs forth from their imaginations. Thus, when the news is good, it is easy for a researcher to tell producers that viewers love the material. However, when a researcher informs the production staff that viewers disliked something they created and suggests revisions, the researcher is in a position analogous to telling parents that their baby is ugly, but could be made more attractive with a few improvements.

Still, although the danger of lapsing into an adversarial relationship does exist, a well-handled relationship is far from combative. Instead, the relationship becomes truly collaborative, with each side contributing its own unique perspective and expertise, and the result is a whole that is greater than either could have created alone. In the case of *Sesame Street*, the production team began to recognize at an early stage the value in having access to researchers who could gather actual reactions from children to inform production decisions, rather than having to rely on subjective "best guesses" (Palmer & Fisch, chap. 1, this volume). As CTW's founder, Joan Ganz Cooney, described it,

> ... *we are talking about a marriage*—not researchers to work as consultants to producers... We were by then talking about a product that would come out of a marriage—living together, dealing together, drinking together, eating together until they all would absolutely understand what the product looked like. (Quoted in Land, 1972, p. 34)

To be productive, the relationship between production and research must be approached as a team effort, united in the mutual desire to create materials that will be as appealing and beneficial for children as possible.

Researchers play a multifaceted role in this process, not only collecting and analyzing data, but also serving as advocates for children and bringing the voice of the child into the production process. Outside of empirical formative research itself, one of the key elements that researchers bring to the process is their expertise regarding children. Through their training and their ongoing contact with children, researchers are uniquely positioned to review scripts and predict children's reactions: the degree to which children are likely to understand the material, where difficulties or misconceptions may lie, potential effects of inadvertent negative modeling, and the likely appeal of the material. More important, researchers must be able to contribute suggestions for ways to improve any potential difficulties through changes in dialogue, visuals, or stories (although the final choice as to whether to make changes, along with decisions about the exact wording or execution of any changes, rightfully rests with the production team). For example, in the anecdote that opened this chapter, it was researchers who suggested the inclusion of Muppets in live-action Street scenes, but it was production people who created the specific characters of Big Bird and Oscar the Grouch.

Yet, although researchers may thus be inclined to approach a relationship with production from the standpoint that "we know children," they also must recognize that an experienced production team is likely to know children too, albeit from a different perspective. Any production team with experience in producing material for children comes with its own set of instincts about what works for children and what doesn't; after all, without such instincts, the team could not have achieved any past success. These instincts often may be correct and should always be respected. At the same time, however, it is the responsibility of researchers, as the true child experts, to supplement those instincts, correct misconceptions, and point to issues that the production team may not have recognized on its own.

The Importance of "Buy-In"

As Cronbach and Associates (1983) observed, "Nothing makes a larger difference in evaluation than the personal factor—the interest of the officials in learning from the evaluation and the interest of the evaluator in getting attention for what he knows" (p. 49). Formative researchers can run themselves ragged collecting and analyzing data for a particular study, but if the production team is not invested in the study (even if the team believes in research more generally), the data are likely to have little impact. After all, if producers feel that the issues addressed by the study are themselves of little importance, there is little reason for them to make costly changes in response to those issues. Thus, it is vital for researchers to make sure that the production team has bought into the importance of each study, even before the study is run. If they have not, then there may be little reason to expend the effort and expense to conduct the study in the first place.

Buy-in is easiest to obtain when a study is conducted to answer a question that has been raised by the production team itself. In such a situation, the producers and writers have a natural interest in and curiosity about data that speak to their own questions, and are likely to pay attention to them. For example, when the *Sesame Street* production team decided to send Oscar's pet worm, Slimey, to the moon in Season 30, they recognized that they needed to know just how much preschool children already understood about space and how much would need to be explained. In response, researchers conducted a study to assess young children's knowledge of space (*Sesame Street* Research, 1997) and the production team used these data as a foundation on which to build their scripts (Truglio et al., chap. 4, this volume).

At other times, however, researchers may identify issues that have not occurred to the production team, and decide that a study is needed to provide further insight. In this case, it is the researchers' responsibility to help the production team understand the importance of the issues being tested, even before the study is under way. Obtaining buy-in in this situation may be as simple as bringing the relevant issues to the attention of the production team; in many cases, the importance of the issues speaks for itself once the issues have been made salient. For example, when researchers recently suggested the importance of conducting a study to determine the best way to cluster segments to maximize children's comprehension of the Letter of the Day, producers quickly recognized the potential value of the suggestion—and, indeed, the data from this study have informed changes in the way segments are organized within each episode of *Sesame Street* (*Sesame Street* Research & Applied Research and Consulting, 1998; Truglio et al., chap. 4, this volume). In other cases, the team may require some convincing to recognize the issues as important, and in some cases, they may never be convinced.

Once buy-in has been obtained and the decision has been made to move ahead with a study, researchers must also think in terms of the production team as they select and design measures for the study. It is rare that there is only one method that can shed light on a given issue, and as we have discussed earlier, many of the considerations that feed into a choice pertain to issues of validity and utility. However, human factors play a role here as well. In particular, individual producers may simply consider some types of data to be more credible or convincing than others, due to their own personal inclinations. For example, at various points through the years, some *Sesame Street* producers have been more inclined toward quantitative data such as attention data as measures of appeal, whereas at other times, other producers have tended to be swayed more by interview responses or qualitative descriptions of behavior during viewing. Thus, in situations where different types of data are likely to yield equivalently valid indications of children's reactions, researchers must also consider which type of data (or which combination of types of data) will be most convincing to producers in informing production decisions.

Presenting Research for an Audience of Nonresearchers

Once a study has been conducted, the effectiveness of the data in informing production depends greatly on the clarity with which those data are presented. Production people typically do not have training as researchers, and cannot be expected to wade through mountains of statistics and research jargon to intuit implications from data. Rather, it is the responsibility of the researchers to digest that information and translate it into a form that will be useful for the production team. Several key considerations are crucial to this process:

- *Keeping it short.* As a rule, everyone involved in production (producer and researcher alike) is inevitably struggling to stay on schedule and is always pressed for time. Short reports are more likely to be read than long ones, and short presentations are more likely to hold the team's interest. If the data cannot be captured adequately in short form, then an executive summary and/or highlights presentation can be extremely useful for those who do not have the time or inclination to peruse the entire report.
- *Avoiding jargon and statistics.* Because production teams typically are not schooled in the social sciences, discussions that rely on unfamiliar terms or heavy uses of statistics are liable to obscure, rather than enhance, meaning (cf. Stalford, 1985). Although inferential statistics may be essential in ensuring a valid analysis of the data, it is not necessary for the statistics themselves to be reported to the producers; for example, it is important for a production team to know that boys liked a particular segment more than girls did, but not that the statistic used to check the difference for significance was a t test.
- *Sticking to what the production team needs to know.* The focus of any report or discussion should be on those aspects of the data that hold concrete implications for production. Data that do not hold implications—no matter how inherently interesting they may be to the researchers themselves—should be mentioned only in passing or, better yet, omitted entirely.
- *Translating data into concrete implications for production.* Where data hold implications for production, those implications should be spelled out explicitly as concrete recommendations. Results should be laid out clearly, to allow producers the opportunity to draw their own conclusions. However, the production team should not be required to untangle all of the implications of a complex data set by themselves. Thus, for example, if data show that children fail to recognize that key words in a segment (e.g., *zebra, zoo, zipper*) all start with the letter Z, researchers might recommend showing each word as on-screen print with the Z in each word highlighted. The production team can then choose to follow the recommendation or use different means to address the issue.

- *Prioritizing implications and recommendations.* Inevitably, some recommendations that emerge from a study will be more important than others. The most important recommendations should be highlighted for the production team, so that they can focus their energies in those directions. In general, a short list of high-priority recommendations is likely to be more effective than a lengthy list of recommendations that have not been prioritized.

Interpreting Data

As in most social science research, researchers craft implications by interpreting the data at hand, synthesizing the data with their knowledge of data from past studies, and extending beyond the data to draw conclusions and pose recommendations. For example, in the hypothetical letter Z example previously mentioned, the data may show that after viewing the relevant segment, only a certain percentage of children recognize that the words *zebra*, *zoo*, and *zipper* all begin with Z; this is the stage of interpreting the data at hand. The finding becomes more meaningful when researchers compare that percentage to past testing and find that the current percentage is lower than that obtained after viewing other letter-based segments. Recognizing a weakness in the current segment, then, researchers must then consider features of the more successful segments that are lacking here; if other segments have used on-screen print but this one has not, then such an addition might be useful.

As carefully as all of this interpretation is handled, however, the researchers must nevertheless remain aware of the fact that it is only their own interpretation and inference. Someone else might interpret the same data differently, or attribute trends to other causes, which can lead to different recommendations for changes. Competing interpretations can arise from within the research team itself, or they may come from producers. In either case, competing interpretations must be considered carefully. Some may not, in fact, be valid; for example, it is not uncommon for a single child's response to strike a chord in a producer's head, even if most of the children in the sample actually responded differently. However, some competing interpretations may actually explain the data better than the interpretation proposed by the researchers themselves. If the goal is the best possible solution to improving the materials under consideration, it is vitally important that researchers remain open to all ideas and interpretations, no matter where they come from.

Mutual Respect

Following from the above point comes the more general principle that, like all human relationships, the relationship among producers and researchers must be handled with sensitivity, tact, and mutual respect. If either side comes to the relationship with the attitude that they are always right, then the relationship cannot function productively.

Thus, when researchers have ideas or suggestions to bring to the table, they must work to inform the production team, but they must do so tactfully. If researchers demand changes in materials, those changes are not likely to be made. But if researchers explain their issues and work with the production team to find solutions, they are far more likely to be effective.

At the same time, no one will always be successful in getting changes made—and rightly so, because no one is always correct. If researchers approach every issue with the same level of zeal, regardless of whether the issues are major or minor, then they can quickly lose their credibility. Instead, researchers must prioritize their issues and know when to let go; conceding on a minor issue today can preserve the credibility needed to impact on a major issue tomorrow.

Conversely, when producers bring questions to the research team, researchers must be prepared to respond promptly, but they also must feel comfortable in saying, "I don't know" when appropriate. Far from showing a deficit in the researchers' expertise, such admissions can help maintain their credibility. However, the admission also must be followed quickly by efforts to do whatever is needed (e.g., conduct a study, consult with colleagues or past literature) to provide an answer that is both accurate and timely.

Finally, all of these points lead to a single common thread: The relationship between production and research must be approached from the standpoint that all of the players are on the same team, and that it is not a case of "us versus them." The ultimate goal is not to be right; it is to produce the best product possible. Such a goal can only be reached by all of the parties involved working hand-in-hand.

CONCLUSION

At its best, formative research becomes a seamless part of the production process, and researchers become as natural a part of the team as any of the production staff. As Joan Ganz Cooney observed nearly 30 years ago, the relationship between production and research on *Sesame Street* is a marriage. Like any marriage, the relationship requires a great deal of work and commitment from all of the parties involved. For formative researchers, this means not only conducting research that is useful, timely, and valid, but also working with the production team to ensure that the data will be effective in meeting the needs of production and informing critical decisions. If these criteria are met, and if researchers join with producers in an air of shared mission and mutual respect, then experience with *Sesame Street* shows that the results can be both fruitful and long-lasting.

REFERENCES

Anderson, D. R., Lorch, E. P., Smith, R., Bradford, R., & Levin, S. (1981). Effects of peer presence on preschool children's television viewing. *Developmental Psychology, 17,* 446–453.

Bernstein, L. (1977). *Measuring the appeal of children's television: A review of research methods and findings* (unpublished research report). New York: Children's Television Workshop.

Big Bag New Mexico Research. (1995). *Acquired materials: New Mexico study* (unpublished research report). New York: Children's Television Workshop.

Briggs, L. J., & Wager, W. W. (1981). *Handbook of procedures for the design of instruction* (2nd ed.). Englewood Cliffs, NJ: Educational Technologies Publications.

Connell, D. D., & Palmer, E. L. (1971). *Sesame Street*: A case study. In J. D. Halloran & M. Gurevitch (Eds.), *Broadcaster/researcher cooperation in mass communication research.* Leeds, England: Kavanagh & Sons.

Cronbach, L. J. (1963). Course improvement through evaluation. *Teachers College Record, 64,* 672–683.

Cronbach, L. J., Ambron, S. R., Dornbusch, S. M., Hess, R. D., Hornik, R. C., Philips, D. C., Walker, D. F., & Weiner, S. S. (1980). *Toward reform of program evaluation: Aims, methods, and institutional arrangements.* San Francisco: Jossey-Bass.

Cronbach, L. J., & Associates. (1983). Ninety-five theses for reforming program evaluation. In G. F. Madaus, M. Scriven, & D. L. Stufflebeam (Eds.), *Evaluation models: Viewpoints on educational and human services evaluation.* Boston: Kluwer-Nijhoff Publishing.

Dale, P. S. (1976). *Language development: Structure and function* (2nd ed.). New York: Holt, Rinehart & Winston.

deVilliers, J. G., & deVilliers, P. A. (1978). *Language acquisition.* Cambridge, MA: Harvard University Press.

Dow, P. B. (1991). *Schoolhouse politics: Lessons from the Sputnik era.* Cambridge, MA: Harvard University Press.

Druin, A. (Ed.). (1999). *The design of children's technology.* San Francisco, CA: Morgan Kaufman.

Eells, K. (1953). Some implications for school practice of the Chicago studies of cultural bias in intelligence tests. *Harvard Educational Review, 23,* 284–297.

Fisch, S. M. (1998). The Children's Television Workshop: The experiment continues. In R. G. Noll & M. E. Price (Eds.), *A communications cornucopia: Markle Foundation essays on information policy* (pp. 297–337). Washington, DC: Brookings Institution Press.

Fisch, S. M., McCann, S. K., Body, K. E., & Cohen, D. I. (1993, April). Can formative research achieve reliability? In L. Martin & S. M. Fisch (Chairs), *Meeting the challenges of formative research: Lessons from the Children's Television Workshop.* Symposium conducted at the annual meeting of the American Educational Research Association, Atlanta, GA.

Flagg, B. N. (Ed.). (1990). *Formative evaluation for educational technology.* Hillsdale, NJ: Lawrence Erlbaum Associates.

Higgins, N., & Sullivan, H. (Eds.). (1990). Children's learning from television: Research and development at the Children's Television Workshop [Special issue]. *Educational Technology Research and Development, 38*(4).

Huston, A. C., & Wright, J. C. (1997). Mass media and children's development. In W. Damon, I. Sigel, & A. Rennings (Eds.), *Handbook of child psychology* (Vol. 4). New York: Wiley.

Joint Committee on Standards for Educational Evaluation. (1981). *Standards for evaluation of educational programs, projects, and materials.* New York: McGraw Hill.

Land, H. W. (1972). *The Children's Television Workshop: How and why it works.* Jericho, NY: Nassau Board of Cooperative Educational Services.

Lesser, G. S. (1974). *Children and television: Lessons from Sesame Street.* New York: Vintage Books/Random House.

Mielke, K. W. (1983). The educational use of production variables and formative research in programming. In M. Meyer (Ed.), *Children and the formal features of television.* Munchen, Germany: Saur.

Mielke, K. W. (1990). Research and development at the Children's Television Workshop. *Educational Technology Research and Development, 38*(4), 7–16.

Scriven, M. (1967). The methodology of evaluation. In R. Tyler, R. Gagné, & M. Scriven (Eds.), *Perspectives of curriculum evaluation* (pp. 39–83). Chicago: Rand McNally.

Scriven, M. (1993). Hard-won lessons in program evaluation. *New Directions for Program Evaluation, 58,* 1–101.

Sesame Street Research. (1990). *Sesame Street females: The facts* (unpublished research report). New York: Children's Television Workshop.

Sesame Street Research. (1995). *The Muppet study, 1995* (unpublished research report). New York: Children's Television Workshop.

Sesame Street Research. (1997). *What do preschoolers know about space?* (unpublished research report). New York: Children's Television Workshop.

Sesame Street Research. (1998a). *Muppet and child character appeal study* (unpublished research report). New York: Children's Television Workshop.

Sesame Street Research. (1998b). *Elmo's World: Assessing the appeal and comprehension of the Ball episode* (unpublished research report). New York: Children's Television Workshop.

Sesame Street Research. (1998c). *Elmo's World "Shoes": Assessing the appeal, engagement, and comprehension* (unpublished research report). New York: Children's Television Workshop.

Sesame Street Research. (1998d). *Elmo's World "Hats": Assessing the appeal, engagement, and comprehension* (unpublished research report). New York: Children's Television Workshop.

Sesame Street Research. (1998e). *Elmo's World "Balls": Assessing the appeal, engagement, and comprehension among first-time and repeat viewers* (unpublished research report). New York: Children's Television Workshop.

Sesame Street Research. (1999). *Elmo's World "Dancing": Assessing the appeal, engagement, and comprehension of repeat viewers over three consecutive days* (unpublished research report). New York: Children's Television Workshop.

Sesame Street Research & Applied Research and Consulting (1998). *Sesame Street letters and numbers cluster study* (unpublished research report). New York: Children's Television Workshop.

Skinner, B. F. (1971). *Beyond freedom and dignity.* New York: Bantam/Vintage.

Stalford, C. B. (1985). Reflections on writing a clear evaluation summary. *Evaluation News, 6*(4), 10–16.

Smith, M. L., & Glass, G. V. (1987). *Research and evaluation in education and the social sciences*. Englewood Cliffs, NJ: Prentice-Hall.

Stufflebeam, D. L. (1983). The CIPP model for program evaluation. In G. F. Madaus, M. Scriven, & D. L. Stufflebeam (Eds.), *Evaluation models: Viewpoints on educational and human services evaluation*. Boston: Kluwer-Nijhoff Publishing.

Stufflebeam, D. L., & Webster, W. J. (1980). An analysis of alternative approaches to evaluation. *Educational Evaluation and Policy Analysis, 3*(2), 5–19.

Tessier, B. (1996). *Sesame Street brand survey results, 1995–1996* (unpublished research report). New York: Children's Television Workshop.

Weston, C., McAlpine, L., & Bordonaro, T. (1995). A model for understanding formative evaluation in instructional design. *Educational Technology Research and Development, 43*(3), 29–48.

4 The Varied Role of Formative Research: Case Studies From 30 Years

Rosemarie T. Truglio
Children's Television Workshop
Valeria O. Lovelace
Media Transformations
Ivelisse Seguí
Children's Television Workshop
Susan Scheiner
Teachers College, Columbia University

Since the inception of *Sesame Street*, the voice of the child has been incorporated continuously into the development of the show. The creators believed that the best way to develop and evaluate a quality educational television program was to consult with the true experts—preschool children—and get their reactions. From the beginning, the creators of *Sesame Street* designed this entertaining, educational show as an experimental research project that would bring together educational advisors, researchers, and television producers as equal partners. This interdisciplinary team approach, referred to as the *CTW Model*, would ensure the quality of both the entertaining and educational components of the show, but most importantly involve children through formative evaluation of segments and whole shows.

The "marriage" between research, content experts, and producers continues today as the cornerstone of the long-term success of *Sesame Street*. Palmer and Fisch (chap. 1, this volume) reviewed the origins of *Sesame Street* research, and Fisch and Bernstein (chap. 3, this volume) discussed the formative research methodologies employed over time. The purpose of this chapter is to highlight several case studies to illustrate ways in which the CTW model is utilized to bring the curriculum to life in *Sesame Street* segments and stories. Some of the curriculum areas developed were raised by the production team;

61

others, stimulated by changes in early childhood education, the changing media environment (e.g., the widespread use of computers), and societal issues (e.g., racial tension).

Throughout the chapter, we discuss the questions we sought answers for, the lessons learned from formative research with preschoolers about the appeal and comprehensibility of segments and stories, and the recommendations provided to *Sesame Street* Production to inform the creation of entertaining and age-appropriate segments and stories. The content areas covered in this chapter are science, literacy, race relations, and specific social issues such as death, love, marriage, and pregnancy.

Science

For *Sesame Street*'s 29th experimental season, the producers decided to revisit the science curriculum. The objective of the "Science of Discovery" curriculum was to link preschoolers' natural curiosity with their love of exploration by illustrating both science content and scientific processes. In collaboration with science education advisors, we examined our existing science curriculum goals and discussed current issues regarding science education for preschoolers. We decided to adopt a scientific inquiry approach to emphasize reasoning skills such as observation, asking questions, and making predictions. The science content included information about plants and animals, the natural environment, "What's alive?," body parts and senses, light and shadows, and space.

In developing scripts, we emphasized that: (a) science is not confined to the laboratory, (b) everyone can do science, and (c) children are naturally curious. Guided by the curriculum, we illustrated that our everyday environment provides a wealth of interesting things to wonder about and to explore, and we varied sex, age, and ethnicity to portray many different kinds of people doing science. Furthermore, we promoted children's natural curiosity by portraying situations in which adult characters encouraged children's questions as they modeled generating and evaluating one or more explanations or answers.

The topic of space had been included in the science curriculum because of an idea for a space-based story arc that had been proposed by Production. However, there was some concern about the age-appropriateness of including space as a content area for preschoolers, so we assessed preschoolers' understanding of space, the moon, astronauts, and space travel *before* developing an 18-week story arc featuring Slimey, Oscar the Grouch's pet worm, as he participates in the "Worm Air and Space Agency's" (WASA) very first "wormed" moon mission. The results of this exploratory study indicated that preschoolers were indeed interested in these topics, and given their limited information about the topics, we had an opportunity to enhance their knowledge, interests, and aspirations. For example, many preschoolers mentioned characteristics of the moon (e.g., it is round, it is seen at night, it is in the sky), but they knew little about how to get to the moon, what astronauts do, or that the moon is in space that is up above the sky (*Sesame Street* Research, 1997). Research not only encouraged moving ahead but also helped writers understand young children's knowledge of space, so that in writing scripts, they would have a sense of the knowledge that they could assume from preschool viewers and the information that they would have to explain.

As with every new curriculum season, we assessed how well we met our goals by conducting two studies, the Science Segment Study and Slimey Goes to the Moon (Truglio, Scheiner, Seguí, & Chen, 1999). The purpose of the Science Segment Study was to assess preschoolers' comprehension of the science lessons, the appeal of the segments, and the extent to which preschoolers participated (e.g., sing, label on screen, laugh) while viewing individual science segments. Nineteen science segments with the following science goals: natural environment, "What's alive?," body parts and senses, light and shadows, space, and observation, were chosen and placed on five test reels containing three to four segments per tape. Test reels were assembled to reflect a mix of goals and formats (e.g., animation and live action).

Children were randomly placed into five groups of 30 (each group consisted of 10 3-, 4-, and 5-year-olds with approximately equal number of boys and girls). Each child viewed one test tape in a group setting and while they viewed each segment, researchers recorded the children's participatory viewing behaviors and their attention to the screen. After viewing each segment, the tape was stopped and the children were interviewed individually to assess comprehension of the material.

In general, children expressed that they liked watching these science segments, many participated by smiling, laughing, moving to music, and singing, and they comprehended the intended lessons of each of the segments (Truglio et al., 1999). Specifically, we learned the following lessons about individual goals and made the following recommendations to guide the production of future segments:

"What's Alive?"

- After viewing a segment during which a tree and several animals were labeled as alive and a range of inanimate objects as not alive, children were confused about whether a tree is alive is alive or not. Given the age of the children, this finding did not surprise our science advisors. Thus, we recommended that future segments for the goal "What's Alive?" should focus on either plants or animals but not mix the two categories.

Light and Shadows

- Children were better able to explain the appearance of a shadow when they could see the shadow's appearance and disappearance as it directly related to the light source. For example, in one segment, the shadow appeared when the light source, a lamp, was turned on and it disappeared when the lamp was turned off. This connection was reinforced in a subsequent scene when a different light source, the sun, was linked to the appearance of a shadow. This was in contrast to the other two segments in which the connection between the light source and the shadow was not as salient. Therefore, we recommended that future "Light and Shadows" segments should emphasize the relation between the light source and the shadow.

Body Parts and Senses

- Almost all of the children correctly labeled the parts of the face after viewing the segments. Many children, however (especially the 3-year-olds), had some difficulty with the functions of these body parts. Therefore, we recommended that future segments emphasize more strongly all the appropriate senses or functions associated with each body part.
- More children correctly named the functions of the eyes, nose, and mouth after viewing a segment with Grover and a little girl named Chelsea than did the children who saw Elmo singing about these functions using artwork (e.g., an abstract painting of the Mona Lisa). One possible explanation is that Chelsea may have been a better model for body parts than the models in the artwork that Elmo was singing about. Another distinction is that Elmo sang about the functions while Grover and Chelsea discussed them. Therefore, we recommended that future "Body Parts and Senses" segments feature an adult or child with (or without) a Muppet; and that segments in which the message is embedded in a song also incorporate a spoken line at the beginning or the end to reinforce the curriculum goal.

The second study, Slimey to the Moon, was a longitudinal study designed to assess children's understanding of space, the moon, astronauts, and space travel, as well as the degree to which their understanding of such concepts changed as a result of exposure to *Sesame Street*'s Slimey to the Moon story arc (Truglio et al., 1999). A longitudinal design is atypical for formative research but to inform future creative decisions, *Sesame Street* Production needed to know if this ongoing storyline format was age-appropriate. The story began with Slimey's fascination with the moon, and proceeded with the mission training, lift-off, the long journey in space, landing on the moon and exploring it, and finally, his jubilant return to earth. Six key shows from the 18-week space story arc were included in this study.

The sample consisted of 119 children from two day-care centers (one low-income and one middle-income). At both the low-income and middle-income centers, children were divided into three groups by age: 3-, 4-, and 5-year-olds. At each center each age group was visited on a weekly basis over a 7-week period. During the first week, individual baseline interviews were conducted prior to viewing *Sesame Street*, to assess their general knowledge of space, the moon, Earth, astronauts, and space travel. Children were also asked about their desire to be an astronaut and go to the moon. Over the next 6 weeks, same-age children viewed each of the six space shows in a group setting. Shows were edited to be approximately 30 minutes in length by including Street scenes (i.e., story segments filmed on the *Sesame Street* set) but removing almost all of the insert segments (i.e., animation, Muppet, and live-action segments that are placed between the Street scenes). All of the Street scenes during which the space story was told were the same as originally aired, and these segments were separated by at least one insert segment about space.

Baseline results revealed that, prior to viewing, preschoolers from the middle-income center had significantly greater knowledge of space and space exploration than did preschoolers from the low-income center. After viewing the six episodes from the Slimey Goes to the Moon story arc, children from the low-income center demonstrated the greatest gains in comprehension. These children gained knowledge about what to call someone who travels to the moon, what astronauts do and how they travel to the moon, what astronauts wear on the moon, and that the planet we live on is called the Earth. Although preschoolers from the middle-income center had a good understanding about space, they also showed some significant increases in their knowledge of how long it takes to get to the moon and what astronauts wear on the moon. Overall, children enjoyed the space shows, remained interested in the story, and most importantly, they acquired more specific knowledge about astronauts and space travel over a period of time (Truglio et al., 1999).

Literacy

For 30 years, *Sesame Street* has created a literate television environment for children where letters, books, writing, and vocabulary words are skillfully featured in each daily visit. It is a world where all children can share the joy of reading. For many children, it serves as the only place where reading is viewed as a critical, important, and necessary element of life.

From the very beginning, Joan Ganz Cooney was convinced that children could learn from "commercials" featuring letters as easily as they learned the names of household detergents. Her goal was to take this "television wasteland" and turn it into an experience that prepared young children for school, with reading as its centerpiece.

Thirty years later, *Sesame Street* continues to be an innovator and literacy continues to be a formative research challenge as the show's curriculum has grown and new creative and educational approaches to teaching letters, book reading, writing, and vocabulary have emerged. (See Lesser & Schneider, chap. 2, this volume for a review of the literacy goals developed for the first season and the subsequent changes over the 30 years.) Through seminars and formative research, two questions have remained in the forefront: What specific literacy skills should be taught to 3-, 4-, and 5-year-olds? and What is the best way to present educational content and messages regarding these goals to maximize learning?

What Specific Literacy Skills Should Be Taught?

In the years since the first seminars conducted in the summer of 1968, 10 additional seminars have been held to address the literacy needs of preschool children. The literacy goals have included both phonics and whole language goals and they have reflected the changes in terminology and approaches to teaching reading through the years. At the end of the 25th Season, Michael Loman, Executive Producer of *Sesame Street* and a former reading teacher, suggested that we devote Seasons 26, 27, and 28 to review literacy goals on *Sesame Street*, to understand how the curriculum evolved, and to update it. The final decision to focus on literacy as a curriculum area was based on changes in educational theory and practice regarding literacy and a movement toward emergent literacy (Adams, 1990; Neuman, 1993).

What Is the Best Way to Present Specific Literacy Skills to Maximize Learning?

As the first segments for the series were produced in 1968, Edward Palmer, Director of Research, and his staff, used his "distractor method" to evaluate one of the first *Sesame Street* letter segments, the *J* commercial (see Palmer & Fisch, chap. 1, this volume for a discussion of this methodology). Based on data concerning children's attention to this segment, several changes were made prior to final production. Initially, the *J* was stationary. But after observing that children paid more attention to the actions of the animated characters, the producers made the *J* itself much more animate, too. Furthermore, although each *J* word appeared on the screen as it was spoken, the children seemed much more aware of the rhyming pattern in the voice-over than of the *J* sounds within it. Because rhyming is an excellent teaching device, the rhyming in the segment was also rewritten to emphasize the *J* sounds within the rhyme and make them more prominent (Lesser, 1974).

Pretesting revealed that very few children could recognize *J* before viewing, but after viewing the revised segment, the majority of the children could recognize and label *J*, especially those who watched the segment more than once. Based on these findings, research recommended that future letter segments should be created with the following production guidelines: (a) make the letter salient and active, (b) use the familiar as a bridge to the unfamiliar, and (c) all activities within the segment should work to reinforce the letter (Lesser, 1974).

Through the years, the research staff tested individual literacy segments to determine children's comprehension of storybook reading segments, vocabulary, writing, sight-words, letters, and letter sounds with great success. The 3-year Emergent Literacy Initiative gave us the opportunity to conduct research on literacy messages across 31 shows (20 in Season 26 and 11 in Season 27). For the purposes of this chapter, we review only the results of the letter recognition studies.

After viewing each episode, children were interviewed individually to assess their ability to identify the letter(s) featured on the show. On average across the 31 shows, less than 20% of the children identified the Letter(s) of the Day. Yet, as one might expect, performance varied widely across the shows. A closer examination of four shows that produced significant gains in preschoolers' recognition of the Letter(s) of the Day provides insight into factors that can contribute to higher levels of learning after one viewing.

It is not surprising that two potential factors pertained to repetition and reinforcement; specifically, emphasizing the Letter of the Day in a number of segments and including the Letter of the Day in both Street scenes and insert segments. For example, in one of the stronger episodes, the Letter of the Day, D, is highlighted in the narrative across three Street scenes, as well as five inserts. The story in the Street scenes involves Rosita watching Baby Bear finish his drawing of the letter D. Impressed, Rosita wants to draw it the same way but gets frustrated because she cannot. She asks Baby Bear to teach her, and he excitedly does so. After viewing this show, 50% of the children recognized D, a significant increase from the pretest (*Sesame Street* Research, 1995a).

Reinforcement of a different kind—reinforcement across consecutive episodes—was provided in two other episodes whose Street scenes were linked in a two-part story that continued over 2 days. In these shows, print played a central role in the story as the *Sesame Street* characters tried to find the owner of a lost dog by making posters. Besides demonstrating the value of print in solving a problem, the letter R was featured in both shows. In Part 1 of the story, the letters of the day were R and B; for Part 2, the letters were R and F. When testing these shows, the same children watched both episodes and were tested on consecutive days to measure changes in learning the letter R over time.

Comprehension data showed that after viewing Part 1, only 20% of the children recognized R as one of the Letters of the Day (*Sesame Street* Research, 1995b). After viewing Part 2, there was a significant increase in learning with 47% of the children recognizing the letter R (*Sesame Street* Research, 1995c). The reinforcement provided by the second episode on the next day appeared to make a significant contribution to children's recognition of the letter.

Another possible factor in promoting letter recognition was the degree to which the letters were embedded in shows whose Street scenes provided a literacy-based context. In these instances, the Letters of the Day were not featured in the Street scenes themselves, but the Street scenes presented a strong foundation of literacy that may have helped attune the children toward the inserts that did present these letters. For example, in one episode, the *Sesame Street* characters enacted a storybook, "The Tree That Wanted to Leave the Park." The program opens with dramatic music and a strong voice-over reading a full screen of print featuring the title of the story and Maria in a costume sitting on a park bench reading the story. Bob, the tree, wants to leave the park because he thinks nobody cares about him. As the story unfolds, the tree learns that: Birds need the tree during spring; the tree is appreciated for shade during the summer; in autumn, the Count counts the tree's fallen leaves; and, in winter, the tree is finally persuaded to stay in the park, year round, after being hugged by a bunch of children dressed as snowflakes.

The letters of the day, X and O, are featured in one or two clusters of inserts segments (i.e., appearing between the Street scenes). After viewing the episode, 53% of the children recognized the letter O and 47% of the children recognized the letter X (*Sesame Street* Research, 1995d). This was a marked difference from three other episodes featuring these letters, in which there was less than 20% letter recognition.

Finally, another possible factor contributing to increased gains in preschoolers' letter recognition was the inclusion of one versus two Letters of the Day in a given episode. In the show in which Baby Bear is drawing the letter D, described above, 50% of the children recognized the letter after only a single viewing, whereas an average of only about 20% correctly identified the letters featured in shows that contained two Letters of the Day.

Based on the results of the previous studies, research recommended that each episode should feature only one Letter of the Day and that this letter be repeated and reinforced in two clusters with three segments per cluster, and, when possible, across Street scenes. Three years later, a separate line of formative research investigated another potential contributing factor, the clustering of letter segments within a single episode.

To explore the relation between letter segment clusters interwoven throughout the show and preschoolers' learning of a specific letter, we modified the letter clustering formats in a previously aired show in which Maria and Luis' daughter, Gabi, struggles with the anxiety of riding her bike without the training wheels. This show was selected because a previous study had shown this story to be highly appealing among preschoolers (*Sesame Street* Research, 1998). The letter D (both upper and lowercase) was the featured letter in the show. There were three versions of the show, each featuring one of the following clustering formats: Format A, the standard format used in the show prior to testing that employed two clusters with three segments about the letter D per cluster; Format B, two clusters with one cluster containing three letter D segments, the other containing two segments; and Format C, three clusters with two segments about the letter D per cluster.

One hundred and eighty-seven children from six day-care centers in New York and Minnesota participated in this study. When the episode was over, researchers conducted individual posttest interviews to assess possible gains in preschooler's letter recognition from pretesting. The strongest gains in letter recognition occurred in the show featuring Format B, which was comprised of one cluster of three letter segments reinforced later in the show with a second cluster of two letter segments. Based on these findings, Format B was adopted as the standard format for presenting letter segments in *Sesame Street* starting in Season 31.

Together, these studies identified five possible factors contributing to preschoolers' comprehension of the Letter of the Day: (a) the number of segments featuring the letter per episode, (b) the inclusion of the letter in both the Street scenes and inserts, (c) the use of the same letter across consecutive shows for reinforcement, (d) the use of a literacy-based storyline context, and (e) the inclusion of only one Letter of the Day per episode.

When combined with prior formative research (e.g., Gibbon, Palmer, & Fowles, 1975), this line of research confirms Palmer's early recommendations for the creation of letter segments. It is during the preschool years that children are just beginning to identify and label letters, as well as gain some understanding of the meaning of these symbols. Because preschoolers are just learning their letters and are facing the tremendous task of learning the upper and lower case of each letter, the letter needs to be salient and reinforced. To enhance the salience of the letter within a segment, it needs to be isolated, labeled, the focus of attention, on screen throughout the segment, and placed in the context of familiar words that begin with the target letter. It is important to expose preschoolers to a range of segments that capture, not only the visual letter symbol, but also the sound or sounds a letter represents; for letters with two sounds, only one sound should be featured within the segment.

Reinforcement and salience can also be promoted through the ways in which individual segments are combined. The decisions to only have one Letter of the Day, rather than two, and to reinforce the letter across two clusters of segments both serve to enhance the salience of the letter.

Finally, comprehension can be promoted through stories that illustrate literacy as important, useful, and enjoyable. When Street scenes featured reading fundamentals that were featured prominently in solving child-relevant problems (e.g., reading a story, writing and reading a poster to solve a problem), preschoolers' knowledge of the letter featured in the show was enhanced. This special attention to the functional value of print served as a bridge from the familiar to the unfamiliar, to help children understand the importance of letters in these shows.

Race Relations

Sesame Street is a celebration of diversity and since its inception, it has modeled racial harmony. In 1989, as a result of rising racial unrest in the United States, a 4-year race-relations curriculum initiative was launched to be more explicit about physical and cultural differences, and to encourage friendship among people of different races and cultures. In collaboration with the production staff, *Sesame Street* Research developed 23 race relations curriculum goals, over the course of 4 years, to promote positive interactions among five cultural groups: African Americans, American Indians, Latino Americans, Asian Americans, and White Americans. Emphasis was placed on the similarities that make us all human and on fostering an appreciation of racial and cultural differences. Through these curriculum goals, preschoolers were encouraged to perceive people who look different from themselves as possible friends, and to bring a child who has been rejected because of physical and/or cultural differences into the group.

During four consecutive seasons, a specific cultural group was selected for each season, and the year was then devoted to conducting research, writing scripts, and producing segments to address the issues raised by each specific group. To gain a deeper understanding of each cultural group and to design *Sesame Street* messages that would be effective for all preschoolers, a curriculum seminar was held each year to bring experts together with the *Sesame Street* staff. Resource guides were created to provide detailed information on each group's history, customs and traditions, foods, and the contributions that each group has made to the arts, science, and sports. In addition, a lecture series provided more personal and in-depth cultural information through the use of speakers, artists, musicians, and performers.

Initially, there was some doubt as to whether race relations was truly an issue for preschoolers. Therefore, the research team conducted an extensive review of the literature (e.g., Clark & Clark, 1939; Cross, 1991; Derman-Sparks, 1989; Graves, 1975; Katz, 1976) and held meetings with experts. From these investigations and discussions, it was clear that preschoolers were not only aware of racial differences but the topic was both appropriate and timely.

In keeping with the tradition of establishing baseline information before goals are written, the *Sesame Street* Research team conducted formative research to determine African American, White, Crow Indian, Puerto Rican, and Chinese American preschoolers' understanding and perceptions of race relations (Lovelace, Freund, & Graves, 1991). More specifically, attention was placed on preschoolers' perceptions of self and other children, parental perceptions, and world views. In all cases, the researchers and the children were racially and ethnically matched. The following are a few of methodologies that were developed to explore the ways in which preschoolers view themselves and the world:

- Face cards with line drawings of five faces depicting "very happy," "happy," "okay," "sad," and "angry" were used to determine how children felt about themselves and their skin.
- A "Make a Neighborhood" game was created to observe how preschoolers would sort pictures of children who differed by race, clothing, and hairstyle into places in the neighborhood. The game pieces included 10 neighborhood structures (i.e., two separate homes, schools, playgrounds, markets, and churches) along with drawings of children of different ethnic backgrounds. The preschoolers were instructed to show the interviewer where each child would go.
- As the *Sesame Street* curriculum expanded over 4 years to include each group, the methodology was adapted. For example, the face cards were used to gauge parental attitudes, such as how the children thought their mothers would feel if they were friends with a child of a different race. In addition, children were asked to look in a mirror and choose (out of a set of five) the crayon that looked most like their skin. Structures in the neighborhood game were changed to be more reflective of areas in which the children lived; the cutout

dolls were changed from African American and White to American Indian, Latino American, or Asian American.

The result of a series of formative studies revealed:

- The majority of White (90%), African-American (87%), and Chinese-American (87%) preschoolers felt good about themselves (*Sesame Street* Research, 1992b, 1993a). However, these children were significantly more positive about themselves than Puerto Rican (63%) and Crow Indian (50%) children (*Sesame Street* Research, 1991, 1993a).
- The majority of the White (77%), Chinese-American (70%), light-skinned Puerto Rican (70%), African-American (60%), and dark-skinned Puerto Rican (57%) children were accurate in identifying the color of their skin (*Sesame Street* Research, 1993a). (The Crow Indian children were not shown crayons, so the information is not directly comparable.)
- The majority of African-American (70%), White (63%), Crow Indian (60%), and Chinese-American (60%) children felt good about the color of their skin. However, only 35% of the Puerto Rican children felt positive about the color of their skin (*Sesame Street* Research, 1992b, 1993a).
- Overall, the children wanted to be friends with children of different races (Table 4.1). The percentages ranged from 50% to 87%. The majority of the Puerto Rican children (72% to 87%) were the most positive about being friends with children of different races. Chinese-American children, however, expressed more reservations about developing interracial friendships. African-American children felt positive about being friends with a White child (72%) and a Chinese-American child (77%), but were less positive about a friendship with a Puerto Rican child (53%). White children also expressed a pos-

TABLE 4.1.
Percentage of Children Who Said They Want to Be Friends With a Child of a Different Race

Children	White Friend	African Amerian/ Black Friend	Puerto Rican/ Spanish Friend	Chinese Friend
White	——	77%	67%	50%
African American	72%	——	53%	77%
Puerto Rican	87%	72%	——	77%
Chinese American	53%	53%	60%	——

itive attitude about being friends with an African-American child (77%), but were less enthusiastic about being friends with a Chinese-American child (50%) or a Puerto Rican child (67%).

- However, although preschoolers were open to being friends with children of different races, they perceived their mothers as less encouraging of such friendships. Percentages ranged from 23% to 50% (*Sesame Street* Research, 1992b). At most, one-half of the African-American, White, Puerto Rican, Crow Indian, and Chinese-American children reported that their mothers would be positive about them having a friend of another race.
- Given the opportunity to create a neighborhood, Chinese-American, African-American, Puerto Rican, and Crow Indian preschoolers integrated all of the neighborhood structures with children from their own group and White children. White preschoolers integrated Chinese-American and White, Puerto Rican and White, and Crow Indian and White children in every structure. However, White preschoolers, in particular 5-year-olds, segregated African-American and White children in all of the structures: homes (80%), schools (80%), playgrounds (80%), churches (90%), and stores (90%).

To improve our understanding of the children's nonverbal responses, small groups of White children were told a story about a group of White children who separated White and African-American children in each of the structures. The children were then asked to help us understand why the children in the story responded as they did. The majority of the White children agreed that African-American and White children should be separated and gave the following reasons to explain the segregation: physical differences, economics, conflict, existing separate housing, others' opinions (Lovelace, Scheiner, Dollberg, Seguí, & Black, 1994; Lovelace, Schneiner, Seguí, & Black, 1995). However, they also said that the separation would lead to sadness for both White and African-American children.

Based on the results of these baseline studies, curriculum goals were written and segments were produced with the intention of hopefully counteracting some of these beliefs. For example, in direct response to the segregation that was noted in the formative research, two segments were created: "Visiting Ieshia" and "Play Date." In "Visiting Ieshia," a White girl visits an African-American girl in her home. "Play Date" shows a similar family visit with an African-American boy in his home and his White friend.

Across two studies, a total of 150 African-American, White, and Puerto Rican preschoolers were observed while viewing these segments and subsequently interviewed. Data indicated that children found the segments to be appealing regardless of race or gender. Moreover, preschoolers identified with and remembered common experiences that the children in the segments shared. Almost all of the children (97%) who viewed "Visiting Ieshia" and most of the children who viewed "Play Date" (87%) recalled something that the children did together: ate, slept, washed their hands, listened to music, played games. The majority of the children stated that the visiting White child felt positive about being at Ieshia's home (70%) and Jamal's home (58%). Almost three-quarters of the preschoolers knew that the White child felt positive about eating the new cultural foods such as grits (70%) and collard greens (73%) (*Sesame Street* Research, 1991; 1993b).

Yet, in spite of these findings, less than one half of the African-American and White children who viewed "Play Date" felt that the African-American mother in the film (48%) and the unseen White mother of the White boy (39%) felt very happy or happy about the visit (*Sesame Street* Research, 1993b). Consistent with the formative research conducted prior to production, preschoolers perceived their mothers as not feeling positively about other race friendships, even after viewing hospitable, friendly, and inviting images of parents in "Play Date." As a result of these findings, it was recommended that in future segments, mothers, fathers, and other family members need to have a more prominent role in expressing positive and supportive feelings about their child's friendships with children of different races before, during, and after these visits. In addition, researchers suggested that conversations between the visiting children's parents, and parent–child conversations be held before and after the visits to show the parents expressing the positive value of making and keeping good friends.

Specific Social Issues

Through the years, *Sesame Street* has dealt with many social issues relevant to preschoolers, some more difficult than others. For the sake of illustration, we discuss only several social topics addressed by *Sesame Street*: death, love, marriage, pregnancy, and divorce.

Dealing With Death. In 1983, *Sesame Street* dealt with the death of its longtime storekeeper, Mr. Hooper. The actor, Will Lee, who played this character died and the producers decided to deal with his death on the show rather than replace him with another actor. This single episode was kept simple, conveying the following key messages: Mr. Hooper is dead; Mr. Hooper will not be coming back; and Mr. Hooper will be missed by all. Due to the sensitive nature of this story, research was conducted prior to its air date and parents were encouraged to watch this episode with their children to answer their children's questions about death according to their own cultural religious beliefs.

Prior to broadcast, *Sesame Street* Research conducted a series of studies to answer four questions for the production staff. The questions were: (a) Will children understand the three key messages about Mr. Hooper's death? (b) How attentive will children be to the storyline? (c) How will parents respond to our treatment of such a sensitive topic on *Sesame Street*? and most important of all, (d) Will children be disturbed by this story either immediately after viewing or during the following week?

Research used three different research methods to address these concerns: (a) children watched only the *Sesame Street* scenes conveying the storyline without inserts and were then interviewed after viewing, (b) children watched the entire show and their attention was recorded, and (c) children and their parents viewed the storyline without inserts, and parents were interviewed 9 or 10 days later (*Sesame Street* Research, 1983; Lovelace, Schwager, Saltzman, 1994).

Preschoolers' comprehension of the key messages was tested with a sample of 31 3-, 4-, and 5-year-olds. The majority of the 4- and 5-year-olds understood that Mr. Hooper was dead and that he was not coming back (73% and 88%, respectively), whereas only about one-fourth of the 3-year-olds responded correctly. Furthermore, virtually all of the 4- and 5-year-olds knew that Big Bird and the adult characters felt sad. The second study in the series, conducted with 24 preschoolers and their parents, indicated that on average, the majority of the children (80%) were attentive during the show.

Parents' reception of the show was overwhelmingly positive and used words such as "well done," "compassionate," "helpful," "honest," and "age-appropriate." Approximately one half of the 21 parents interviewed stated that they discussed death with their children after viewing the show, and none of the parents reported any negative immediate or delayed reactions in their child.

Love, Marriage, and Pregnancy.   For the 19th season of *Sesame Street* in 1988, the production team decided to have Maria and Luis (two of the existing human characters) fall in love and get married (Lovelace, Perez, Communtsis, & Freud, 1990). The subsequent year their daughter, Gabi, was born. To inform the production of segments on these topics, formative research with preschoolers was incorporated early in the process, before producing any material, to assess preschoolers' existing knowledge and misconceptions about love, marriage, family configurations, and pregnancy. With the exception of pregnancy, there were no children's books for preschoolers for most of these topics, and there were virtually no relevant research studies on young children's knowledge of these topics at the time. For pregnancy, research began with reviews of children's books written on conception, descriptions of early childhood sex education curricula, and research studies on children's understanding of "where babies come from."

Throughout the development of these stories, formative research helped target scripts directly to children's prior knowledge, allowing the writers to focus their attention on areas in which children's knowledge was weakest. Moreover, these studies provided baseline data that were later used for comparison, once segments were produced and tested for comprehension.

A total of 30 preschoolers were individually interviewed to assess their understanding of "love." Most preschoolers (77%) were not able to define what love is. When they did give an acceptable response, their definition referred to physical actions such as kissing, hugging, giving presents (e.g., flowers), and people they love. Almost two thirds of the children associated the symbol of a heart with the spoken word "love." Being angry was clearly the activity that children thought was least likely to be associated with love (*Sesame Street* Research, 1988a).

The recommendations to production were: (a) to define love as a special feeling that you have for someone you like and care for very much; (b) to show that love relationships include good and bad times; therefore, when arguments or conflicts are presented, more time should be spent on the resolution than the actual conflict, and to reassure the children that Maria and Luis still love each other although they were angry, they should make up with kissing, hugging, and giving flowers; and (c) to use the symbol of the heart to reinforce the messages about love because children understand this symbol so well.

The concept of marriage was also difficult for preschoolers to define. Approximately one half of the children (16 out of 30 preschoolers) gave appropriate examples of who can get married, and all responded yes to the question "Can anyone get married?" However, most of the children were not able to define what marriage is or why people get married (*Sesame Street* Research, 1988a). When asked what the man or woman does after they get married, children named more roles for the wife than for the husband. Kissing was most salient in children's descriptions of the husband's role, whereas having a baby was the most frequently described aspect of the wife's role.

Children gave broad definitions of families and appropriate family configurations regardless of where the family members live or whether they were blood relatives. The key component of family was love; if there was no love, there was no family.

Recommendations to Production about marriage and family included defining marriage as a promise between a grown-up man and woman to love and care for each other, share their lives, and make a family. Researchers suggested that it would be helpful for child viewers to see Luis and Maria discussing their plans to live together and become a family and for them to discuss how they will share household chores and the care of children.

Once the love and marriage segments were produced, they were tested for comprehension. Studies on these segments showed that, compared to baseline data, viewers were better able to define love and marriage (with kissing still emerging as the most salient indictor of love). In addition, whereas almost all of the children in the baseline study believed that people who were angry with each other did not still love each other, 67% of the children who viewed a segment in which Maria and Luis argued and then made up understood that they still loved each other even when they were angry (*Sesame Street* Research, 1988b).

Before producing the material about Maria's pregnancy, a total of 60 preschoolers participated in interviews to assess their knowledge about pregnancy. Most preschoolers (57%) were unable to define the term "pregnant," and 60% knew that the baby moves while inside the mother. Two thirds stated that the baby could hear, but they did not know how the baby breathed or ate inside the mother. The majority of the preschoolers (70%) stated that the baby was in the mother's stomach, belly, or tummy before it was born, and 93% did not know where the mommy's womb was (*Sesame Street* Research, 1988c).

Once segments on Maria's pregnancy were produced, comprehension testing showed a dramatic impact on preschoolers' understanding of pregnancy. Compared to baseline data collected prior to production, preschoolers who viewed the segments on pregnancy demonstrated a greater knowledge of the subject. Preschoolers more often defined "pregnant" in terms of having a baby (63%, compared to 43% in the baseline data), understood that the baby could move inside its mother (90%, vs. 60% baseline), and there were slight increases in their knowledge about where the baby grows in a woman (83%, vs. 70% baseline) and that the baby eats (20%, vs. 7% baseline) and breathes (10%, vs. 0% baseline) (*Sesame Street* Research, 1989).

Divorce.   Since the late 1960s, research has played an instrumental role in determining whether to air or whether to retire (i.e., no longer air) specific segments or shows. In 1992, research findings led to the decision not to air a newly-produced show that attempted to deal with the issue of divorce by having the parents of Snuffy and Alice (a pair of Muppet Snuffleupaguses) get a divorce. Given the divorce rate in the United States, it was believed that exploring this topic was appropriate. In consultation with content experts and developmental psychologists, every word of the script was reviewed. The show was fully produced and subsequently tested for comprehension and attention with a sample of 60 preschoolers across four day-care centers (*Sesame Street* Research, 1992a).

Although the subject of divorce was approached with great sensitivity in the show, the results of the study showed several unintended negative effects. Many of the children did not understand that Snuffy and Alice's parents still loved them despite the divorce, they were unclear where Snuffy's parents (particularly his father) lived, and many believed that his father ran away and Snuffy and Alice would never see their father again. The majority of the preschoolers asserted that an argument between parents would lead to a divorce, despite Gordon's reassuring discussion about the relationship between arguments and divorce.

Based on these data, the research and production teams and the CTW corporate staff decided that it was unwise to risk the possibility of negative effects among the mass viewing audience. Therefore, despite the cost of producing the show, this show was never aired—a decision clearly made by listening to the voices of children and by putting their needs first.

Conclusion

Since the late 1960s, formative research on *Sesame Street* has played a vital and varied role in implementing a comprehensive preschool curriculum that addresses the whole child, and in bringing it to life through highly entertaining segments and stories. Formative research has allowed us to be successful in responding to the production staff's interests and *Sesame Street's* mission to help the whole child develop and grow in today's complex world.

Previous chapters in this volume have discussed other roles that the *Sesame Street* Research Department plays throughout production (Lesser & Schneider, chap. 2, this volume; Palmer & Fisch, chap. 1, this volume). These roles include developing the *Sesame Street* curriculum with assistance from content advisors and modifying it on a yearly basis, to reflect each season's curriculum focus. Over the years, the curriculum has covered a wide range of cognitive and social/emotional curriculum areas, as well as special topics, such as death, marriage, and pregnancy. As scripts are written, the Research Department reviews each one and recommends modifications regarding age-appropriateness and child relevance.

This chapter, on the other hand, has highlighted our work with the true experts—the children—to inform Production about how best to increase the educational effectiveness of the show. The insight we have gained from children has been invaluable. Although preschool children are similar in so many ways, our research made us aware of age differences and the need to be sensitive to the diverse races, cultures, languages, and disabilities. We learned that it is important to be positive about this diversity and to celebrate it. When a segment or show is tested with preschoolers and they rate it as unappealing or their comprehension is weak, we assume the "failure" and never place blame on the target audience. We learn through our mistakes and then integrate that learning into the development of the show to enhance its educational effectiveness.

Much of the success of *Sesame Street* is attributed to the respectful collaboration between Research and Production, and it is through this working collaboration that we hope to make a positive difference in the lives of our preschoolers. We at *Sesame Street* are committed to helping all children develop an excitement about learning and a positive appreciation and respect for all people.

REFERENCES

Adams, M. J. (1990). *Beginning to read: Thinking and learning about print, a summary.* Center for the Study of Reading, Cambridge, MA: MIT Press.

Clark, K. B., & Clark, M. P. (1939). The development of consciousness of self and the emergence of racial identity in Negro preschool children. *Journal of Social Psychology, 10,* 591–599.

Cross, W. (1991). *Shades of black.* Philadelphia, PA: Temple University Press.

Derman-Sparks, L., & the ABC Task Force. (1989). *Anti-bias curriculum.* Washington, DC: NAEYC.

Gibbon, S. Y., Palmer, E. L., & Fowles, B. R. (1975). *Sesame Street, Electric Company* and reading. In J. Carroll & J. Chall (Eds.). *Towards a literate society* (pp. 215–256). New York: McGraw-Hill.

Graves, S. B. (1975). *Racial diversity in children's television: Its impact on racial attitudes and stated program preferences.* Unpublished doctoral dissertation, Harvard University, Cambridge, MA.

Katz, P. A. (1976). The acquisition of racial attitudes in children. In P. A. Katz (Ed.), *Toward the elimination of racism* (pp. 213–241). New York: Pergamon Press.

Lesser, G. S. (1974). *Children and television: Lessons from Sesame Street.* New York: Vintage Books/Random House.

Lovelace, V. O., Freund, S., & Graves, S. B. (1991, April). *A Sesame Street perspective: Preschooler's understanding of race relations.* Paper presented at the biennial meeting of the Society for Research in Child Development, Seattle, WA.

Lovelace, V. O., Perez, M., Communtsis, G., & Freund, S. (1990, June). Paper presented at the annual meeting of the International Communication Association, Dublin, Ireland.

Lovelace, V. O., Scheiner, S., Dollberg, S., Seguí, I., & Black, T. (1994). Making a neighborhood the *Sesame Street* way: Developing a methodology to evaluate children's understanding of race. *Journal of Educational Television, 20*(2), 69–78.

Lovelace, V. O., Scheiner, S., Seguí, I., & Black, T. (1995, August). *Making a neighborhood the Sesame Street way.* Paper presented at the annual meeting of the American Psychological Association, New York.

Lovelace, V. O., Schwager, I., & Saltzman, E. (1984, August). *Responses to death on Sesame Street from preschoolers and parents.* Paper presented at the annual meeting of the American Psychological Association, Toronto, Canada.

Neuman, S. B. (1993). *Language and literacy learning in the early years: An integrated approach.* Ft. Worth, Texas: Harcourt Brace.

Sesame Street Research. (1983). *Study on show #1839* (unpublished research report). New York: Children's Television Workshop.

Sesame Street Research. (1988a). *First comes love, then comes marriage, then comes Maria and Luis with a baby carriage* (unpublished research report). New York: Children's Television Workshop.

Sesame Street Research. (1988b). *Love ... the continuing saga* (unpublished research report). New York: Children's Television Workshop.

Sesame Street Research. (1988c). *Pregnancy* (unpublished research report). New York: Children's Television Workshop.

Sesame Street Research. (1989). *Pregnancy (part 4): The bottom line* (unpublished research report). New York: Children's Television Workshop.

Sesame Street Research. (1991). *Visiting Ieshia* (unpublished research report). New York: Children's Television Workshop.

Sesame Street Research. (1992a). *Study on show #2895, Snuffy's parents get a divorce* (unpublished research report). New York: Children's Television Workshop.

Sesame Street Research. (1992b). *Puerto Rican, African-American, White, and Crow Indian self-awareness and race relations* (unpublished research report). New York: Children's Television Workshop.

Sesame Street Research. (1993a). *Chinese-American, African-American, White, and Puerto Rican Children's self-awareness and race relations: Part I* (unpublished research report). New York: Children's Television Workshop.

Sesame Street Research. (1993b). *Play date: Two boys play and eat* (unpublished research report). New York: Children's Television Workshop.

Sesame Street Research. (1995a). *Research portfolio, show #3356: Rosita wants to draw a "D" just like the one Baby Bear drew* (unpublished research report). New York: Children's Television Workshop.

Sesame Street Research. (1995b). *Research portfolio, show #3351: Luis finds a lost dog and puts up posters to locate owner* (unpublished research report). New York: Children's Television Workshop.

Sesame Street Research. (1995c). *Research portfolio, show #3352: The owners finally arrive and Gabi makes a new friend* (unpublished research report). New York: Children's Television Workshop.

Sesame Street Research. (1995d). *Research portfolio, show #3272: The tree who wanted to leave the park* (unpublished research report). New York: Children's Television Workshop.

Sesame Street Research. (1997). *What do preschoolers know about space?* (unpublished research report). New York: Children's Television Workshop.

Sesame Street Research. (1998). *Executive summary: Sesame Street letters and numbers cluster study* (unpublished research report). New York: Children's Television Workshop.

Truglio, R. T., Scheiner, S., Seguí, I., & Chen, L. (1999, April). *Sesame Street's science of discovery*. Poster session presented at the biennial meeting of the Society for Research in Child Development, Albuquerque, NM.

II Impact
of *Sesame Street*

5 A Review of Research on the Educational and Social Impact of *Sesame Street*

Keith W. Mielke
Children's Television Workshop (retired)

THE ROLE OF RESEARCH AT CTW

From its very conception in 1968 at the Children's Television Workshop (CTW), *Sesame Street* was to be a different kind of children's television series. Probably the most obvious differences in the beginning were its high production values and the topics it covered. But there were also important and innovative differences behind the scenes, such as in the goals CTW set for itself, and the commitment it made to find out through research if they had been achieved.

The earliest research on *Sesame Street*'s effects was either done in-house at CTW or commissioned by CTW to outside research groups. Later, academic researchers added their work to the pool of evidence about the effects of this series. Collectively, there is now more research on the effects of *Sesame Street* than for any other television program or series in the entire history of the medium. Only recently, major studies have added the dimension of long-term effects to this body of knowledge (Huston et al., chap. 8, this volume; Wright, Huston, Scantlin, & Kotler, chap. 6, this volume; Zill, chap. 7, this volume). The majority of this chapter, however, focuses on the earlier *Sesame Street* work that staked the claim, so to speak, that it was possible for television to make a major contribution to the education of young children. The initial research grew directly out of the goals set for the series, so the discussion begins there, with goals.

Goals of *Sesame Street*

The most common and general goal for any television series, whether commercial or noncommercial, is to reach the largest possible audience within some target category, such as "women 18 to 39 years of age," or "children 6 to

11 years of age." CTW also had a target-audience goal for *Sesame Street*, but it was not drawn from typical commercial marketing practice. In its broadest expression, the target audience was to be all preschool children. Within that, the target age range was 3 to 5 years of age, with the bull's eye being age 4. But there was still further specification. Special efforts were to be made to ensure that the audience was racially and geographically diverse, and included children from communities where it was typical to find low income, high unemployment, poor housing, insufficient health care, and poor academic performance (Ball & Bogatz, 1970; Mielke, 1994; Polsky, 1974). *Sesame Street* was therefore distinctive even in the common basics of setting goals for audience reach.

With most television programming, the goals start and end with audience size and composition, but not with *Sesame Street*. Special effort was made to analyze the educational needs of the target audience, and then to create appropriate educational goals for this unique preschool project (Lesser, 1974; Lesser & Schneider, chap. 2, this volume). A challenge to the early planners was to avoid thinking in traditional classroom terms, and to think instead about what the medium of *television* could do with the pedagogical power of high production values, and the distribution power of national broadcasts.

As Lesser and Schneider (chap. 2, this volume) have explained, a series of five curriculum seminars in 1968 led to the adoption of five broad areas of goals for *Sesame Street*: social, moral, and affective development; language and reading; mathematical and numerical skills; reasoning and problem solving; and perception.

As a quick-take image, the media sometimes refer to *Sesame Street* as being about "letters and numbers," and that is partially correct. The cognitive learning area (extending beyond letter and number recognition, to include topics such as classifying and reasoning) is definitely a high priority, and it did get top billing in the premiere season. However, "social, moral, and affective" goals were included from the start, and the curriculum has been expanding and evolving ever since.

Goal-Based Research

In a commitment not common then or even now, CTW opted to be accountable not only for attracting its target audience, but also for having an educational effect. There was no map to follow, no model to emulate. Before *Sesame Street*, there was little popularity of public television among inner-city and low-income viewers, or research to suggest that preschool children, viewing mostly at home, could learn much of educational value from a television series.

The self-imposed burden of proof thus fell to the innovators to make their case with data-based evidence. This had been anticipated. The proposal for the creation of CTW itself envisioned " ... two separate research efforts that came to be known as 'formative research' and 'summative research'" (Polsky, 1974, p. 48). The summative research was "...to determine how effectively the program is teaching the children it does reach" (p.49). The effects of *Ses-*

ame Street were thus to be determined through summative research, and the research questions were to be derived primarily from the stated goals of the project (i.e., seeing if the series did what it set out to do).

Michael Scriven (1967) had introduced the terms *formative evaluation* and *summative evaluation* into the literature only 1 year previously. Scriven used *formative evaluation* to refer to the testing of work while it's still in its formative stages, so that the feedback can be used to improve the product; and *summative evaluation* as applying to a final evaluation of a completed work. These concepts fit well with CTW's management plan, and the terms *formative* and *summative* became an integral part of its corporate parlance. Although CTW has not distinguished consistently among the terms *evaluation, research,* and *evaluation research,* through the years the formative-summative distinctions have been maintained. In 1968, the original formative work for *Sesame Street* was assigned to one team, the summative work to another (Polsky, 1974).

The formative research that has been conducted in support of the *Sesame Street* television series is discussed at length in several chapters in this book (Fisch & Bernstein, chap. 3, this volume; Palmer & Fisch, chap. 1, this volume; Truglio, Lovelace, Seguí & Scheiner, chap. 4, this volume). The following discussion draws on summative studies that investigated the impact of *Sesame Street* on children's academic knowledge and skills and their social behavior.

IMPACT ON ACADEMIC KNOWLEDGE AND SKILLS

Evaluation of Seasons 1 and 2

Planning. Before any production had begun, CTW arranged for the Educational Testing Service (ETS) of Princeton, New Jersey to design and conduct the summative evaluation for the premiere season of *Sesame Street*. With everyone on the project working from scratch, there was an unusual opportunity in the premiere season for the summative evaluator to be involved in the creation of the original goals. It was also possible for the production planners to grapple with how the results of their intentions might actually be measured later on.

Two decades after his initial work with the *Sesame Street* evaluation (Ball & Bogatz, 1970), Sam Ball, the principal investigator, reflected on a few of the challenges he faced in creating goals, instruments, and the research design (Ball, 1990). He recalled the hesitation of some curriculum advisors to be specific in stating educational goals in measurable terms. Given workable goals, there was the enormous task of creating research instruments that could yield useful measures under conditions of unusual difficulty. Relatively untrained testers would have to collect voluminous data from a large sample of economically, geographically, and ethnically diverse children who were only 3 to 5 years of age. Then there was the challenge of the research design itself.

Ball " ... opted for a true experimental design because this was the best way of unequivocally showing causal relationships between a treatment and its effects" (Ball, 1990, pp. 14–15).

The general, core idea was to compare a large sample of *Sesame Street* viewers (treatment group) with nonviewers (control group) on several goal-based topics that were treated in the series. A secondary assignment was to look for side effects. The experimental design, with its many variables and sample subdivisions, unsurprisingly, was anything but simple (Ball & Bogatz, 1970). Both before and after broadcast of the full 26-week first season, children were tested extensively in areas such as knowledge of the alphabet and numbers, names of body parts, recognition of forms, knowledge of relational terms, and sorting and classification skills.

Without direct control over voluntary viewers, the researchers hoped that the treatment group, encouraged to view, would in fact view, and that the control group, receiving no such encouragement, would not view. Ironically, the high appeal of the series served to weaken the experimental design: The control group unexpectedly viewed the new series in large numbers, making the planned comparisons uninterpretable. Because of this, the researchers had to devise other ways to analyze the data, such as comparing results across four levels of actual viewing, regardless of the child's initial assignment to treatment or control groups. The four levels of viewing were derived by dividing the sample into four quartiles, depending on the amount of *Sesame Street* they viewed: the highest 25% watched *Sesame Street* more than five times per week, the next highest 25% viewed four to five times per week, the next 25% viewed two to three times per week, and the lowest 25% rarely or never viewed the series.

The second-year evaluation (Bogatz & Ball, 1971) again featured an experimental design, but this time it handled the problem of control group "contamination" by selecting control-group households where *Sesame Street* could not be received. Another part of the second-year evaluation was a follow-up on some carry-over respondents from the first study.

Data.   Vast amounts of data were generated in the course of the two large-scale evaluations, spanning a wide range of curriculum areas, such as letters, numbers, sorting, classification, and labeling body parts. A single example of a specific finding—a child's ability to correctly name a rectangular shape—will be cited here just to give a feel for one of the elements in the multitude of "raw ingredients" that Ball and Bogatz processed in order to reach their more general conclusions. At the end of the first season, heavier viewers did better than light viewers or nonviewers in their ability to name the rectangular shape correctly: 64% of the heaviest *Sesame Street* viewers could correctly name the rectangular shape at the end of the first season, as compared to 43% of the next heaviest viewers, 34% of the next lower group, and 15% of the group who watched the least. The pretest-to-posttest percentage *gains* in being able to do this also increased with the amount viewed; spread across the same four levels of viewing, high to low, the percentage gains were: 53%,

31%, 21%, and 7%, respectively. From hundreds of such specific data-based findings, analyzed in multiple ways, and showing instances where learning gains did and did not occur, Ball and Bogatz (1970) forged their general conclusions, characterizing the series as a whole in its first two seasons.

The three most general statements of outcomes of the first-season evaluation, and generally replicated in the second season, were:

- Children 3 to 5 years of age who watched the most learned the most; their "gain scores" increased stepwise upward as viewing went stepwise upward.
- Topics getting more screen time on the show (e.g., letters) were learned better than were topics receiving less screen time.
- Children viewing in the informal home setting gained as much as children viewing in school under the supervision of a teacher.

These general effects tended to hold up across various subdivisions of children (e.g., by gender, age, geographic location, socio-economic status, etc.).

In the second-year evaluation, teachers were asked to rank their incoming students in kindergarten, first grade, or Head Start, on seven dimensions of school readiness, without knowing anything about these students' level of viewing *Sesame Street* in the previous year. By sorting those rankings into levels of prior viewing, it was seen that teachers rated heavier viewers higher on general readiness for school, quantitative readiness, positive attitudes toward school, and relationships with peers (Bogatz & Ball, 1971).

Sesame Street in Social Context.   In the mid-1970s, Cook and others reanalyzed the ETS evaluation data for *Sesame Street*'s first 2 seasons (Cook et al., 1975). They reached more modest conclusions about the learning effects of *Sesame Street*, after removing what they considered to be the learning effects not of the series per se, but of "encouragement to view," which was the procedure used to define and obtain the treatment or "viewing" group. Somewhat oversimplified, the argument of Cook et al. was that the encouragement itself enhanced the learning, and therefore accounted by itself for some but not all of the observed learning gains. Yet, reporting on a separate analysis designed to break out the effects of "encouragement" on the observed learning gains, Ball and Bogatz (1975) stated: "We, as did Cook et al., found *viewing* apart from encouragement to be a significant factor" (p. 394).

Encouragement to View in Naturalistic Contexts.   A comment is in order about the concept of *encouragement*. Although there might be a rationale for minimizing or trying to isolate *encouragement* effects in a research design, in the real world, encouragement to pursue educational activity is a desirable and natural thing, a routine part of good parenting. In a child's experience, viewing is an integral part of the ever-present physical and social contexts in which the viewing occurs. This is what makes it so difficult to isolate all the different reasons why a child may or may not learn something taught on *Sesame Street*. Metaphorically speaking, the programming is always an ingredient in the mix, a thread in the fabric. The *Sesame Street* producers cannot control the social and physical environment in the home, yet that environment is a critical influence on what's possible for the child or the program to accomplish. When parents use all the various means at their command to help a child learn, that could well include encouragement to view *Sesame Street*. In fact, CTW actively promotes "encouragement to view" through outreach programs, parent guides, materials for child-care settings, promotional campaigns, alliances with other mission-compatible organizations, and productions in other media. (Descriptions of some of these initiatives, along with the relevant research, are described by Yotive & Fisch, chap. 10, this volume.) The "credit" for learning is fundamentally a shared credit.

The ETS summative evaluation reports for *Sesame Street*'s first season (Ball & Bogatz, 1970) and again for the second season (Bogatz & Ball, 1971) were landmark studies. They not only provide the majority of the early evidence on the educational effects of *Sesame Street*, they are also cited widely in the entire literature of television's effects. These ETS evaluations were the last domestic attempts to compare "before *Sesame Street*" with "after *Sesame Street*" by way of a large-scale experimental design with viewing and control groups. The baseline conditions could not be found after the second year because the series had become so widely viewed; true control children (i.e., children who had never been exposed to *Sesame Street*) were quickly becoming a rarity. By its second season, *Sesame Street* was reaching between 3 and 4 million children, including the targeted but difficult-to-reach inner-city viewers (Lesser, 1974; Mielke, 1994). As a consequence, later large-scale studies would tend to use statistical designs and methods for estimating cause-effect relationships, rather than trying to establish groups of "viewers" and "nonviewers."

Language Acquisition

A Longitudinal Study.   We turn now to other research studies on the cognitive effects of *Sesame Street*. The first of these deals with language acquisition (Rice, Huston, Truglio, & Wright, 1990). This was not an evaluation of *Sesame Street* per se, but a theoretically based study that included the viewing of *Sesame Street*. It was known that children actively processed information, and that they watched a lot of television, but it was not known if children actually acquired new vocabulary from the dialogue modeled on the television programs that they viewed at home. The researchers did the study in the home environment, with all its typical distractions, because that's where most of the viewing takes place. *Sesame Street* was chosen because of its appeal to preschool children, and its emphasis on educational goals.

In a 2-year longitudinal study, engaging 326 children and their families in the Topeka, Kansas area, the authors examined vocabulary acquisition among children 3 to 7 years old. Their approach was to collect five "waves" of (1-week) viewing diaries in 6-month intervals. The diaries covered every member of the family, and were buttressed by home-based interviews about such things as rules and typical practices for watching television in the home. The effect, vocabulary acquisition, was measured by way of the Peabody Picture Vocabulary Test (PPVT), which has norms established for ages 2 through adult.

Data were collected not only for what television shows were viewed, but also for other variables that could be relevant to language acquisition, such as the education level of the parents, the presence or absence of older siblings, and the parents' attitudes toward television generally. Statistical methods were used to isolate the linkage of a single factor to vocabulary level while controlling or statistically removing the influence of the other factors. In this way, earlier viewing of *Sesame Street* was used to predict later (PPVT-measured) vocabulary, with the effects of such influences as parents' education being statistically removed.

In summary, these were the major outcomes:

- For younger children, starting at ages 3 to 3 1/2, *Sesame Street* viewing was a significant predictor of vocabulary scores at age 5. Such viewing, however, did not predict 5 to 5 1/2-year-olds' vocabulary measured at age 7 (because the older children had outgrown the show).
- Unlike *Sesame Street*, children's viewing of programs without specific educational intent, such as most cartoons, was not associated with increased vocabulary.
- Most viewing occurred without coviewing parents, implying that children could learn vocabulary even without their parents viewing the programs with them.
- The associations of increased vocabulary with *Sesame Street* viewing held, regardless of parent education, family size, child gender, or parental attitudes toward television.

The researchers speculated as to why only *Sesame Street*, and not the other kinds of shows, led to increased vocabulary. Perhaps it was because *Sesame Street* consciously uses simple language and formats designed to encourage physical and mental participation, frequently pairing new words with representative pictures, and using songs to provide repetition in an entertaining way.

Home Video Study. Another study, also pertaining to language acquisition, dealt with the use of *Sesame Street* home videocassettes in the natural home setting (Rice & Sell, 1990). Twenty children, ages 2 to 5, and their families participated in this 1-year study. Four *Sesame Street* cassettes—"I'm Glad I'm Me," "The Alphabet Game," "Learning About Letters," and "Count It Higher"—were given to families for home use.

Researchers collected information from parents on family-video use, and recorded observations in the homes as the children viewed the cassettes. They tested the children before and after the period of home viewing on cognitive skills thought to be potentially affected by viewing. Measures included the Brigance K & 1 Screening for kindergarten and first grade, the recognition of numerals section of the Brigance Diagnostic Inventory of Basic Skills, and other materials designed to assess the skills taught by the videos.

The researchers documented gains in children's vocabulary, letter recognition, number recognition, and printed word identification. They interpreted the learning effects as " ... rather remarkable, given that the children averaged only two-and-one-half to three hours of viewing each tape, over 11 weeks, in a situation with competing social activities" (p. 2). Rice (1990) noted that the cassettes seemed to encourage discussion that could have helped to reinforce educational content and messages: "Children talk about the cassette, they label the characters and things, and they repeat parts of the songs and dialogue. The parents also comment on the tapes and relate the tapes to other experiences of the child" (p.45).

Summary

Subsequent research has served to confirm and extend the pattern of data that emerges from the studies dealing with *Sesame Street*'s impact on academic knowledge and skills, described earlier. In particular:

- A 3-year longitudinal study, conducted by researchers at the Center for Research on the Influences of Television on Children (CRITC) at the University of Kansas (now at the University of Texas at Austin), found that *Sesame Street* viewing was positively associated with subsequent performance in reading, mathematics, vocabulary, and school readiness. These effects were significant even after the effects of socio-economic status(SES), mothers' education, and educational quality of home environment were removed statistically (Wright et al., chap. 6, this volume).
- An analysis of data from a national survey conducted for the U.S. Department of Education found significant correlations between *Sesame Street* viewing and preschoolers' ability to recognize letters of the alphabet, and tell connected stories when pretending to read. In addition, when they subsequently entered first and second grade, children who had viewed *Sesame Street* as preschoolers were also more likely to be reading storybooks on their own, and less likely to require remedial reading instruction (Zill, chap. 7, this volume).
- Perhaps most notably, a "recontact" study by researchers from CRITC and the University of Massachusetts at Amherst employed a sample of high school students whose television viewing as preschoolers had been tracked approximately 10 to 15 years earlier. The results of the study showed that adolescents who were frequent viewers of *Sesame Street* at age 5: had significantly better grades in English, science, and mathematics; read more books for pleasure;

and had higher motivation toward achievement (Huston et al., chap. 8, this volume).

Each of these three studies is discussed in greater detail in subsequent chapters of this volume.

IMPACT ON SOCIAL BEHAVIOR

Much has been written and researched about the negative social effects of television, particularly as applied to violent portrayals on television and subsequent aggressive behavior of viewers. There is a much smaller literature on the positive potential of television to encourage prosocial behaviors such as cooperation, sharing, empathy, and valuing others. Because such prosocial learning is obviously important for the child, the parent, and later on to the success of the child's entry into school, the question arises as to why there is not more research available.

At least one reason is that prosocial learning effects, although easy to talk about, are difficult to measure with precision. Lesser (1974) referred to early research with Head Start as a possible model for the *Sesame Street* evaluation: "Although five of the seven stated goals of Head Start stress social and emotional benefits (self-concept, self-discipline, positive attitudes toward family and society, self-confidence, self-worth), these were ignored in the evaluation because no good measures of them were available" (p. 147). Ball and Bogatz (1975), referring to a criticism that their evaluation did not contain more affective measurements, stated: "The measurement of affect is difficult, and specific suggestions of other measures we might have used will be warmly welcomed" (p. 396).

The television research literature on social effects generally indicates that both prosocial and antisocial television portrayals are associated with consequential behaviors in children (Comstock & Paik, 1991). Prosocial modeling leads to more prosocial behavior and less antisocial behavior. For reasons not fully understood, young children in prosocial research studies tend not to generalize a modeled prosocial principle to a different situation, but they can express the behavior in contexts and situations similar to those modeled in the portrayal. This holds for research on *Sesame Street* as well (Dorr, 1990).

Empirical Data

The earliest study on *Sesame Street* and prosocial learning was conducted by Paulson (1974), and focused on cooperation. The study drew from an entire season of *Sesame Street* programs, with an experimental design of 36 viewers and 42 nonviewers. For measures of effects, Paulson used the Oregon Preschool Test of Interpersonal Cooperation (OPTIC), a picture recognition test, and observations from free play. The OPTIC measures social behavior by placing two children into a series of specially designed situations, then scoring the extent to which the children cooperate with each other. Consistent with findings from other studies, *Sesame Street* viewers cooperated more than those who did not view, when tested in situations similar to those presented on the programs. Also, children who viewed were more likely than the nonviewers to recognize examples of cooperation presented on the show, to judge the cooperative solutions as best, and use the word *cooperation* in an appropriate manner.

Leifer (1975) compiled nine videotapes of prosocial *Sesame Street* segments, three for each of three experimental conditions (differing in how the prosocial content was presented; e.g., showing valued/devalued behavior, showing consequences, etc.). Fifty-three children were: (a) tested individually, (b) observed as they participated in structured tasks, (c) observed in social behavior occurring naturally, and (d) observed in their attention to the videotapes themselves. In general, the results showed positive prosocial learning effects, but only when the measures closely resembled the behaviors modeled in the videotapes.

Bankart and Anderson (1979) did a small-scale field observational study of the impact of prosocial television (*Sesame Street*) on free play of preschool children in a day-care setting. Viewing *Sesame Street* was not associated on their measures with increased prosocial behavior, but it was related to decreased aggressiveness.

More generalized effects of *Sesame Street* viewing were found by Zielinska and Chambers (1995), who conducted research in eight Montreal day-care centers. Across eight days, a sample of 150 children watched *Sesame Street* segments that were either (a) cognitive or (b) prosocial in content. Observations were made during follow-up activities that were either (a) cooperative in nature or (b) individualistic; further observations were made during free play. Data from these observations were coded with an eye toward several classes of prosocial behavior: positive interaction, cooperation, helping, giving, sharing, turn taking, comforting, and affection.

The results of the study showed that viewers of the prosocial segments were highest in prosocial behaviors during planned activities. Viewers of prosocial segments who also participated in cooperative follow-up activities were lowest in antisocial behavior during free play.

Summary

Together, these studies suggest that *Sesame Street* can exert a significant impact on children's social behavior, but the research evidence is not as strong as it is with cognitive effects, nor are there as many studies in the literature. Some studies have found exposure to *Sesame Street* to affect social behavior only in situations comparable to those shown on the series (e.g., Leifer, 1975), while others have also found effects on children's social behavior in other situations (e.g., Zielinksa & Chambers, 1995).

CONCLUSION

The focus on educational goals in measuring the success of *Sesame Street* is also a decision *not* to examine other areas of real or potential evidence of impact. *Sesame Street* can, of course, have impact and be evaluated in areas other than its educational goals. For example, Cook and Curtin (1986), citing *Sesame Street's* professional awards, favorable reviews from media critics, global acceptance, parental testimonials, longevity, and pioneering leadership in combining entertainment with education, stated: "By almost any criterion, *Sesame Street* has been a success" (p. 3). Through the years, *Sesame Street* has also been a contributing participant in many broad, social issues that lie beyond its formal curriculum and research assessment, such as "putting public television on the map," or "laying the groundwork for new legislation," or "contributing to a general upgrade of the kindergarten curriculum." Similarly, if groups of economists, historians, and anthropologists were asked to study the effects of *Sesame Street*, their research questions probably would not be drawn from the educational goals for the series, but from their own distinctive traditions, theories, and methods of inquiry. The significance of *Sesame Street* is greater than its educational effectiveness discussed here.

From the standpoint of educational impact, early research on the cognitive effects of *Sesame Street* laid to rest the truly basic question of feasibility; that is, whether it was possible to achieve worthwhile outcomes from preschoolers' voluntary home-based viewing of educational television programming. The answer is yes. Taken as a whole, these early research studies show that preschool children can and do learn cognitive skills and information from *Sesame Street*. The greater their exposure to purposive educational programming such as *Sesame Street*, the more they learn, and that opportunity extends to all children, regardless of their parents' station in life. At the same time, children also demonstrate learning of prosocial skills modeled on *Sesame Street*, particularly when children can express it in a form similar to the way in which it was modeled in the program. Children's learning from *Sesame Street* occurs within a web of other influences in the social and physical environment, where parental encouragement and participation in the child's viewing can help increase the learning.

Early learning is crucially important, not only for its obvious immediate advantage, but even more importantly for its long-term advantage. One can envision a series of steps and choice points that begin in the formative preschool years, and extend into adulthood. The concern is that failing on that first step can lead to failure on the others, and the hope is that success early on will make possible success later. Early childhood education can give the child a cognitive advantage at step one, say, in mastering the introductory material taught in first grade. In turn, this helps the child successfully complete the upper grades, and so on. Long-term advantages of early childhood learning are not a form of predeterminism, but a logical and plausible sequence of enhanced chances for success.

Comstock and Paik (1991) set out the conservative challenge that *Sesame Street* demonstrate positive influence of preschool viewing into the mid-elementary and even high school years, and recent research has shown that even this high a criterion of success could be reached (Huston et al., chap. 8, this volume). Such findings speak to the potential power of educational television as a whole, and of *Sesame Street* in particular.

REFERENCES

Ball, S. (1990). *The first evaluation. Sesame Street research: A 20th anniversary symposium*. New York: Children's Television Workshop.

Ball, S., & Bogatz, G. (1970). *The first year of Sesame Street: An evaluation*. Princeton, NJ: Educational Testing Service.

Ball, S., & Bogatz, G. (1975). Some thoughts on this secondary evaluation. In T. D. Cook, H. Appleton, R. F. Conner, A. Shaffer, G. Tamkin, & S. J. Weber (Eds.). *Sesame Street revisited*. New York: Russell Sage Foundation.

Bankart, C. P., & Anderson, S. S. (1979). Short-term effects of prosocial television viewing on play of preschool boys and girls. *Psychological Reports, 44*, 935–941.

Bogatz, G., & Ball, S. (1971). *The second year of Sesame Street: A continuing evaluation*. Princeton, NJ: Educational Testing Service.

Comstock, G., & Paik, H. (1991). *Television and the American child*. New York: Academic Press.

Cook, T. D., Appelton, H., Conner, R. F., Shaffer, A., Tamkin, G., & Weber, S. J. (1975). *Sesame Street revisited*. New York: Russell Sage Foundation.

Cook, T .D., & Curtin, T. R. (1986). An evaluation of the models used to evaluate television series. In G. Comstock (Ed.), *Public communication and behavior, Volume I*. New York: Academic Press.

Dorr, A. (1990). *Social and emotional effects of Sesame Street. Sesame Street research: A 20th anniversary symposium*. New York: Children's Television Workshop.

Leifer, A. (1975). *How to encourage socially valued behavior*. Paper presented at the biennial meeting of the Society for Research in Child Development, Denver, CO.

Lesser, G. (1974). *Children and television: Lessons from Sesame Street*. New York: Random House.

Mielke, K. (1994). *Sesame Street* and children in poverty. *Media Studies Journal, 8*(4), 125–134.

Paulson, F. (1974). Teaching cooperation on television: An evaluation of *Sesame Street* social goals programs. *AV Communication Review, 22*(3), 229–246.

Polsky, R. (1974). *Getting to Sesame Street: Origins of the Children's Television Workshop*. New York: Praeger.

Rice, M. L. (1990). Educational effects of *Sesame Street* home videos. *Sesame Street research: A 20th anniversary symposium*. New York: Children's Television Workshop.

Rice, M. L., Huston, A. C., Truglio, R. T., & Wright, J. C. (1990). Words from *Sesame Street*: Learning vocabulary while viewing. *Developmental Psychology, 26*(3), 421–428.

Rice, M., & Sell, M. (1990). *Executive Summary: Exploration of the Uses and Effectiveness of Sesame Street of Home Videocassettes*. Lawrence, Kansas: Center for Research on the Influences of Television on Children.

Scriven, M. (1967). The methodology of evaluation. In R. Tyler, R. Gagne, & M. Scriven (Eds.), *Perspectives of curriculum evaluation*. AERA Monograph Series on Curriculum Evaluation. Chicago: Rand McNally.

Zielinska, I. E., & Chambers, B. (1995). Using group viewing of television to teach preschool social skills. *Journal of Educational Television, 21*(2), 85–99.

6 The Early Window Project: *Sesame Street* Prepares Children for School

John C. Wright
Aletha C. Huston
Ronda Scantlin
University of Texas at Austin
Jennifer Kotler
Georgetown University

Sesame Street was launched in the late 1960s during a period of social ferment and optimism about the ability of our society to bring the benefits of prosperity and opportunity to all of its people. The War on Poverty rested on the premise that the disadvantages of poverty could be overcome by providing the poor with the skills and capabilities needed for success. Interventions for young children, including Head Start and other early education initiatives, were a major part of this effort. If children in poor families could be prepared for school by early education programs, it followed that they could also learn from television. And, of course, television had the great advantages of availability in millions of homes, appeal to young children, and low cost per child per year (relative to other educational initiatives). (For further discussion of the motivations that underlay the creation of *Sesame Street*, see Palmer & Fisch, chap. 1, this volume.)

Because *Sesame Street* was breaking new ground in many respects, a strong evaluation was included in the first 2 years of broadcasting. No one was sure that such a program could attract viewers, especially among the poor and ethnic minority children who were its target audience. Equally important, there was little basis for knowing whether children would learn anything of value from televised instruction that they watched voluntarily and often irregularly at home.

The evaluations were conducted by an independent research team at the Educational Testing Service (Ball & Bogatz, 1970; Bogatz & Ball, 1971; cf. Mielke, chap. 5, this volume). Their research designs were experiments—that is, they identified families with children in the age range of 3 to 5 and randomly assigned them to a "program" group that was encouraged to watch *Sesame Street* or to a control group that was not informed about the new program. In the first year of broadcasting, the program was more popular than anyone had expected, so the control group watched it even without encouragement. The experimental part was defeated by the instant success of the program, but although they could not find enough people who never watched the show to make a categorical comparison, the more kids watched the better the outcomes. In the second year of evaluation, the researchers studied two communities in which public television was available only on UHF channels or by cable, which most poor families could not access on their television sets (Bogatz & Ball, 1971). The "encouraged" group was given cable or UHF capabilities, and the control group was not, so the experiment was successful the second time around in creating large differences in children's viewing.

The results of these studies provided solid evidence that children could learn preacademic skills from *Sesame Street*. Children in the "encouraged" groups gained more on tests of literacy, number skills, concepts, and other cognitive skills taught by *Sesame Street* than did children in the control group. The gains occurred for children from different racial and ethnic groups, for both boys and girls, and for children from different regions of the country. A hint of trends to come was the fact that, although children of all ages learned, 3-year-olds gained more than did older children. At that time, the target age for the program was 4. Everyone underestimated what very young children could learn from television.

Despite the very high quality of the evaluation design, some members of the research community questioned its conclusions (Cook et al., 1975). They pointed out that the "treatment" for the experimental group included parental encouragement as well as children's viewing, so parents may have been alerted to watch with their children and to rehearse some of the program content. Therefore, the positive results could not be attributed solely to viewing the program. Some of the gains might have come from the parental attention and support. For the small number of children in the control group who viewed the program without accompanying parental encouragement, the gains in cognitive skills were limited to specific knowledge about letters and numbers. There is other evidence that adults who watch the program with the child can enhance what children learn. The question that remained was whether children could learn significant and lasting intellectual skills without adult mediation.

These investigators also argued that *Sesame Street* was not closing the gap between rich and poor; in fact, it might even be enlarging it. When children from disadvantaged homes watched, they learned as much as did the more advantaged children. However, in the absence of parental encouragement, children from economically advantaged homes watched more regularly than did children from disadvantaged homes. That was during the first season of broadcasting, when the program was unknown and many poor families did not have access to public television. In the years since then, *Sesame Street* has become familiar to parents and children in all parts of the United States (as well as in many parts of the world), and most people now have the television equipment and the proximity to a public television station needed to receive it. In a representative national sample surveyed by Westat (Zill, chap. 7, this volume), children from families across the income spectrum watched equally often.

With success came other questions and criticisms. Some questioned whether television was a suitable medium to promote learning, even with the best of content. Healy (1990) argued, for example, that the visual nature of television dominates children's attention and cognitive processing, making it less likely that they will acquire language skills from viewing. Others suggested that children might learn rote content (e.g., reciting the alphabet), but not more abstract conceptual skills that would carry over into the school years. Singer (1980) criticized the rapid pace of the program, arguing that it did not provide time to process information at more than a superficial level. Finally, some argued that even good television is a poor substitute for more direct learning experiences that might be available to young children. They worried that parents would use *Sesame Street* as a "baby-sitter" and that time spent viewing would displace more active and creative ways of spending time.

This chapter is focused on a short-term longitudinal study of children from low-income neighborhoods called the "Early Window Project" (Wright & Huston, 1995). It was conducted by the faculty, students, and staff of the Center for Research on the Influences of Television on Children, called "CRITC," at the University of Kansas, and, as of 1996, at the University of Texas at Austin. Since the founding of CRITC in 1978, we have been investigating many of these issues. Some of our early studies provide relevant background for the Early Window Study. First, we and colleagues examined the formal features and spoken language in *Sesame Street*, comparing it to other children's programs to determine its typical pace, level of action, use of visual and auditory special effects, and use of language. These analyses of programs from the late 1970s indicated that *Sesame Street* was less rapidly paced than commercial entertainment cartoons, and that PBS programs for children in general provided many times the number of minutes per week in each category of educational programming than was provided by educational programs on commercial television (Neapolitan & Huston, 1994).

Mabel Rice, an expert on children's language, did detailed analyses showing that the spoken language on *Sesame Street* was presented according to principles that should enhance children's understanding and acquisition of new vocabulary (Rice, Huston, & Wright, 1982). Far from detracting from language, the visual portions of the program were used to help children understand the words used. Words were used in conjunction with visuals (e.g., "jumping" spoken while animated figures jumped); words said slowly and were repeated; and language was carefully tailored to the level of the young viewers who were the target audience.

Both the audiovisual formal features and the language used on *Sesame Street* were distinctly different from those used in cartoons and other programs designed for children. The formal features were less frenetic and more integrated with content; and there was more speech that was presented in ways likely to be comprehended by young children. These analyses supported our initial assumption that all television is not alike.

Research in Daniel Anderson's laboratory demonstrated conclusively that children attended to the language in *Sesame Street*, often using its comprehensibility as a basis for deciding whether or not to attend visually to a segment (Anderson & Levin, 1976). Moreover, they understood verbal content when it was combined with visual presentations better than when it was not.

We next conducted a longitudinal study from 1980 to 1983, and found evidence that children learned vocabulary from viewing at home. We collected viewing diaries over a 2-year period, following one group from ages 3 to 5 years old and a second group from ages 5 to 7 years old. Children's receptive vocabulary was tested at the beginning and the end of the 2-year period with the Peabody Picture Vocabulary Test. On the basis of extensive interviews with parents, we had information about parents' education, family structure, other children in the family, parents' attempts to encourage and regulate different types of television viewing, and children's experiences in preschool and child care (Huston, Wright, Rice, Kerkman, & St. Peters, 1990). Because some of these family characteristics were correlated with viewing, we controlled them statistically. That is, our analyses were designed to find out whether children who watched *Sesame Street* frequently gained more vocabulary in 2 years than children who rarely watched the program, even when they were statistically equated for parents' education and other family characteristics. The answer was yes for children followed from age 3 to age 5. It appears that viewing *Sesame Street* contributed to children's vocabulary development during the preschool years. There was no evidence of further gains from age 5 to age 7, probably because children in that age range are beyond the level of the target audience (Rice, Huston, Truglio, & Wright, 1990).

THE EARLY WINDOW STUDY

By the late 1980s, *Sesame Street* had been on the air for nearly 20 years, but no large-scale evaluation of its effects had been done since the initial studies by ETS. When Children's Television Workshop (CTW) received an unrestricted grant from the MacArthur Foundation to study the program, Keith Mielke, the Vice President for Research, and Valeria Lovelace, the Director of *Sesame Street* Research, invited us (Wright & Huston) to conduct a longitudinal study to investigate the effects of the program on children's academic and social competencies. It was understood that the evaluation would be independent of CTW and that we would have the right of publication regardless of the findings. A technical report on the findings has in fact been published as well (Huston, Wright, Marquis, & Green, 1999). With those assurances and agendas, the Early Window Study was launched.

In 1989, it was no longer possible to use an experimental design in which children could be randomly assigned to view or not to view because virtually all U.S. preschoolers were familiar with *Sesame Street*. Therefore, we elected to use a longitudinal design that was similar to our earlier studies, but with several important differences: (a) children were followed for 3 years from age 2 to 5 or 4 to 7 in an effort to capture very early viewing on one end and the first year or 2 of school on the other, (b) the sample was drawn from low-to-moderate income families from three ethnic groups—African American, White, and Latino, (c) several tests of school-related skills were collected annually, (d) we measured the quality of home environment by direct observation in order to separate the influence of the learning environment provided by parents and activities at home from that provided by television, (e) two different types of viewing information were collected—24-hour time-use diaries recorded several times a year, and annual reports of viewing frequencies.

The Early Window Project had three major goals: to describe viewing patterns for its low-income sample by age, gender, and family characteristics; to investigate how time spent viewing was related to time in other activities; and to determine whether early viewing of *Sesame Street* was related to later school readiness.

Design

As shown in Fig. 6.1, children were 2 or 4 years old at the beginning of the study, and they were 5 or 7 at the end. Each year, families came to the project

Year	1990	1991	1992	1993
Cohort 1 Age	2	3	4	5
Cohort 2 Age	4	5	6	7
Office Visits	Wave 1	Wave 2	Wave 3	Wave 4
Home Visits	Wave 1	Wave 2	Wave 3	Wave 4

Bi-Monthly Time-Use Phone Diaries | Period 1 | Period 2 | Period 3 |
 ⟵——⟶ | ⟵——⟶ | ⟵——⟶ |

FIG. 6.1. Design of the study.

office for testing, observation, and interviews, and had a home visit from our staff. These four annual assessments are called "waves" of data. Although they were spread out over 4 years of data collection, for any one family the pattern was as shown.

The 3 years elapsing between waves are called "periods," so that Period 1 is between Waves 1 and 2, and so on. Throughout each period, approximately every 2 months, each family completed a telephone interview to record a diary of everything the child did on the previous day. These diaries were distributed over weekdays and were also collected on the occasions of office visits and home visits. To be included in the analyses, a family had to participate for at least one whole period (1 year) with a completed wave before and after it.

Sample

More than 250 families with a preschool child participated during the years from 1990 through 1993. The families were recruited from census tracts in Kansas City, Missouri and Kansas City, Kansas and from Lawrence, Kansas where the median incomes were lowest.

Table 6.1 describes the volunteer sample across the four waves of data collection. There were nearly equal numbers of boys and girls. About 40% of the families were African American, about 40% were White, and about 20% were Latino. A small number of families were Native American or other ethnic groups. About 18% used Spanish as the primary language in the home.

Both mothers and fathers had, on the average, 13 years of education, which means high school plus additional education or training of about 1 year. On the Census Bureau's Socioeconomic Occupational Scale (0 to 100), both parents' current or most recent job averaged about 27, a skilled blue collar level. A majority of the mothers had, or were seeking, a regular paid job outside the home.

The income/needs ratio is defined as the family's actual income divided by that income for a family of their composition located at the poverty threshold. The average income/needs ratio for this sample averaged about 1.73 except in the last year. In 1991, this was equivalent to an annual income of $23,894 for a family of four and $18,983 for a family of one adult and two children. About 46% of the families had received one or more forms of means tested assistance within the past 3 years.

Measures

Television Viewing. Information about children's viewing was drawn primarily from the time use diaries that were collected using a method that is standard in many studies of time use by children and adults (Juster & Stafford, 1985). The parent was asked to consider the previous day and describe the child's activities in order from midnight to midnight. For all activities except sleep, the parent was asked where the child was (home, school, other) and who else was there. The primary activity was the first activity

TABLE 6.1
Characteristics of the Sample

Attribute	Description	Wave			
		1	2	3	4
Gender:	Boys	118	132	114	107
	Girls	118	128	115	112
Ethnic Group:	African American	91	107	75	73
	Hispanic American	40	44	43	40
	European American	96	100	94	90
	Native American	4	6	10	10
	Other	5	3	7	6
Primary Language:	English	199	219	192	184
	Spanish	37	41	37	35
Demography:	Mom-years of education	13	13	13	13
	Dad-years of education	13	13	13	13
	Income/need ratio	1.7	1.7	1.8	1.9
	Mom-occupational status	26	28	29	29
	Dad-occupational status	25	28	29	28
	Family received means-tested assistance in past 3 years	48%	44%	46%	46%

named in a time interval (e.g., eating breakfast). For each primary activity, the parent was asked, "Was X doing anything else?" If so, it was considered a secondary activity. When television was named as a primary or secondary activity, the interviewer asked what program the child was watching.

Amount of viewing was defined as the total number of minutes spent in primary or secondary viewing in each 24-hour diary. The score for a 1-year period was the average of all weekday diaries collected during that year up to and including the office visit for the next wave. Weekend diaries were treated separately because viewing on weekends and that on weekdays followed different patterns. This measure was corroborated by the annual global ratings by the parents in their interview. They answered questions like "How many hours per week would you say that (child's name) watched educational or informational programs for children?" Clearly the diaries provided far more detail and richness than did the global ratings. But their results converged.

The time use diaries were also coded for time spent with books, educational activities, video games, play, and other activities.

Family Demographics and the Quality of Home Environment.

These were measured each year during the office and home visits. The Home Observation Measure of the Environment (Caldwell & Bradley, 1984), usually abbreviated as the "HOME," was used to measure the quality of the home environment. This standard instrument is a measure of the degree to which the child's home environment provides stimulation and support for cognitive and educational development and a mentally and emotionally healthy context for the child. It includes maternal affection, language, and intellectual stimulation to the child, as well as available toys and play areas, and opportunities for contacts with people and places outside the home. It predicts IQ and school performance of children from a wide range of socioeconomic backgrounds, income levels, and ethnic groups. Our home visitors were trained by experts from the University of Arkansas, where the instrument was devised. They maintained reliabilities of at least 80% agreement.

Language and School Readiness Skills.

Children's initial language skills were measured at Wave 1. Because the 2-year-olds were too young for most of the standardized tests, we used the Primary Language Scale (PLS) to get a general index of verbal skill. The 4-year-olds were given the Peabody Picture Vocabulary Test (PPVT- Revised), which measures receptive English vocabulary. It requires the child to point to one of four pictures on a page that illustrates or exemplifies a spoken word.

Academic and language skills were measured at Waves 2, 3, and 4 with standardized measures. The Woodcock-Johnson Tests of Achievement were used to measure reading and number skills. All children received the Letter Word Recognition Subtest, which measures recognition of icons, letters, and words. Children who reached a criterion on the Letter Word section were given the Passage Comprehension Subtest, a measure of reading comprehension. Math skills were assessed by the Applied Problems test, which involves counting, inequalities, and simple arithmetic. For the younger children only, general school readiness was assessed by the Bracken Basic Concepts Test of School Readiness. The test includes knowledge of colors, shapes, letters, numbers, spatial, and size relations. All children were given the PPVT-R.[1]

---

[1]Standard scores based on the published test norms for the child's chronological age were used for all four tests. The Woodcock-Johnson tests and the Peabody Picture Vocabulary have standard scores based on a mean of 100 and a standard deviation of 15. The Bracken Basic Concepts Test is scored on a scale with a mean of 10 and a standard deviation of 3.

Testers and interviewers were multiracial and multicultural. For children from Spanish-speaking families, a fully bilingual person whose first language was Spanish administered all tests. If the child appeared more fluent in Spanish than English, or if the child stated a preference for speaking Spanish when asked, Spanish translations were used except when the test assessed proficiency in English (e.g., reading and vocabulary). The Peabody Picture Vocabulary Test was administered first in English because we were interested in whether they had learned English vocabulary from viewing *Sesame Street*. The Spanish version of the PPVT was later administered during the home visit in order to assess Spanish-language vocabulary.

RESULTS

Age, Sex, and Family as Predictors of Viewing

The longitudinal design enabled us to investigate how viewing changes with age, whether boys and girls have different patterns of viewing, and how parent and home environmental characteristics are related to viewing *Sesame Street*. In our earlier study, viewing peaked at age 4 and declined steadily after that (Huston et al., 1990). Boys and girls watched for about the same amounts of time. Children with younger brothers and sisters watched more *Sesame Street* and peaked at a later age than did children with older brothers and sisters. The age changes were not all due to changing interest in the program, but also to the fact that older children spent more time in preschool and school. Even as preschoolers, the more time children spent in preschool or child care, the less time they watched *Sesame Street*, probably because they had less opportunity for viewing than did children who were home all day. In that study, there were no differences in viewing between children of more and less well-educated parents.

In the Early Window Study, the average child in the sample watched *Sesame Street* for slightly more than 2 hours per week at 2 to 3 years of age, with declines to about 1 hour per week at 4 to 6 years of age, and further declines after that. The patterns are shown in Fig. 6.2. Children watched other educational programs, but *Sesame Street* was the most frequently viewed; it occupied about 80% of the total time devoted to educational programs. As children got older, however, they shifted to other educational programs including *Reading Rainbow, Mr. Wizard's World*, and *3-2-1 Contact*. There were not consistent differences between boys and girls.

When interpreting these numbers, it is important to keep in mind that the sample is relatively small and was not selected to represent U.S. families in general. It is a volunteer sample of urban, Midwestern, low-income families. The sample is useful for generalizations about temporal patterns and covariations of viewing with other variables, but inferences about average viewing for children across the nation are not appropriate. (For data drawn from a national sample, see Zill, chap. 7, this volume.)

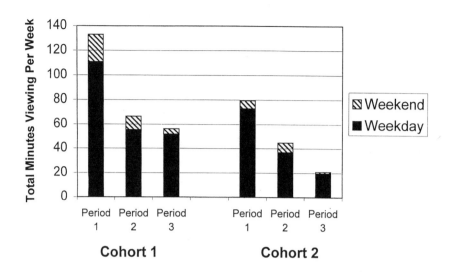

FIG. 6.2. Total weekly viewing of *Sesame Street*.

Children's early viewing patterns predicted later viewing. Although most children watched less frequently as they got older, those who were frequent viewers as very young children continued to watch relatively often in comparison to children who had rarely watched when they were 2 or 3 years of age.

Children who watched *Sesame Street* and other child informative shows were not heavy television viewers in general. They spent *less* time with cartoons and general audience programs than did children who were infrequent viewers of educational programs.

We did extensive analyses of home and family variables for the first period of data collection, when the children were 2 to 3 and 4 to 5 years old. One of the most striking findings was that children in Spanish-speaking families watched more *Sesame Street* than did children in families whose first language was English. Spanish-speaking mothers were slightly less well-educated than the non-Spanish mothers, and their children were less apt to be in child care, but the difference remained even when these variables were taken into account. Children in these families did not watch more non-informational television, only more child informative programming. The Spanish-speaking families in our sample were typically first generation; most were from Mexico. Some parents said they considered *Sesame Street* especially helpful for learning English, themselves.

Parent education, family income, and parents' occupational status were positively related to viewing. Of these, maternal education was the best predictor of children's viewing.

Children in high-quality family environments, as measured by the HOME scale, watched more *Sesame Street* than did those in low-quality environments, particularly in the age range from 2 to 3. Parents who provided intellectual stimulation and nurturance to their children had children who were apt to watch *Sesame Street* at age 2 to 3, and other children's educational programs in the later preschool years. These parents apparently encouraged *Sesame Street* when their children were very young, but moved on to other informational programs for children by the time the children were 4 or 5 years of age.

When mothers are employed, and children are in child care, opportunities to watch *Sesame Street* are sometimes limited because the program is broadcast during the day. We collected viewing information from child-care settings, and, as expected, children in child care watched television less often than did children at home. As in our earlier study, children who spent time in child care watched less *Sesame Street* than those who were cared for by their mothers most of the time (Huston et al., 1990).

Children with older brothers and sisters watched less *Sesame Street* than children who were the oldest in their families, probably because older siblings selected other programs for joint viewing. The impact of older siblings was especially strong for 4-year-olds who appeared to be moving away from interest in the program for developmental reasons.

Sesame Street Viewing and Other Ways of Using Time

The time-use diaries permitted us to examine how *Sesame Street* viewing was related to the time children spend in other activities. We addressed the possibility that television (even good television) displaces other more valuable activities, particularly reading and other educational activities, as well as the reverse hypothesis that well-designed television can stimulate children's interest in books rather than drawing them away. Several popular children's programs, including *Story Time* and *Reading Rainbow* are specifically designed to pique children's interest in reading. Evaluations of *Reading Rainbow* have shown large increases in library and bookstore requests for books featured on the program (Bianculli, 1994; Fetler, 1984).

From the time-use diaries, we calculated the amount of time children spent in "reading," that is, looking at books, magazines, and other print media; being read to by an adult or older child; and actually reading.

Second, we calculated time spent with "educational activities," which included paper work, writing, drawing, singing, puzzles and games for learning, preschool curricular activities, educational or scientific hobbies, trips to museums, the zoo, historical sites, lessons and practice in art, music, or dance. Time in school was not included because children do not have a choice about the allocation of that time.

Video and computer games were of special interest because of their new popularity, and because in some respects they share the entertainment appeal of watching television. Although some of these may have been educational, the majority of time was spent on "Nintendo" and "Sega"™ platforms which typically do not have educational content.

Individual Differences Among Children.   In each of the 3 years of
the study, high viewers of *Sesame Street* spent *more* time reading and engaging
in educational activities than did low viewers. *Sesame Street* viewing did *not*
displace print use and educational activities; rather, it may have enhanced
them. (By contrast, children who spent a lot of time watching cartoons and
adult programs, relative to others in our sample, spent *less* time in educational
activities and reading). Children who spent a lot of time on video games
watched less *Sesame Street* than did children who spent little or no time on
video games.

Individual Change Over Time.   These analyses of the relationships
between media use and other activities provide a picture of how children differ. Those children who watched a lot of *Sesame Street* also spent time on reading and educational activities; they devoted little time to video and computer
games. But, differences among children do not tell us much about an individual child's time allocations. Both the displacement hypothesis and the "en-
hancement" hypothesis suggest that high or low viewing should lead to a
change in an individual's time in other activities. For example, if *Sesame Street*
displaces reading and educational activities, a child who increases viewing
over time would decline in reading and educational activities.

To test this possibility, we used each diary collected over the 3-year period
to calculate curves or patterns of viewing and of time in other activities for
each child. We compared the time spent viewing child educational programs
with time spent in reading and other educational activities. The question we
asked was: When an individual's educational viewing increases or decreases,
does that child's time in reading and educational activities increase or de-
crease? The answer was that neither happened consistently. Individual
changes in viewing were not accompanied by systematic changes in reading
and educational activities.

We examined three other types of activity in these analyses: video games
and computers, play, and social activities (talking, outings, and meals).
Changes in viewing educational programs were not related to changes in time
spent on video games and computers or in social activity. Viewing educational programs and play varied together. When one increased, the other increased; when one declined, the other declined. As play varied positively with
viewing all types of television, this finding probably indicates that children
tend to play while watching television.

The Bottom Line: Basic Learning Skills
and School Readiness

Educational television is designed to achieve a wide range of educational goals
for children in both the cognitive and social domains. It is not limited to preparing children for school in the narrow sense of basic kindergarten-level

facts and skills, although that has always been one of the important objectives of *Sesame Street*.

The final section of this chapter is concerned with analyses of the degree to which viewing *Sesame Street* at one period predicts test performance at later points in time (i.e., later waves). For the most part the simple correlations between viewing and test scores are positive. That is, children who watched *Sesame Street* performed better than those who did little or no *Sesame Street* viewing.

However, we know that families who are better educated and who provide a stimulating and supportive home environment for their young children are also likely to be the families who encourage their children to watch *Sesame Street*. Differences in school readiness and test score performance could be due to family characteristics rather than to the *Sesame Street* viewing with which they are statistically associated.

Our analyses were designed to separate the cumulative contributions of family and environmental variables from those of television viewing. Accordingly in order to level the playing field, four basic characteristics of the family were identified as critical because they were associated with both viewing and test performance. They were mothers' years of education, family income/needs ratio, the HOME score, and the primary language spoken in the home (English or Spanish).[2]

We also needed to level the playing field by taking account of each child's prior attainments at the start of the study, so we used our best estimate of the children's initial mental abilities at Wave 1 as a control variable. For the 2-year-olds, it was their score on the Primary Language Scales at Wave 1. For the 4-year-olds, it was their score on the Peabody Picture Vocabulary Test at Wave 1.

In all of the analyses, these four family variables, plus initial vocabulary were controlled. That is, children's outcome scores were statistically corrected for the effects of initial linguistic skills, maternal education, income, primary language, and HOME score. Then we evaluated whether the amount of viewing was still related to the corrected outcome score measured one to three years later. That is, did *Sesame Street* viewing make a difference in children's performance above and beyond the effects of their own initial skills and the characteristics of their families?

Viewing *Sesame Street* in the early preschool years, from ages 2 to 3 was a consistent positive predictor of preacademic skills up to and including age 5. The patterns are shown in Figs. 6.3 and 6.4. These figures show the approximate advantage (positive) or disadvantage (negative) on the outcome measures experienced by a child who viewed 25 minutes a day as compared with a

---

[2]Language turned out to be a "suppressor variable" in that Hispanic American children often viewed *Sesame Street*, but, having English as a second language, performed less well than the average native English speaking children in the sample. Thus, for extraneous reasons, they represented high viewers with low outcome scores.

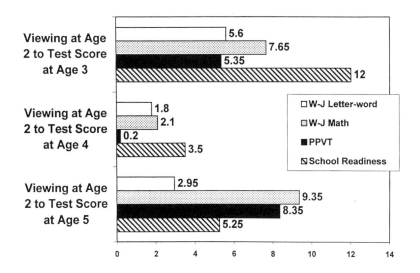

FIG. 6.3. Cohort 1: Viewing *Sesame Street* predicting test score
(advantage [+] or disadvantage [-]).

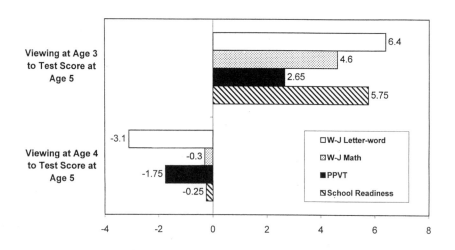

FIG. 6.4. Cohort 1: Viewing *Sesame Street* predicting test score
(advantage [+] or disadvantage [-]).

child who did no viewing, after the control variables have been taken into account.[3] The outcome measures have been scaled to resemble IQ scores. That is the average score is 100, and the 95% of the kids tested fall in a range from 70 to 130. The advantage of having watched 25 minutes a day of *Sesame Street* was typically about five points on these school readiness scales. Teachers' ratings of how ready to learn children were when they first attended school also showed significant positive effects of *Sesame Street* viewing.

Viewing *Sesame Street* at age 2 was positively associated with reading, math, vocabulary, and school readiness skills at age 3. More interesting, the high early viewers of *Sesame Street* (age 2 to 3) still had an advantage over lower early viewers 3 years later at age 5. This advantage was less apparent in the middle year (age 4), but followed a similar pattern (see Fig. 6.3).

Viewing between ages 3 and 4 was also positively related to school readiness and reading skills at age 5, though strangely not at age 4. Beyond age 4, there was no apparent effect of viewing for the group shown in Fig. 6.4 or for the children followed from ages 4 to 7.

CONCLUSIONS

Consider first the criticisms by Cook et al. (1975) of the first evaluation of *Sesame Street*. One was that the effects of viewing were mixed with the effects of parental encouragement. The present study clearly indicates that the acquisition of the skills in the program's curriculum does not require the involvement of parents, desirable as that may be, but occurs as a result of viewing alone. A second criticism was that *Sesame Street* helps disadvantaged children, but helps advantaged children more, thus increasing rather than narrowing the gap between privileged and deprived children. Our findings are that advantaged kids gain no more than disadvantaged kids per hour of viewing, but that disadvantaged kids do not watch enough to get the maximum benefits of viewing the program. The implication is clear: We need to do some "encouragement to view" as we work with the parents of disadvantaged children. Preschool teachers and home care providers also need to be encouraged to expose their charges to *Sesame Street* and other children's educational programs. Such outreach efforts are reported by Yotive and Fisch (chap. 10, this volume).

Hopefully these results will contribute to the effectiveness of outreach efforts by PBS and its affiliated stations to inform and motivate parents of chil-

---

[3]In the statistical analyses, all viewing times were converted to the square root of the number of minutes per day (averaged across all diaries in that period) in order to make the distributions suitable for the analyses used. This meant that we could illustrate the effects of 5 units of viewing (the approximate equivalent of 25 minutes per day of viewing) in order to give the reader a concrete idea of the magnitude of the effects. Note that 50 minutes of viewing would not have twice the impact of 25 minutes it would be equivalent to approximately 7 units. In order to double the magnitude of the effect shown for 5 units of viewing, one would have to watch 100 minutes a day, corresponding to 10 units of viewing.

dren who might be at risk of not being as prepared for school success as they might be if they were regulars on "the *Street*."

Another source of criticism is the concern that *Sesame Street* might lead to reduced or delayed language development, as a consequence of its immense audiovisual appeal. But this concern was not supported by the present study. On the contrary, it indicates that children are learning a great deal from *Sesame Street*, not simply memorizing letters and numbers, and are developing a positive attitude toward learning itself, including ready-to-learn attitudes, prereading skills, general concepts, and useful vocabulary.

Another lesson from these data is that television is not a monolithic entity with homogeneous effects on children regardless of their television diet. McLuhan was wrong: The *medium* is not the message—the *message* is the message; and thereby we arrive at a major corrective for popular opinion about television and children: It matters, very much, what you watch. Among the very same children for whom watching *Sesame Street* and other educational programs made a significant positive contribution to school readiness compared to not watching, viewing commercial entertainment cartoons had a sometimes significant *negative* effect on the same outcomes. Moreover, heavy viewers of *Sesame Street* and other educational children's programs were not heavy viewers in other categories of television, nor less likely to spend time in reading and other educational activities. In fact these regular viewers of *Sesame Street* spent less time watching cartoons and prime time adult dramas; less time playing video games; more time reading or being read to; and more time in other educational activities than did infrequent viewers of *Sesame Street*.

In summary, early viewing of educational children's television does appear to contribute to children's school readiness. For the most part the relationships between viewing educational programs and test scores are positive: The more young children watched *Sesame Street* and other educational programs, the more ready for school they were 1 to 3 years later. The impact of this early viewing was stronger than that of viewing the same programs at a slightly older age. It was the viewing by the 2- and 3-year-olds, more than that of the 4- and 5-year-olds, that seemed to enhance readiness for school. This younger preschool audience is especially important because they are less likely to be in a center type of child care, a center with a preacademic curriculum, than are the older preschoolers. Such strong, early influences are more important than later ones in that they initiate an early developmental trajectory that is higher and leads to growing advantage for their beneficiaries. It is therefore likely that these early gains will initiate a chain of influence that will benefit the child in many new ways in later development. It is the younger preschoolers for whom *Sesame Street* is an early window of opportunity for long-term gain.

A follow-up study of high school achievement of youngsters who had watched different amounts of educational programming as preschoolers indicates the persistence of some of these early positive effects. Clearly, the content of instructional *Sesame Street* segments was not what benefited children later in their school careers. Rather it was almost certainly a pattern of positive attitude toward school and school learning, a confident readiness to learn, and the mastery of basic understandings about concepts and communication that made the difference (Huston, Anderson, Wright, Linebarger, & Schmitt, chap. 8, this volume).

Viewing of *Sesame Street* made a positive contribution to these outcomes that was above and beyond the contributions of the child's home and history. It is important that the differences in outcome associated with early *Sesame Street* viewing occurred even when initial language skills, parents' education, family income, and the quality of the home environment were statistically equated.

Watching *Sesame Street* and other educational programs for children is part of a larger package of experiences that support school readiness. It is not an incidental part of the package, but one that makes a measurable, independent contribution to children's acquisition of school related skills. In sum, *Sesame Street* is an important part of a balanced television diet for young children. To prepare for school we all need our pencils, our notebooks, our thermos, and yes, our cumulative experience with *Sesame Street*.

REFERENCES

Anderson, D. R., & Levin, S. R. (1976). Young children's attention to *Sesame Street*. *Child Development, 47,* 806–811.

Ball, S., & Bogatz, G. A. (1970). *The first year of Sesame Street: An evaluation*. Princeton, NJ: Educational Testing Service.

Bianculli, D. (1994). *Teleliteracy: Taking television seriously*. New York: Touchstone.

Bogatz, G. A., & Ball, S. (1971). *The second year of Sesame Street: A continuing evaluation*. Princeton, NJ: Educational Testing Service.

Caldwell, B. M., & Bradley, R. H. (1984). *Home Observation for Measurement of the Environment*. Little Rock, AR: University of Arkansas.

Cook, T. D., Appleton, H., Conner, R. F., Shaffer, A., Tamkin, G., & Weber, S. J. (1975). *Sesame Street* revisited. New York: Russell Sage.

Fetler, M. (1984). Television viewing and school achievement. *Journal of Communication*. 34(2), 104–118.

Healy, J. M. (1990). *Endangered minds: Why our children don't think*. New York: Simon & Schuster.

Huston, A. C., Wright, J. C., Rice, M. L., Kerkman, D., & St. Peters, M. (1990). The development of television viewing patterns in early childhood: A longitudinal investigation. *Developmental Psychology, 26,* 409–420.

Huston, A. C., Wright, J. C., Marquis, J., & Green, S. (1999). How young children spend their time: Television and other activities. *Developmental Psychology 35,* 912–925.

Juster, F. T., & Stafford, F. P. (1985). *Time, goods, and well being*. Ann Arbor, MI: Institute for Social Research, University of Michigan.

Neapolitan, D. M., & Huston, A. C. (1994). *Educational content of children's programs on public and commercial television*. Lawrence, KS: Center for Research on the Influences of Television on Children, University of Kansas.

Rice, M. L., Huston, A. C., Truglio, R., & Wright, J. C. (1990). Words from *Sesame Street*: Learning vocabulary while viewing. *Developmental Psychology, 26,* 421–428.

Rice, M. L., Huston, A. C., & Wright, J. C. (1982). The forms and codes of television: Effects on children's attention, comprehension, and social behavior. In D. Pearl (Ed.), *Television and behavior: Ten years of scientific progress and implications for the eighties.* (pp 24–38). Washington, DC: Government Printing Office.

Singer, J. L. (1980). The power and limits of television: A cognitive-affective analysis. In P. Tannenbaum (Ed.), *The entertainment functions of television.* Hillsdale, NJ: Erlbaum.

Wright, J. C., & Huston, A. C. (1995). *Effects of educational TV viewing of lower income preschoolers on academic skills, school readiness, and school adjustment one to three years later.* Report to Children's Television Workshop. Center for Research on the Influences of Television on Children, University of Kansas, Lawrence.

7 Does *Sesame Street* Enhance School Readiness?: Evidence From a National Survey of Children

Nicholas Zill
Westat

The school readiness of young children is an area of considerable interest and debate in current educational policy. The first of the U.S. National Education Goals states, "By the year 2000, all children in America will start school ready to learn" (National Education Goals Panel, 1998, p. vi). The Goal was first agreed to by President Bush (1990) and the nation's Governors in 1990 and later written into law by the 103rd Congress in the "Goals 2000: Educate America Act" of 1994 (U.S. House of Representatives, 1994, p. 7). Although there is disagreement over what "readiness" means and what role it should play in enrollment decisions, there is general agreement within the educational community that how a child does in school depends in part on things that happen before he or she ever sets foot in a classroom (Resource Group on School Readiness, 1991; West, Germino-Hausken, & Collins, 1993).

In the influential book, *Ready to Learn: A Mandate for the Nation*, the late Ernest Boyer (1991) wrote that "Next to parents, television is, perhaps, a child's most influential teacher" (p. 25). According to Boyer, television can advance school readiness by raising parents' awareness about the importance of providing children with emotional support and intellectual stimulation during the preschool years. It can also contribute directly to children's readiness through programming that promotes an interest in school and teaches basic intellectual and social skills. Boyer specifically praised *Sesame Street* and other programs for children offered by the Public Broadcasting System. But he argued that educational television could and should play even more of a role in promoting school readiness. Congress agreed, passing "The Ready to Learn

Act of 1994," which provides funds to encourage new and expanded programming for young children and their parents.

The appropriate role for television in the nurturing of young children is a topic not without controversy. Some critics want to reduce young people's exposure to television greatly, preferring that children spend more time in interaction with their parents, books and other learning materials, and real-world experiences (Winn, 1985). Some critics contend that viewing *Sesame Street* teaches children to watch television (Tashman, 1994). *Sesame Street* has also received criticism for its fast pace and relatively brief segments, the argument being that this promotes short attention spans and a craving for stimulation (e.g., Healy, 1990).

In recent years, conceptions of school readiness have moved away from a heavily cognitive orientation toward greater emphasis on social and emotional aspects of children's development (Kagan, Moore, & Bredekamp, 1995). This has led some to question *Sesame Street*'s strong focus on the learning of basic literacy and numeracy skills. Of course, since its inception, *Sesame Street* has hardly neglected the social and emotional aspects of children's development, including considerable material dealing with self perceptions, sensitivity to others' feelings, and the frustrations and anxieties of childhood.

For their part, American parents generally are quite happy with *Sesame Street* and other PBS children's programs, feeling they are a positive influence on their youngsters. As focus group studies conducted for Children's Television Workshop (CTW) have shown, these programs are one group of television shows that most parents are glad to let their children watch (Tessier, 1995).

Sesame Street has received numerous awards and been widely praised for contributing to children's school readiness and raising public awareness about the importance of providing children with intellectual and cultural stimulation during the preschool years. As other chapters in this volume show, a variety of research studies have examined both the short- and longer-term effects of *Sesame Street* viewing on children's cognitive development (Mielke, chap. 5, this volume; Huston, Anderson, Wright, Linebarger, & Schmitt, chap. 8, this volume; Wright, Huston, Scantlin, & Kotler, chap. 6, this volume). But previous research has not studied *Sesame Street* viewing and its correlation in the context of a nationally representative sample of young children.

The discussion about television's role in promoting school readiness could benefit from data on how much educational television programming young children currently watch, how exposure varies across social groups and geographic areas, and whether such viewing seems to be associated with enhanced school readiness. An opportunity to gather national data on the viewing of *Sesame Street* and other PBS programs by young children in the United States arose during the design of the 1993 National Household Education Survey (NHES).

The NHES is a periodic national telephone survey conducted by the survey research firm Westat for the National Center for Education Statistics of the U.S. Department of Education. One of the topics that the 1993 survey focused on was school readiness. Information was obtained on a sample of

10,888 children, including 4,423 preschoolers, 2,126 kindergartners, and 4,277 first and second graders (Brick et al., 1994). It seemed logical to include a few items in the survey questionnaire to gauge current viewing of selected PBS programs by preschoolers and kindergartners, because of the prominent role that television plays in the lives of young children. The survey also asked about the previous viewing of the most widely known of the shows, *Sesame Street*, by kindergartners, first, and second graders before they started their formal schooling. This would not only permit estimates to be made of the extent of such viewing by children of different ages and social backgrounds, but also allow correlations to be drawn between educational television viewing and other aspects of the child's home environment and development (Zill, Collins, West, & Germino-Hausken, 1995). Further information on the survey methodology is presented in the appendix to this chapter.

Because of their natural interest in data on the audience for *Sesame Street* and other PBS children's programs, the Children's Television Workshop (CTW) and the Corporation for Public Broadcasting (CPB) commissioned Westat to analyze the relevant items and their demographic and developmental correlates and prepare reports on the findings (Zill, Davies, & Daly, 1994; Zill & Davies, 1994). The analysis of the survey findings on *Sesame Street* was intended to answer four major questions. They were as follows:

1. How extensively is *Sesame Street* viewed by America's preschool and kindergarten children?

2. How much does *Sesame Street* viewing vary by child and family characteristics, such as age, sex, race, and Latino origin, by geographic areas, and across areas with relatively high to relatively low concentrations of child poverty? Is the program being seen by children from families who may provide their offspring with limited stimulation and supportive home environments, due to low parent education or family income levels, lack of parental facility with the English language, or other disadvantages?

3. Do preschoolers who currently watch *Sesame Street* show a higher frequency of developmental accomplishments, such as being able to count to 20 or identify letters of the alphabet, than those who do not watch the show?

4. Do elementary schoolchildren who watched *Sesame Street* before they started kindergarten have more advanced development or fewer achievement and adjustment problems in school than those who were not *Sesame Street* viewers?

RESULTS

Patterns of *Sesame Street* Viewing by Young Children in the United States

According to reports from parents, viewing *Sesame Street* was a common activity for over 6.6 million American preschool children, and nearly 2.4 million kindergartners. The program's widespread appeal is evidenced by the finding that 77% of preschool children were watching *Sesame Street* once a week or more at the time of the survey, and 86% of kindergarten, first-, and second-grade students were reported to have watched the program at least once a week for a period of 3 months or more prior to beginning school.

Viewers of *Sesame Street* were likely to view other PBS children's programs as well. Over 7.6 million American preschool children (88%) and nearly 3.2 million kindergartners (80%) watched at least one of four public television children's programs asked about in the 1993 NHES (i.e., *Sesame Street*, *Barney and Friends*, *Mister Rogers' Neighborhood*, and *Reading Rainbow*). Seventy-three percent of preschoolers and 61% of kindergartners were reported to watch two or more of the programs on a regular basis.

Sesame Street, which is among the oldest of the PBS children's programs, remained the most popular of these four programs aimed at the young child audience. Among preschoolers, 77% watched *Sesame Street* once a week or more, 69% watched *Barney*, 45% watched *Mister Rogers' Neighborhood*, and 39% watched *Reading Rainbow*, which is aimed at an early elementary school audience. Among kindergartners, *Sesame Street* and *Barney* were tied, with 60% watching each show regularly, while 40% watched *Reading Rainbow*, and 32%, *Mister Rogers' Neighborhood*.

Findings on the frequency of viewing among subgroups of the child population showed that the demographic reach of *Sesame Street* is extremely broad. It includes children from families with relatively low parent education and income levels, and families living in neighborhoods with high concentrations of child poverty. These families typically do not make as extensive use of educational materials and informational services as families with higher education or income levels.

Sesame Street was viewed by large proportions of young children from racial and ethnic minorities, and by those whose mothers did not speak English as their first language. Thus, the NHES data indicated that PBS programming was reaching most of the children who could be considered at risk of school failure, based on the socioeconomic and experiential factors typically used to identify such children. Among the highlights of the viewership findings were the following:

- *Sesame Street* reached majorities of young children in virtually all demographic groups. *Sesame Street*'s broad coverage of the young child audience extended to most demographic subgroups, with majorities of children from all areas, ethnic groups, and socioeconomic strata having regular exposure to the program. This included the economically disadvantaged children for whom the program was originally developed.
- Children from the poorest communities were most likely to be regular viewers. Still another indication of *Sesame Street*'s success in reaching high-risk children was that, among preschoolers living in areas with relatively high concentrations of child poverty (20% or

more), 83% were viewers of *Sesame Street*. This was greater than the viewing percentages found in areas with less child poverty.

- Younger children were more likely to watch *Sesame Street* regularly. There was a decline in *Sesame Street* viewing as preschool children approached school age, and a further drop when they started kindergarten. Parents reported that 80% of 3-year-olds watched the program regularly, compared with 75% of 4-year-old and 69% of 5-year-old preschoolers. Sixty-two percent of 5-year-olds who were in kindergarten viewed the program, compared with 54% of 6-year-old kindergartners.
- Children of highly educated parents stopped viewing *Sesame Street* earlier than children of less educated parents. Over most of the range of parent education levels, there was relatively little variation in the frequency of children's *Sesame Street* viewing. This was one indication that the program was succeeding in reaching at-risk children, inasmuch as a low parent-education level is one of the strongest markers of a child's being likely to experience difficulties on entering school. However, the proportion of current viewers was considerably smaller among children whose parents had at least 1 year of graduate school. But the retrospective reports of these parents showed that these children were as likely as other children to have been viewers at some point prior to school entry. They simply stopped watching sooner, probably because they mastered the skills being "taught" on *Sesame Street* at younger ages, and hence found the program less engaging.
- Children whose parents did not read to them regularly were less likely to watch *Sesame Street*. One risk group that did not watch *Sesame Street* quite as often was comprised of children whose parents had not read to them in the past week. Only about two thirds of these preschoolers were regular viewers of *Sesame Street*. Although this was a healthy majority, it was considerably smaller than the 77% of viewers among preschoolers whose parents read to them on a daily or almost daily basis.
- Eighty-five percent of early elementary pupils from low-income families watched *Sesame Street* prior to starting school. The NHES found that *Sesame Street* viewing varied relatively little across family income categories. This was another indication of the program's success at reaching high-risk preschoolers and kindergartners, because poverty-level or near-poor family incomes are strong markers of a child's educational risk.
- Ninety percent of African-American elementary students and nearly 90% of Latino pupils viewed *Sesame Street* prior to starting school. Differences in program viewing across racial and ethnic groups were also modest. Larger majorities of African-American preschoolers (87%) and Latino preschoolers (77%) than of European-American preschoolers (74%) were reported to be current viewers of the pro-

gram, and all but about 10% of elementary-school students from these minority groups were reported to have watched the program prior to school entry.

- Eighty-three percent of early elementary students with Spanish-speaking mothers watched *Sesame Street* prior to starting school. Young children whose mothers are not native English speakers can be at a disadvantage when they reach school because they may not have had as good a chance to acquire oral language and literacy skills in English at home as children whose mothers are native English speakers. The NHES data indicated that most children of nonnative English speaking mothers were exposed to *Sesame Street*. For example, 77% of preschool children with Spanish-speaking mothers and 67% of those whose mothers spoke an Asian language were current viewers of the program. Furthermore, more than 80% of elementary students from all the minority language groups were reported to have watched the program prior to school entry.

Associations Between *Sesame Street* Viewing and Children's Emergent Literacy and Numeracy

The NHES found evidence that the widespread viewing of *Sesame Street* and other educational children's programs on PBS seemed to be benefiting preschoolers as far as their development of school-related skills was concerned. The relationship between *Sesame Street* viewing and signs of emergent literacy and numeracy was stronger among children from low-income families than among those from more affluent families. A significant association between program viewing and emergent literacy and numeracy remained after controlling for possible confounding factors such as parent education, family income, race, preschool program participation, and frequency of parental reading to the children.

Preschool Viewers of *Sesame Street* More Likely to Show Signs of Emergent Literacy.
Four-year-old preschoolers who viewed *Sesame Street* were compared with their age-mates who did not watch the program on selected signs of emergent literacy and numeracy that were reported by their parents. These included telling connected stories when pretending to read, recognizing letters of the alphabet, counting to 20 or more, and writing and drawing rather than scribbling. Children who were reported to have viewed *Sesame Street* once a week or more were also more apt to be described as having accomplished most of these tasks than those who did not watch. For example, 64% of the viewers could count to 20 or more, compared with 57% of the nonviewers. And 59% of the viewers, compared with 52% of the nonviewers, could recognize most letters of the alphabet. Also, 76% of the viewers told connected stories when pretending to read, compared with 71% of nonviewers. In addition, children who viewed one or more of the PBS chil-

dren's programs were compared with their age-mates who did not view any of the programs on various signs of emergent literacy and numeracy. Viewers of the PBS shows were more likely to have accomplished the developmental tasks than nonviewers.

Developmental Differences Between Viewers and Nonviewers More Marked Among Low-Income Children. The 4-year-olds in the survey were divided into those from families whose incomes were below the official poverty threshold and those from families not in poverty. As has been found in previous studies (Zill et al., 1995), children from low-income families were less likely than those from more prosperous families to be reported as having displayed signs of emergent literacy and numeracy. For example, 43% of the low-income children, compared with 63% of the middle-income, could recognize most letters; and 48% of the low-income children, versus 68% of the middle-income, could count to 20 or higher.

Sesame Street viewing was more strongly associated with the signs of emergent literacy and numeracy among the 4-year-olds from low-income families than among the more "advanced" children from higher-income families. For example, 68% of the low-income children who watched *Sesame Street* programs told connected stories when pretending to read, whereas 55% of low-income children who did not watch did so. By contrast, among middle-income children, *Sesame Street* viewing was not related to the children's ability to tell connected stories when pretending to read. This same pattern occurred with regard to children's ability to count to 20. (See Fig. 7.1 for percentages.)

However, with respect to the task of recognizing letters of the alphabet by name, there was a statistically significant difference between *Sesame Street* viewers and nonviewers among middle-income children: 64% of middle-income viewers knew their letters, compared with 56% of middle-income nonviewers. On this task, low-income viewers and nonviewers did not differ significantly: 43% of the former knew their letters, compared with 41% of the latter (Fig. 7.1).

Although the low-income children who watched *Sesame Street* showed more signs of emergent literacy than low-income children who did not watch, they were still considerably less likely to show these signs than were the children from middle-income families. For example, 68% of low-income children who watched *Sesame Street* told connected stories when pretending to read, whereas 78% of both middle-income viewers and nonviewers did so (Fig. 7.1). Thus, the skills that children may learn from educational television do not completely make up for the disadvantages they have with respect to children who come from more affluent families.

Sesame Street Viewing Continues to Be Linked to Emergent Literacy When Family Background Factors Are Taken Into Consideration. The National Household Education Survey was a cross-sectional survey, rather than a controlled evaluation or a prospective panel study. Thus, there is the

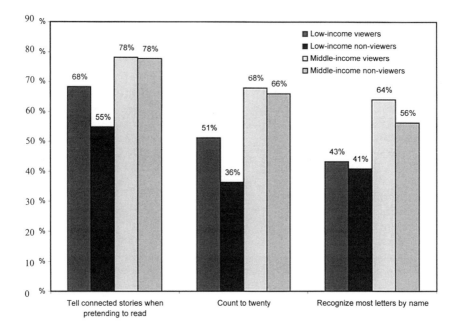

FIG. 7.1. Low-income viewers of *Sesame Street* show more signs of emergent literacy than low-income nonviewers, but fewer than middle-income viewers or nonviewers. Source: Zill, N. (1994). Analysis of data on 4-year-old preschoolers from 1993 National Household Education Survey, National Center for Education Statistics.

possibility that observed differences between *Sesame Street* viewers and nonviewers may be due to factors other than program viewing as such. The NHES study used regression analysis to adjust for the effects of several child and family background variables that are known to relate to children's intellectual development. Differences in emergent literacy and numeracy associated with *Sesame Street* viewing were found after controlling for these factors.

A composite index of emergent literacy and numeracy was used as the dependent variable in the regression analysis. Six separate signs of emergent literacy were combined into a summary score by counting the number of accomplishments that each preschool child was reported to have done. The index ranged from zero to 6 in value, and was comprised of recognizing most letters, counting to 20 or higher, telling connected stories when pretending to read, identifying colors, writing and drawing rather than scribbling, and writing own name.

The mean emergent literacy scores were 4.26 for all 2,000 4-year-old preschoolers in the survey sample; 4.54 for the 1,625 4-year-olds from middle-income families; and 3.50 for the 375 children from low-income families.

(These sample numbers are the unweighted *Ns*. After weights were applied, low-income children constituted nearly 27% of all 4-year-olds).

As just noted, children of highly educated parents are less likely to watch *Sesame Street* in the later preschool and kindergarten ages, although parents report that they did watch the program when younger. In order not to exclude these children from the *Sesame Street* viewer group, this group was defined as children who watched any of the four PBS children's programs asked about in the NHES. Factors entered into the regression equation along with *Sesame Street* or other PBS viewing were whether the parents read to the child not at all, only once or twice, or three or more times in the previous week; whether the child ever attended a center-based preschool program; the child's age, sex, race, and Latino origin; parent education and family income levels; whether both parents were present in the home, whether the mother's primary language was Spanish, another non-English language, or English; whether the child was the oldest or only child in the family; the number of children under the age of 9 in the household; and whether the child's mother worked full-time, full-year, part-time or part-year, or not at all during the previous 12 months.

Viewing *Sesame Street* once a week or more often was a significant predictor of the child's score on the emergent literacy and numeracy index after these other factors were controlled. Children who watched PBS programs had index scores nearly half a point higher, on average, than 4-year-olds who did not watch the program. By way of comparison, 4-year-olds who had attended Head Start, prekindergarten, or other center-based preschool programs had index scores two thirds of a point higher than those who had not attended such programs, all other factors being held constant.

Among 4-year-olds from low-income families, regular viewing of PBS children's programs was associated with an emergent literacy score more than eight tenths of a point higher, on average, than that for low-income children who did not view any of the programs regularly. This was equivalent to the score index boost associated with preschool program participation among these children. Among 4-year-olds from middle-income families, regular PBS program viewing was associated with a statistically significant but smaller increment in emergent literacy scores, less than three tenths of an index point.

Thus, statistical analyses supported the conclusions that viewing of *Sesame Street* is linked to emergence of early literacy and numeracy skills in preschoolers and that the link is stronger among children from impoverished families than among those from more advantaged family backgrounds.

Associations Between Watching *Sesame Street* and Children's Performance and Behavior in Elementary School

The NHES found evidence that first- and second-grade students who were reported to have watched *Sesame Street* prior to school entry were better readers than their classmates who had not watched the program. On the other hand,

Sesame Street viewers did not differ reliably from nonviewers in the frequency of having to repeat a grade, falling in the lower half of the class, or receiving negative feedback from teachers.

Children Who Watched Sesame Street Show Greater Ability to Read and Fewer Reading Problems in First and Second Grade.

First and second graders who were reported to have watched *Sesame Street* before they began kindergarten were significantly more likely to be able to read storybooks on their own, and significantly less likely to be receiving special help in school for reading problems. Among students who had watched the program, 91% could read storybooks on their own, whereas only 84% of nonviewers could read. Conversely, 19% of viewers, as opposed to 26% of nonviewers, were getting special help in school for reading problems.

The observed differences in pupil reading facility associated with *Sesame Street* viewing remained significant when family background differences between viewers and nonviewers were statistically controlled. Factors entered into the regression analysis along with *Sesame Street* viewing were the child's age, sex, race, and Latino origin; parent-education and family-income levels; whether the mother's primary language was Spanish or another non-English language; whether the child was the oldest or only child in the family, and the number of children under the age of 9 in the household; the number and type of parents present in the household; whether the child's mother worked full-time, full-year, part-time, or part-year, or not at all during the previous 12 months; and whether the child ever attended a center-based preschool program.

After adjusting for the effects of these other factors, the odds of being able to read storybooks were nearly twice as great for *Sesame Street* viewers as for nonviewers, whereas the odds of getting special help for reading problems were only 71% as great for viewers as for nonviewers.

First and Second Graders Who Watched Sesame Street Do Not Show Less Grade Repetition or Better Academic Standing.

A history of *Sesame Street* viewing was not associated with indicators of academic performance and classroom adjustment in the early elementary grades. The indicators examined were whether the child had to repeat a grade; whether the parent rated the child's academic standing as in or below the middle of the class; and whether the parent received negative feedback from the child's current teacher about his or her academic performance or behavior in class. In regression analyses with these indicators as the dependent variables, the regression coefficients representing the effects of *Sesame Street* viewing were generally in the "right" direction but were not sufficiently large to be deemed reliably different from zero.

SUMMARY AND CONCLUSIONS

Data from the 1993 National Household Education Survey were used to examine the extent to which young children from different family backgrounds and areas of the United States watch the educational television program *Sesame Street* and other PBS programs for children. The survey data were also analyzed to determine whether viewing of these programs is associated with signs of emergent literacy and numeracy in preschool children, with the development of reading skills in elementary school children, and with fewer academic and behavior problems in elementary students.

The study found ample evidence that *Sesame Street* is being viewed by large numbers of young children in all major demographic groups, including most of the children who can be considered at risk of experiencing difficulties once they reach school. In contrast to many other educational aids, which are more likely to be used by families with more education and income, viewing of *Sesame Street* and other PBS children's programs is just as common or only slightly less common among children of parents who had less than a high school education or poverty-level or near-poverty incomes as among children of parents with more education and higher incomes. Young children who live in communities with high concentrations of child poverty are even more likely to be viewers of *Sesame Street* than preschoolers and kindergartners living in areas with less child poverty.

The study found that *Sesame Street* viewers were more likely to show signs of emergent literacy in the preschool years. The association between program viewing and emergent literacy was stronger among children from poverty-level families than among children from middle-income families. Program viewers were also more likely to be reading storybooks on their own in the first and second grades, and less likely to be receiving special help in school for reading problems. However, *Sesame Street* viewers were neither more nor less likely than nonviewers to have repeated a grade, to have been described as being in the bottom half of the class, or to have received negative feedback from their teachers.

Although the survey data seem to support the contention that regular viewing of *Sesame Street* and other educational television programs can aid children's preparation for school, some caveats are in order. First of all, the survey was obviously not a controlled educational experiment in which children were randomly assigned to experimental or control groups. Families whose offspring watched *Sesame Street* were self-selected and the differences in the children's development may have been due to other factors that were correlated with but not caused by *Sesame Street* viewing (or nonviewing).

The study attempted to control for potential confounding factors by carrying out regression analyses that took the effects of parent education, family income, race, minority language status, frequency of parental reading to the child, and other background variables into account. Significant differences between viewers and nonviewers remained after these statistical controls. It is certainly possible, however, that other factors were at work that were not captured in the regression analyses. For example, it is possible that children who did not watch *Sesame Street* came from families that were educationally deprived in ways that were not fully represented by measuring the parents' education levels and frequency of reading to the child.

Nonetheless, it seems reasonable to accept the supposition that the developmental differences between viewers and nonviewers observed in the NHES are at least partly due to the educational effects of the children's programs. We should bear in mind, though, that preschoolers from low-income families who watched *Sesame Street* were still behind their peers from middle-income families in recognizing letters, counting to 20, and other signs of emergent literacy and numeracy. Clearly, whatever good it may be doing, educational television is not a cure for the handicapping effects of coming from an educationally or economically impoverished family.

This finding underscores the need for program development, demonstration projects, and research to uncover ways in which educational television might be made even more beneficial to children who come from disadvantaged family backgrounds. It also emphasizes the need for efforts such as *Sesame Street* PEP (Preschool Educational Program), which trains child care providers to make use of *Sesame Street* and related activities to enrich the daily experiences of young children who are in their charge (Yotive & Fisch, chap. 10, this volume). Similar training programs for parents from low-education and language-minority backgrounds might help to extend the already significant effects of *Sesame Street* for these children. The survey findings reinforce the late Ernest Boyer's call for public and commercial television to do more in aiding parents to be their children's first teachers and in helping young children get ready for school.

APPENDIX:
SURVEY METHODOLOGY AND DATA RELIABILITY

The National Household Education Survey (NHES) is a data collection system conducted by Westat for the National Center for Education Statistics (NCES). Designed to address a wide range of education-related issues, the NHES collects data on high-priority topics on a rotating basis. Data for this report are from the 1993 NHES School Readiness component (Brick et al., 1994). Data collection took place from January through April of 1993. The sample was selected using random digit dialing (RDD) methods, and the data were collected using computer assisted telephone interviewing (CATI) technology. When appropriately weighted, the sample is designed to be nationally representative of all civilian, noninstitutionalized persons in the target age range in the 50 States and the District of Columbia, not just those living in telephone households.

The School Readiness Interview

The School Readiness component of the 1993 NHES sampled 3- to 7-year-olds and 8- and 9-year-olds enrolled in second grade or below. Two instruments were used to collect information on the variables related to the school readiness of these children. The first instrument, a screener administered to an adult member of the household, was used to determine whether any children of the appropriate ages lived in the household, to collect information on each household member, and to identify the appropriate parent/guardian to respond for the sampled child. If one or two eligible children resided in the household, interviews were conducted about each child. If more than two eligible children resided in the household, two children were randomly sampled as interview subjects. A School Readiness (SR) interview was conducted with the parent/guardian most knowledgeable about the care and education of each sampled child, usually the child's mother.

Educational Television Questions in the NHES

Although the 1993 NHES was not specifically designed to study the impact of educational television programming, the survey does afford an opportunity to gauge current viewing patterns of young children and the extent to which viewing of educational television programming is associated with school readiness and developmental accomplishments of American children. The success of these television programs in reaching children who may be considered at-risk for developmental and school difficulties is another subject that is addressable with the survey.

Because of time limitations and the need to address several other readiness-related topics in the survey, the number of questions devoted to viewing of public television children's programs was quite small. Specifically, the 1993 NHES asked parents of preschoolers and children in kindergarten about regular viewing of *Sesame Street, Barney and Friends, Mister Rogers' Neighborhood,* and *Reading Rainbow.* The question wording was:

"Please tell me whether (CHILD) watches any of the following television programs *once a week or more,* either at home or someplace else: *Sesame Street?*; *Mister Rogers' Neighborhood?*; *Barney and Friends?*; *Reading Rainbow?*"

Parents of children in kindergarten, first, and second grade were asked a retrospective question about *Sesame Street* viewing only:

"Before starting (kindergarten/first grade), did (CHILD) watch *Sesame Street* either at home or someplace else, at least once a week for a period of three months or more?"

There was also a series of questions about the total amount of television viewing the child did during different time periods of the day on weekdays, and the total hours of viewing on Saturdays and Sundays.

Sample Sizes and Response Rates

The 1993 NHES survey completed screeners with 63,844 households, of which 9,936 contained at least one child eligible for the SR component. A sample of 12,905 children was selected for the SR component from these households. The response rate for the screener was 82%. The completion rate for the SR interview, or the percentage of eligible sampled children for whom interviews were completed, was 90%, or 10,888 interviews. Thus, the overall response rate for the SR interview was 74% (the product of the screener response rate and the SR completion rate).

The total SR population was divided into three segments, each of which was asked a somewhat different sequence of questions. The preschool segment was composed of children age 3 and older who were not yet enrolled in kindergarten. The number of cases in this group was 4,423. The kindergarten segment consisted of children who were currently enrolled in kindergarten. The number of cases in this group was 2,126. The primary school segment consisted of children enrolled in first or second grade. The number of cases in this group was 4,277.

Data Reliability

Estimates produced using data from the 1993 NHES are subject to two types of error, sampling and nonsampling errors. Nonsampling errors are errors made in the collection and processing of data. Sampling errors occur because the data are collected from a sample rather than a census of the population. For most of the percentage estimates presented in this chapter, the margin of error due to sampling is plus or minus 3 percent.

In general, it is difficult to identify and estimate either the amount of nonsampling error or the bias caused by this error. In the 1993 NHES, efforts were made to prevent such errors from occurring, and to compensate for them where possible. For instance, during the survey design phase, focus groups and cognitive laboratory interviews were conducted for the purpose of assessing respondent knowledge of the topics, comprehension of questions and terms, and the sensitivity of items. The design phase also entailed over 500 staff hours of CATI instrument testing and a pretest in which over 275 interviews were conducted.

An important nonsampling error for a telephone survey is the failure to include persons who do not live in households with telephones. About 90% of all 3- to 7-year-olds live in households with telephones. Estimation procedures were used to help reduce the bias in the estimates associated with children who do not live in telephone households (Brick & Burke, 1992). The population controls used to develop the weights for the NHES were based on Census Bureau figures that include families that live in nontelephone households. In weighting up groups that are underrepresented in a telephone survey, the assumption is made that members of those groups who were in telephone households at the time of the survey sample are similar to members who were not. This may or may not be the case, depending on the characteristic being estimated.

Another potential source of nonsampling error is the fact that most of the information about the child and family were collected from the same parent respondent. Thus, possible response biases on the part of that respondent (for example, a tendency to answer affirmatively to questions) might cause different items to appear more highly correlated than they really are. Some of the questions in the survey, such as the question as to whether the child had watched *Sesame Street* prior to starting school, are based on retrospective recall over a period of years. Responses to such questions tend to have more error than responses to questions dealing with circumstances or events in the present or immediate past. Finally, there may be some bias introduced because respondents are told that the survey is being conducted for the U.S. Department of Education. Parents may feel a need to respond in a way that is consistent with their views of what parents ought to be doing to help the development and learning of their children. While these provisos should be kept in mind, experience with past surveys indicates that the NHES findings are generally consistent with results of other federal surveys conducted by the Census Bureau and other agencies, and with smaller-scale educational studies that use in-person rather than telephone data collection methods.

REFERENCES

Boyer, E. (1991). *Ready to learn: A mandate for the nation.* Princeton, NJ: Carnegie Foundation for the Advancement of Teaching.

Brick, J. M., & Burke, J. (1992). *Telephone coverage bias of 14- to 21-year-olds and 3- to 5-year-olds.* Washington, DC: U.S. Department of Education, National Center for Education Statistics.

Brick, J. M., Collins, M. A., Nolin, M. J., Ha, P. C., Levinsohn, M., & Chandler, K. (1994). *National Household Education Survey of 1993: School readiness data file user's manual* (NCES Publication No. 94–193). Washington, DC: U.S. Department of Education, National Center for Education Statistics.

Bush, President George H. W. (1990). State of the Union Address, January 31, 1990.

Healy, J. M. (1990). *Endangered minds: Why our children don't think.* New York: Simon & Schuster.

Kagan, S. L., Moore, E., & Bredekamp, S. (Eds.) (1995). *Reconsidering children's early development and learning: Toward common views and vocabulary. Goal 1 Technical Planning Group Report 95–03.* Washington, DC: National Education Goals Panel.

National Education Goals Panel. (1998). *The national education goals report: Building a nation of learners, 1998.* Washington, DC: U.S. Government Printing Office.

Resource Group on School Readiness. (1991). An interim report from the Resource Group on School Readiness. In National Education Goals Panel (Ed.), *Measuring progress toward the National Education Goals: Potential indicators and measurement strategies* (pp. 1–16). Washington, DC: National Education Goals Panel.

Tashman, B. (1994, November). Sorry, Ernie. TV isn't teaching. *New York Times*, Op Ed page.

Tessier, E. (1995). *Sesame Street* focus groups report (unpublished, internal research report). New York: Children's Television Workshop.

U.S. House of Representatives. (1994, March). *Goals 2000: Educate America act. Conference report.* Washington, DC: U.S. Government Printing Office.

West, J., Germino-Hausken, E., & Collins, M. (1993). *Readiness for kindergarten: Parent and teacher beliefs.* Washington, DC: U.S. Department of Education, National Center for Education Statistics.

Winn, M, (1985). *The plug-in drug: Television, children, and the family.* New York: Penguin Books.

Zill, N., Collins, M., West, J., & Germino -Hausken, E. (1995). *Approaching kindergarten: A look at preschoolers in the United States.* Washington, DC: U.S. Department of Education, National Center for Education Statistics.

Zill, N., & Davies, E. (1994). *Public television children's programs: Are they helping young children get ready for school?* Rockville, MD: Westat.

Zill, N., Davies, E., & Daly, M. (1994). *Viewing of Sesame Street by preschool children in the United States and its relationship to school readiness.* Rockville, MD: Westat.

8   *Sesame Street* Viewers as Adolescents: The Recontact Study

Aletha C. Huston
University of Texas at Austin

Daniel R. Anderson
University of Massachusetts

John C. Wright
University of Texas at Austin

Deborah L. Linebarger
University of Kansas

Kelly L. Schmitt
University of Pennsylvania

Sesame Street helped to change the television viewing patterns of many American children in the last generation. Since the late 1960s, *Sesame Street* and its international coproductions have been staples of young children's television viewing, not only in the United States, but also in many countries worldwide (Cole, Richman, & McCann Brown, chap. 9, this volume).

Specific curriculum goals have always been a central feature in the model for designing and producing *Sesame Street*. Although these goals have varied across a broad range of topics, teaching academic and prosocial skills have remained central objectives throughout the more than 30 years of the program's existence. On the whole, it is successful in teaching basic literacy and numeracy skills as well as spatial and temporal concepts, sociocultural understanding, and general information (see Mielke, chap. 5, this volume; Wright, Huston, Scantlin, & Kotler, chap. 6, this volume).

In this chapter, we carry the evaluation question one step further to show that the early advantages conferred by viewing *Sesame Street* are still observable when children reach adolescence. Specifically, adolescents who were frequent viewers at age 5 had better grades in high school, read more books for pleasure, had higher levels of achievement motivation, and expressed less aggressive attitudes than did teens who had rarely viewed the program at age 5.

BACKGROUND

Why Might Effects of Early Viewing Last?

For the most part, evaluations of *Sesame Street* have been relatively atheoretical. They have been designed to determine what works, what children learn, what children attend to, and so on. But, if we are to understand how and why viewing a preschool television program might lead to long-term effects on children's development, we need to gain a better understanding of the processes by which viewing effects occur. Several hypotheses or models have been proposed.

Early Learning Model. The most straightforward model, and the one that seems to guide the planners of *Sesame Street*, is what we term the *early learning model*. It is based on the assumption that children in the preschool years benefit from learning basic skills and information from a variety of experiences, including well-designed television. Children learn from exposure to material that is presented in ways they can comprehend and that they find interesting (Anderson & Field, 1983; Huston & Wright, 1989). Learning is cumulative, so that a child who gains basic understanding of symbols and numbers, for example, is then positioned to learn symbol and number combinations, manipulations, and so on. According to this hypothesis, these learning experiences during the preschool years influence not only academic skills, but also the motivational, attitudinal, and behavioral patterns with which children enter formal schooling.

Many observers believe that experiences in the first few grades of school are critical in determining children's ultimate academic trajectories. Children who enter school with good skills in the prerequisites for reading, and, to a lesser extent, the prerequisites for math, begin a trajectory that is likely to reach success. Children with good skills are likely to be placed in higher ability groups and to be perceived as more competent by teachers than children with low levels of preacademic skills. As a result, teachers may give them more individual attention and may expect more from them. They are likely to feel successful and to be motivated to do well (Entwisle, Alexander, & Olson, 1997).

There is a body of evidence showing long-term consequences of experiences in the first grade, particularly ability grouping and teachers' interactions with children. In the Beginning Schools Study, one of the most extensive longitudinal investigations of early schooling, children's initial placements in first-grade reading ability groups predicted achievement over the entire year and beyond. Because first-grade reading tests are not very reliable, teachers make these placements using observations of children's basic skills, motivation, interest, participation, attention span, and nonaggressive behavior (Entwisle et al., 1997).

Early competence in academic and other types of skills may also affect the interests and activities that children choose to pursue on their own. In developmental psychology, we have come to recognize that children take an active role in their own development, particularly as they get older. They choose activities, practice skills, and respond to opportunities, a phenomenon called *niche picking* by some experts (Huston, Carpenter, Atwater, & Johnson, 1986; Scarr & McCartney, 1983). For example, young children who know some letters and words and who know that books contain stories and information may choose to look at books, ask adults to read them, and play with materials that enhance literacy. An older child who can read fluently is more likely to read for pleasure than one who cannot. These activities in turn provide practice that increases competence, and may also put children in the company of peers with mutual interests. As a result, the child is likely to find intellectual and social rewards for involvement in learning through reading and to develop a lifelong appreciation of literacy. Even in infancy, one of the effects of exposure to a stimulating child-care setting is to make infants more active in their environments so that they seek and elicit reactions from others as well as taking advantage of toys and objects that offer a variety of possibilities for action (Burchinal, Campbell, Bryant, Wasik, & Ramey, 1997).

In the early learning model, three facets of early development are implicated as pathways by which long-term consequences of educational media may occur: (a) learning preacademic skills, particularly in reading and language; (b) developing motivation and interest; and (c) acquiring behavioral patterns of attentiveness, concentration, nonaggressiveness, and absence of restlessness or distractibility. Differences in these characteristics when children enter school are likely to be magnified over time because they set children on different developmental trajectories of school achievement and because they lead children to select and seek different opportunities for learning. This hypothesis is similar to the explanation proposed by Barnett (1995) for long-term influences of other early childhood educational interventions.

Aggression and Social Competence. A related hypothesis proposed by Huesmann and Eron (1986) emphasized the role of aggressive behavior as a negative influence on long-term achievement. According to that hypothesis, children with high levels of aggression are likely to exhibit problems of inattention and disobedience that interfere with classroom learning and create negative reactions among teachers and peers. These disadvantages are magnified over time as children experience failure and have negative interactions with others. One goal of *Sesame Street* and other educational programs for children is to teach social competence, tolerance of diversity, and nonaggressive means of resolving conflict. To the extent that they succeed, social competence and nonaggressive behavior might be another avenue through which long-term effects would be sustained.

Rapid Pace and Other Formal Features.   Critics of *Sesame Street* have been less sanguine about its likelihood of leading to positive consequences for children. One frequently voiced criticism is that the rapid pace and entertaining quality of the program leaves children little or no time to process information at more than a superficial level. According to this view, children may learn information by rote (e.g., reciting the ABCs), but are unlikely to acquire skills at a deeper or more conceptual level. Moreover, these critics propose, frequent viewing could lead children to develop patterns of short attention span and a superficial, nonreflective learning style. In the long run, then, one might expect negative influences on learning and school achievement, particularly when children reach more advanced levels of the subject matter being taught. One would also expect negative influences on creative and reflective thinking styles because children do not experience opportunities to elaborate and manipulate information in depth over time (Greenfield, 1984; Singer, 1980; Singer & Singer, 1981).

There is little evidence that viewing *Sesame Street* has negative effects on attention span or conceptual learning at the preschool level (see reviews by Anderson & Collins, 1988; Huston & Wright, 1997). Nonetheless, it is possible that such effects could appear as children reach later childhood and adolescence.

Interference With Language.   Some critics have argued that the medium of television is ill suited for teaching intellectual and academic skills, particularly those that are dependent on language, because its salient visual qualities interfere with children's processing of language. Even programs with educational content like *Sesame Street* are, according to this view, unlikely to be useful and may be harmful to intellectual development because they lead children to rely on visual rather than linguistic ways of understanding the world, with the result that children are not exposed to complex forms of language (Healy, 1990). The available data also fail to support this hypothesis. Several investigations have shown positive relations between viewing and children's vocabulary and verbal skills (cf. Huston & Wright, 1997).

Some observers have also proposed that television reduces imagination and creativity because it provides concrete visual images rather than requiring children to generate their own images as they must do with radio and books with few illustrations (Greenfield, 1984). The evidence about this hypothesis is mixed for television in general; it has not been tested with respect to *Sesame Street* in particular.

Do Some Groups Benefit or Lose
From Exposure More Than Others Do?

Sesame Street was originally designed with an eye toward children from economically disadvantaged homes and neighborhoods because children from these environments often reached school with few preacademic skills. *Sesame*

Street might be especially valuable for children in low-income families because their homes and neighborhoods offer relatively few opportunities to learn the skills and information taught by the program. Parents who are well educated and economically comfortable may provide an enriched and stimulating environment for their children, and they have access to high-quality child care and preschool programs that poorly educated and low-income parents often lack.

The evidence regarding this hypothesis is mixed. In the evaluations conducted during the first 2 years of *Sesame Street* (Ball & Bogatz, 1970; Bogatz & Ball, 1971), children from economically disadvantaged and advantaged homes showed equivalent gains in cognitive skills when they watched the program frequently, but the sample did not include many highly educated, affluent families.

Long-Term Effects.   The four hypotheses about possible short- and long-term effects of viewing *Sesame Street* lead to quite different predictions. The early learning and reduced aggression models suggest positive effects on learning and behavior that have the potential to snowball when children reach school. The theories proposing that viewing can lead to superficial information processing or to inhibition of verbal and abstract skills suggest negative effects that could be magnified as the demands of education shift from rote, visual learning to abstract and reflective thinking. Although the available data support positive effects on literacy, numeracy, and vocabulary acquisition in the preschool years, it is still possible that positive effects could disappear and that some of the negative effects proposed by critics could become apparent as children progress through school.

THE RECONTACT STUDY

The Recontact Study was designed to answer some of the questions about the long-term correlates of early television viewing. In 1994, we interviewed adolescents, ages 15 to 19 years old, who had participated in one of two similar investigations when they were preschoolers. The two original studies were conducted by Daniel Anderson in Springfield, Massachusetts and by John Wright and Aletha Huston in Topeka, Kansas (Anderson, Field, Collins, Lorch, & Nathan, 1985; Huston, Wright, Rice, Kerkman, & St.Peters, 1990). Although the two studies had different designs, both collected multiple detailed diaries of all the television viewed by the children when they were 5 years old. Extensive interviews were conducted with parents, and tests of vocabulary were given to the children.

Both studies were guided by the assumption that all television is not alike. In the viewing diaries, the names of programs viewed and the people watching with the children were recorded. In the study by Anderson and his colleagues (1985), time-lapse videotapes of the television viewing room were recorded in 99 of the children's homes during one of the 10-day periods in which the parents maintained the viewing diaries. Analysis of those video-tapes showed that the diaries were reasonably accurate in reporting the children's television viewing. We are therefore confident that we have detailed and accurate records of the children's early television viewing. As one might expect, *Sesame Street* was popular among these children. They watched it on average for 2.20 hours a week and only 16% did not watch *Sesame Street* during the diary periods.

In 1994, with funding from the Markle Foundation of New York, we located and interviewed most of the children from both samples, who were by then in high school. Our purpose was to examine the long-term relationships between early television viewing and high school achievement, motivation, creativity, and attitudes about a variety of topics.

We were quite successful in finding the original participants. Of the 655 children in the original investigations, we located 92% and were able to interview 570, or 87%, by telephone. The interview focused on a variety of issues, including: academic progress; motivation to achieve in English, mathematics, and science; creativity; and aggressive attitudes. In addition to the interview, we obtained official transcripts of high school grades for most of the participants. When we compared the teens' reports of their own grades to the high school transcripts that we obtained for 86% of them, we found that the teens were accurate but had slightly overstated their own achievement. We adjusted the reported grades accordingly for the remaining 14% of the children for whom we did not have school transcripts.

The primary analyses concerned the relationship of television viewing at age 5 to the academic achievement, motivation, and other characteristics of the sample when they were in high school. For the larger study, we are analyzing all types of television programming, but in this chapter we present the findings for *Sesame Street* in particular. The major question is: How do adolescents who were frequent viewers of *Sesame Street* at age 5 differ from teens who had viewed the program rarely in their preschool years?

One problem in drawing inferences about the "effects" of early viewing in a study of this kind is that home viewing is not random. Some families encourage viewing more than others do, and some children have more interest than others. In an earlier analysis of the Kansas sample, two factors were the most important influences on the amount of time children spent watching *Sesame Street*. The more time children spent in preschool or out-of-home child care, the less they watched *Sesame Street*, probably because they were away from home during the times it was broadcast. And, children with older brothers and sisters watched less than those with younger siblings. Older siblings draw 5-year-old children into viewing other programs, while younger brothers and sisters make it more likely that others in the family will view *Sesame Street* (Piñon, Huston, & Wright, 1989). In analyses of other samples, children of well-educated parents watch more frequently than do those whose parents have less education, and girls watch slightly more than boys (Huston & Wright, 1997).

Some of these same family characteristics are also associated with academic achievement and the other outcomes of interest in the Recontact Study. Therefore, correlations between *Sesame Street* viewing and these outcomes could be due to the family and child characteristics that influence both. To account for differences among families and children, our statistical analyses considered parents' education level, sex, and the birth order of the children. We also included site (Massachusetts vs. Kansas) because there might be geographic differences and the Massachusetts sample was somewhat older on average at the time of the interview. The question these analyses answer is: For children with equivalent parents' education, sex, site, and birth order, do those who watched *Sesame Street* frequently 10 years earlier differ from those who did not?

Academic Achievement

We analyzed high school grades in English, mathematics, and science because these are core subject matter areas and are likely to be taken by all students (although the levels vary). The grade point average (GPA) used was the average across these three subjects on a 4.0 scale where A = 4, B = 3, C = 2, D = 1, and F = 0. (When schools used other scales, grades were converted to a 4.0 scale).

After taking parents' education, child's sex, site, and birth order into account, the more children watched *Sesame Street* at age 5 years, the better were their high school grades. Not only were the average grades better, but grades were better in each of the core subject areas of English, mathematics, and science. In Fig. 8.1, teens were divided into four equal groups or quartiles on the basis of their *Sesame Street* viewing at age 5. The average GPA for members of each group is shown. Teens who had watched least often (less than 1/2 hour a week) obtained an average GPA of 2.51. Those who had watched most often (more than 3.25 hours a week) achieved an average GPA of 2.90.

Figure 8.1 also shows that the positive relationship of *Sesame Street* viewing to high school grades was substantially larger for boys than for girls. Boys in the lowest viewing group had an average GPA of 2.32 compared to 2.86 for the highest viewing group. Girls' GPAs ranged from 2.67 for the lowest viewing group to 2.95 for the highest viewing group. It is noteworthy that boys' grades were generally lower than those of girls, but the difference almost disappeared for teens in the highest viewing group.

In separate analyses of English, mathematics, and science grades, viewing was positively and significantly associated with GPA in each subject matter area for boys. For girls, viewing was significantly and positively associated with grades in science, but the association, while positive, was not statistically significant in English and mathematics.

We also tested the hypothesis that *Sesame Street* might be a more important predictor of achievement for children whose parents had low levels of education than for those with highly educated parents. There was no evidence that this occurred. Viewing predicted achievement about equally well regardless of parent education.

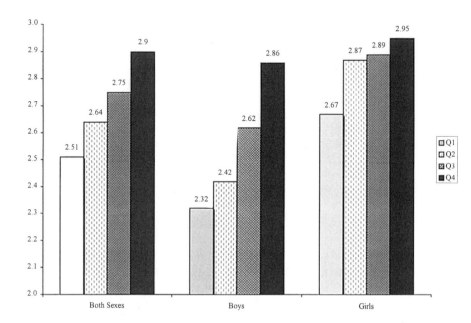

FIG. 8.1. Grade point averages in English, math, and science for adolescents who viewed different amounts of *Sesame Street* at age 5. *Note.* The four groups represent different quartiles of the amount of *Sesame Street* viewing. Average hours per week were: $Q_1 \leq .5$; $Q_2 = .51$ to 1.62; $Q_3 = 1.63$ to 3.25; $Q_4 \geq 3.26$

Leisure Reading

Some critics of *Sesame Street* have predicted that early viewing would reduce interest in reading. We asked the teens several questions about their leisure time reading of books, such as how much time they spent reading books and what books they had read in the last year. Contrary to critics' predictions, the more time spent viewing *Sesame Street* at age 5, the more leisure reading teens did. The difference was highly significant after controlling for parents' education, sex, site, and birth order. For example, teens with the lowest levels of *Sesame Street* viewing (Q1) reported that they had spent an average of 6.73 hours reading books in the last month compared to 10.81 hours for those in the highest viewing level (Q4). Those in the lowest viewing group (Q1) could recall an average of 3.43 titles of books they had read compared to 4.16 for the teens in the highest group (Q4).

Achievement Motivation

Although the relations of early viewing to later academic achievement are gratifying for consumers and producers of *Sesame Street*, they are in some ways difficult to explain. Obviously, the specific content and skills that children may have learned from viewing at age 5 have no direct relevance to knowledge of course content by the time they reach high school. The early viewing hypothesis suggests that a boost in initial skills starts a process of success in school that cascades over time. It is also possible that exposure to academic subject matter increases children's interest and sense of competence, which in turn leads them to learn from a variety of sources, in and out of school, and to find greater rewards and satisfaction in so doing.

One way of answering this question was by examining achievement motivation among the teens in the sample. Our approach was based on a long tradition of research in achievement motivation showing that one needs to consider two components: beliefs about one's own competence, and the value attached to achievement in a particular domain (Eccles, Wigfield, & Schiefele, 1997). We asked teens questions about their *competence beliefs* in each subject matter area (English, mathematics, and science) with such questions as "How good in English/math/science are you?" and "How well would you do in an advanced course in English/math/science?" The *value* associated with each subject matter area was assessed with questions about how useful and worthwhile it is to learn about English, mathematics, or science.

The results were similar to those for academic achievement. With controls for parent education, sex, site, and birth order, frequent *Sesame Street* viewers had higher levels of perceived competence in all three subject matter areas than did infrequent viewers. It appears, however, that students' beliefs simply reflected their school experience—those who got better grades perceived themselves as more competent.

By contrast, *Sesame Street* viewing was also a significant predictor of the *value* that boys attached to achievement in mathematics and science and the *level* of the mathematics courses they elected to take, above and beyond any effects that viewing may have had on school grades. With grades statistically controlled, frequent viewers assigned more value to what can be learned in mathematics and science and they took (or expected to take) more advanced mathematics courses than infrequent viewers did. These patterns did not occur for girls.

Creativity

Because some theories have predicted that the rapid pacing and rich visual images of *Sesame Street* would reduce imagination and creative thought, we attempted to measure two aspects of creativity. One of these is fluency of ideas—the ability to generate a variety of possibilities when solving a problem. The specific questions ask the teen to think of different ways to use such common objects as a key or a shoe. A person who can name several uses, particularly "unusual" uses (e.g., using a shoe to store a marble collection) gets a high score on this measure. Second, we measured teens' participation in creative activities and classes (e.g., art, dance, and theater).

For the most part, frequent *Sesame Street* viewers were neither more nor less creative than infrequent viewers. There was no relation of *Sesame Street* viewing to fluency of ideas. *Sesame Street* viewing did predict participation in creative activities and classes, but only for certain subgroups of teens. These findings do not support the hypothesized negative effects of viewing on creativity. Wherever significant relationships to creativity were found for *Sesame Street*, they were positive.

Aggressive Tendencies

Although people often assume that the primary goal of *Sesame Street* is to teach academic skills, the program also has a strong emphasis on positive social behavior and social competence. One consequence could be that children learn to deal with conflicts and difficult situations in nonaggressive ways. In the teen interview, we asked a set of questions measuring indirect aggression, verbal aggression, irritability, and physical aggression. These were combined as an index of aggressive tendencies.

For boys, but not for girls, *Sesame Street* viewing at age 5 predicted low levels of aggressive tendencies in the teen years. Boys who were frequent viewers scored lower on our questions about aggression than did boys who watched infrequently.

Summary of Findings

Adolescents who often watched *Sesame Street* as preschoolers, compared with those who rarely watched the program, had higher grades in English, mathematics, and science; spent more time reading books outside of school; perceived themselves as more competent in school; placed higher value on achievement in mathematics and science; elected more advanced mathematics courses; and expressed lower levels of aggressive attitudes. Many of these relations between *Sesame Street* viewing and teen behavior were stronger and more consistent for boys than for girls. There was little relation between *Sesame Street* viewing and creativity, but there was no evidence for a negative effect on creativity. All of these patterns occurred when groups were statistically equated for parents' level of education, birth order, site, and sex.

CONCLUSIONS

Watching *Sesame Street* was associated with favorable outcomes in adolescence. The Recontact Study results provide strong support for the early learning model, and they contradict the hypotheses that *Sesame Street* is harmful to abstract and verbal thinking ability or to creativity. Of course, it is always possible that inherently more able children watch *Sesame Street* more frequently, but our controls for parent education, birth order, site, and sex render this and alternative explanations somewhat less likely. In any case, these results provide no evidence for negative long-term effects of viewing.

In fact, it may be surprising to some that we found any association suggesting long-term effects of viewing. Obviously, watching *Sesame Street* cannot directly improve high school grades. High school examinations do not test students on number and letter identification or identifying which things are not like others in an array of objects. Rather, we believe that a related series of processes can be initiated by watching educational programs in the preschool years. Children who watch *Sesame Street* enter school not only with good academic skills, but also with a positive attitude toward education. As a result, teachers consider them bright and well-behaved, expect high levels of achievement, place them in advanced groups, and give them positive feedback. Teachers may be especially responsive to positive classroom behavior and academic skills in young boys. Early school success, in turn, fosters better learning and greater enthusiasm about school, leading to a trajectory of long-term achievement.

Children's skills and interests guide their choices of activities outside school as well as their openness to experiences that are available around them. We sometimes overestimate the effects of adult guidance while underestimating the role of children's own agency in deciding how to spend their time and energy. If children learn cognitive and academic skills and develop interests in new topics as a result of viewing *Sesame Street*, they may choose play and leisure activities (e.g., reading) that allow them to use and expand their knowledge. One of the largest and most consistent differences between frequent and infrequent *Sesame Street* viewers in this study was the amount of leisure reading they reported doing as teens. Early experience with *Sesame Street* may contribute to an early interest in books that forms a long-term pattern of reading for pleasure.

The positive relations of *Sesame Street* to positive outcomes were greater for boys than for girls. Boys did not watch educational programs more than girls did in the early 1980s. Other research with *Sesame Street* indicates that attention and comprehension are typically the same for both sexes (Anderson & Collins, 1988).

One explanation for the greater benefit that boys apparently received is drawn from the broader notion that interventions are most effective for groups who are at risk for failure to develop in a domain. In the early years, boys are generally less mature than girls, and they do less well in school throughout childhood and adolescence. More often, boys have both academic and behavior problems in school, and their average levels of aggression are higher than are girls'. In American society, boys are socialized to be active and aggressive while girls are encouraged to be compliant and responsive to adults. As a consequence, boys may benefit more from the kinds of instruction provided by programs such as *Sesame Street* because they are less likely than girls to receive these messages from other sources in their environments. In fact, the patterns of school grades in Fig. 8.1 suggest that *Sesame Street* viewing allowed boys to catch up with girls or that girls did not need it as much as boys did. Among children who rarely watched *Sesame Street*, boys had much lower grades than girls did; for frequent viewers, boys' and girls' grades were similar.

Thirty years after *Sesame Street* began, it has become an institution of childhood throughout much of the world. Its unprecedented success in attracting large audiences of preschool children paved the way for many other educational programs in the 1970s and again in the 1990s. Its success in reaching and teaching children undoubtedly contributed to U.S. governmental requirements that broadcasters include educational and informative programs for children in their schedules. The Recontact Study adds a piece to the puzzle, providing the first evidence that *Sesame Street* viewing has long-term associations with adolescent achievement.

Public policy about children's television in the United States has waxed and waned since the introduction of the medium. Yet evidence continues to accumulate that educational television programs can provide children with important foundations for learning at a fraction of the cost of any other form of education. It behooves us as a nation and as a world community to sustain and support the kind of programming with *Sesame Street*'s educational value and to expand our efforts to use television to promote the development of children.

REFERENCES

Anderson, D. R., & Collins, P. A. (1988). *The impact on children's education: Television's influence on cognitive development.* Washington, DC: U.S. Department of Education.

Anderson, D. R., & Field, D. E. (1983). Children's attention to television: Implications for production. In M. Meyer (Ed.), *Children and the formal features of television* (pp. 56–96). Munchen: Saur.

Anderson, D. R., Field, D. E., Collins, P. A., Lorch, E. P., & Nathan, J. G. (1985). Estimates of young children's time with television: A methodological comparison of parent reports with time-lapse video home observation. *Child Development, 56,* 1345–1357.

Ball, S. J., & Bogatz, G. A. (1970). *The first year of Sesame Street: An evaluation.* Princeton, NJ: Educational Testing Service.

Barnett, W. S. (1995). Long-term effects of early childhood programs on cognitive and school outcomes. *The Future of Children, 5,* 25–50.

Bogatz, G. A., & Ball, S. (1971). *The second year of Sesame Street: A continuing evaluation.* Princeton, NJ: Educational Testing Service.

Burchinal, M. R., Campbell, F. A., Bryant, D. M., Wasik, B. H., & Ramey, C. T. (1997). Early intervention and mediating processes in cognitive performance of children in low-income African-American families. *Child Development, 68,* 935–954.

Eccles, J. S., Wigfield, A., & Schiefele, U. (1997). Motivation to succeed. In W. Damon (Series Ed.) & N. Eisenberg (Vol. Ed.), *Handbook of Child Psychology: Vol. 4. Social, emotional, and personality development* (5th ed, pp. 1017–1096). New York: Wiley.

Entwisle, D. R., Alexander, K. L., & Olson, L. S. (1997). *Children, schools, and inequality.* Boulder, CO: Westview Press.

Greenfield, P. M. (1984). *Mind and media: The effects of television, video games, and computers*. Cambridge, MA: Harvard University Press.

Healy, J. M. (1990). *Endangered minds: Why our children don't think*. New York: Simon & Schuster.

Huesmann, L. R., & Eron, L. D. (Eds.). (1986). *Television and the aggressive child: A cross-national comparison*. Hillsdale, NJ: Lawrence Erlbaum Associates.

Huston, A. C., Carpenter, C. J., Atwater, J. B., & Johnson, L. M. (1986). Gender, adult structuring of activities, and social behavior in middle childhood. *Child Development, 57*, 1200–1209.

Huston, A. C., & Wright, J. C. (1989). The forms of television and the child viewer. In G. A. Comstock (Ed.), *Public communication and behavior* (Vol. 2, pp. 103–159). Orlando, FL: Academic Press.

Huston, A. C., & Wright, J. C. (1997). Mass media and children's development. In W. Damon (Series Ed.), I. Sigel, & K. A. Renninger (Vol. Eds.), *Handbook of child psychology: Vol. 4. Child psychology in practice* (5th ed., pp. 999–1058). New York: Wiley.

Huston, A. C., Wright, J. C., Rice, M. R., Kerkman, D., & St. Peters, M. (1990). The development of television viewing patterns in early childhood: A longitudinal investigation. *Developmental Psychology, 26*, 409–420.

Piñon, M. F., Huston, A. C., & Wright, J. C. (1989). Family ecology and child characteristics that predict young children's educational television viewing. *Child Development, 60*, 846–856.

Scarr, S., & McCartney, K. (1983). How people make their own environments: A theory of genotype —> environment effects. *Child Development, 54*, 424–435.

Singer, J. L. (1980). The power and limits of television: A cognitive-affective analysis. In P. Tannenbaum (Ed.), *The entertainment function of television*. Hillsdale, NJ: Lawrence Erlbaum Associates.

Singer, J. L., & Singer, D. G. (1981). *Television, imagination and aggression: A study of preschoolers*. Hillsdale, NJ: Lawrence Erlbaum Associates.

Extending *Sesame Street*: Other Settings, Other Media

9 The World of *Sesame Street* Research

Charlotte F. Cole
Beth A. Richman
Susan A. McCann Brown
Children's Television Workshop

Sesame Street is a shared experience for children throughout the world. With more than 120 million viewers in more than 130 countries, Children's Television Workshop (CTW) can be regarded as the single largest informal educator of young children in the world. One of the distinguishing aspects of the *Sesame Street* international experience is that when children view *Sesame Street*, many view versions of the program that have been developed by local producers and educators. Our 19 different adaptations of the series feature unique characters and sets and have at their foundations their own curricula that have been designed to meet the educational needs of children of a given country (Gettas, 1990). The result is that when children view *Sesame Street*, they view a program that has the same essence as the series produced in the United States, in a context that reflects local values and educational priorities. The cultural specificity of the international adaptations of *Sesame Street* is at the heart of their success, both with respect to the programs' appeal and their educational impact.

As with the domestic production of *Sesame Street*, curriculum development and research have been an integral part of the creation of these international coproductions, which are developed using a model of production that involves collaboration among producers, researchers, and educational content specialists. This chapter focuses on the research aspect of this process, providing an overview of how it contributes to the making of culturally relevant, educational, and entertaining programs for young children.

THE COPRODUCTION MODEL

The globalization of *Sesame Street* began in the early 1970s, shortly after the series' initial broadcast in 1969 in the United States. Producers from Brazil, Mexico, Canada, and Germany approached CTW independently, seeing the value of *Sesame Street*, but wanting programs that would specifically address the educational needs of the children of their own countries. To create the series that the producers imagined, CTW devised a flexible production plan that has continued to evolve over time and is now used to develop all of our international productions of *Sesame Street*. Although this model was fairly simple—initially, producers enhanced dubbed versions of the program with instructional cutaways and local language voice-overs—eventually a full model emerged. As in the United States, a triune of individuals is involved: *Producers* are responsible for the creative elements of the production, *educational content specialists* set the curricular priorities, and *researchers* represent the voice of the child and provide information about the program's effectiveness. Studio sets reflective of a given culture are created by local production teams and inhabited by characters developed specifically for each adaptation. Live-action videos and animations are produced in-country, giving the local viewers characters and venues that have direct relevance to their own lives. For example, the production in Mexico, which was one of the first productions to use the model in its fullest form, takes place in a colorful Plaza populated by Abelardo, a bright green parrot, a grouch character named Poncho Contreras, and others. At least one half of the material broadcast is created by the local producer, whereas 50% or less of the program's content is material dubbed from CTW's international library of segments. These segments are selected by each local production team for their pertinence to a given program's educational goals and for their general contribution to the production.

Each of the 19 productions listed in Table 9.1 was developed using a variant of a highly flexible process called the CTW Model (see Truglio & Fisch, chap. 1, this volume). The table highlights the history of our coproductions, summarizing information about our production and broadcast partners. It also includes facts such as the language(s) of each series and the number of seasons produced. Note that the degree of localization on some of the productions has evolved over time, with some countries producing a greater percentage of local material over time. For a chronological history of the *Sesame Street* International coproductions, please refer to Table 9.2.

In working with producers in another country, our intention is not to impose our American sensibilities, but to provide, instead, a framework for a series that will be created in-country by a local production team. As noted in Fig. 9.1, which outlines our production process, we begin by determining the feasibility of and need for the production; this information is pursued through formal and informal research. We seek to determine if there is support for the project in the education community, among government entities, and within the broadcast and production realms. Once we have satisfactorily addressed these concerns and located the right production part-

TABLE 9.1
History of Sesame Street International Coproductions

Country of Origin	Series Title	Coproducer	Broadcaster[a]	Language	Date First Broadcast or Produced	Number of Seasons Produced	Currently in Production and/or Broadcast
Brazil	Vila Sésamo	TV Globo[b]	TV Globo/ TV Cultura	Portuguese	10/23/72	2	No
Canada	Sesame Park/ Sesame Street Canada[c]	CBC (Canadian Broadcasting Corporation)	CBC (Canadian Broadcasting Corporation)	English (with some French segments)	Sesame Park: 10/96 Sesame Street Canada: 1/73	Sesame Park: 4[d] Sesame Street Canada: 22	Yes
China	Zhima Jie	Shanghai TV	Shanghai TV[e]	Mandarin	2/2/98	1	Yes
Egypt	'Alam Simsim	Karma Productions	Egyptian Television	Arabic	2000	1	Yes
France	1, rue Sésame	T.F. 1 (Television Francaise 1)	T.F. 1 (Television Francaise 1)	French	4/3/78	2	No
Germany	Sesamstrasse	NDR (Norddeutscher Rundfunk)	NDR (Norddeutscher Rundfunk)	German	1/8/73[f]	28[g]	Yes

(Continued)

TABLE 9.1 (Continued)

Country of Origin	Series Title	Coproducer	Broadcaster	Language	Date First Broadcast or Produced	Number of Seasons Produced	Currently in Production and/or Broadcast
Israel	Rechov Sumsum	IETV (Israel Educational Television)	IETV (Israel Educational Television)	Hebrew	9/12/83	4	(See below)
Israel/ Palestinian Territories	Rechov Sumsum/ Shara'a Simsim	IETV/Al-Quds University's Institute of Modern Media	IETV (Israel Educational Television)[h]	Hebrew and Arabic	4/1/98	1	Yes
Kuwait[i]	Iftah Ya Simsim	AGSJPPI (Arabian Gulf States Joint Program Production Institute)	AGSJPPI (Arabian Gulf States Joint Program Production Institute)	Arabic	9/29/79	3	No
Mexico[j]	Plaza Sésamo	Televisa	Televisa	Spanish	11/72[k]	6[l]	Yes
The Netherlands	Sesamstraat	NPS (Nederlandse Programma Stichting)	NOS/NPS (Nederlandse Omroepprogramma Stichting)/ (Nederlandse Programma Stichting)[m]	Dutch	1/4/76	23	Yes

Country	Show	Production	Broadcaster	Language	Date	Season	Muppets
Norway	*Sesam Stasjon*	NRK (Norsk Rikskringkasting)	NRK (Norsk Rikskringkasting)	Norwegian	2/25/91	4	Yes
Philippines	*Sesame!*	HSDC (Human Settlements Development Corp)	HSDC (Human Settlements Development Corp)	Tagalog and English	12/19/83	1	No
Poland	*Ulica Sezamkowa*	Euromedia	Polish TV	Polish	10/27/96	2	No
Portugal[n]	*Rua Sésamo*	RTP (Radiotelevisão Portuguese E.P.)	RTP (Radiotelevisão Portuguese E.P.)	Portuguese	11/6/89	3	No
Russia	*Ulitsa Sezam*	Video Arts	NTV (Telecompaniya NTV) and ORT (Obstchestvennoye Rossiiskoye Televideniye)	Russian	NTV: 10/22/96 ORT: 9/97	1°	Yes
South Africa Television	*Takalani Sesame*	Kwasukasukela	SABC (South Africa Broadcast Corporation)	Multi-lingual	7/2000 anticipated	To be produced	Yes
South Africa Radio[p]	*Takalani Sesame*	Vuleka Productions	SABC (South Africa Broadcast Corporation)	Zulu (with some English segments)	10/2000 anticipated	To be produced	Yes

(Continued)

151

TABLE 9.1 (Continued)

Country of Origin	Series Title	Coproducer	Broadcaster	Language	Date First Broadcast or Produced	Number of Seasons Produced	Currently in Production and/or Broadcast
Spain	*Barrio Sésamo (Barri Sèsam)*	TVE (Televisión Española)	TVE (Televisión Española)	Castilian/Catalan[q]	12/24/79	6[r]	Yes
Sweden	*Svenska Sesam*	SR-2 (Sveriges Television)	SR-2 (Sveriges Television)	Swedish	10/31/81	1	No
Turkey	*Susam Sokagi*	TRT (Turkish Radio and Television)	TRT (Turkish Radio and Television)	Turkish	10/89	2	No

[a] For the purposes of this table, we have only noted the names of the originating broadcasters.

[b] TV Cultura cooperated in the production of *Vila Sésamo.*

[c] *Sesame Park* is the Canadian coproduction currently in production and broadcast in Canada. *Sesame Street Canada* was the U.S. version of *Sesame Street,* broadcast in Canada, which featured some Canadian segments.

[d] The 5th season of *Sesame Park* is currently in production.

[e] *Zhima Jie* has aired in over 40 local markets comprising over 70% of all TV households in China.

[f] The early version of *Sesamstrasse* incorporated newly produced German animation and live action segments into the U.S. version of the series, which was dubbed into German. The first *Sesamstrasse* show was broadcast on January 8, 1973. Five years later, in 1978, *Sesamstrasse* included studio segments (featuring German puppets) and Germany became a 50–50 coproducer.

[g] The 29th season of *Sesamstrasse* is currently in production.

(Continued)

[h] A 15-minute version of the program called *Shara'a Simsim*, containing primarily Arabic segments, is broadcast on Al-Quds Educational Television in the Palestinian Territories.

[i] In addition to Kuwait, *Iftah Ya Simsim* was developed for broadcast in 16 Arab-world countries.

[j] *Plaza Sésamo* is broadcast in Spanish-speaking Latin America and Puerto Rico. Since April 3, 1995, it has also aired in the U.S.

[k] *Plaza Sésamo* was first broadcast in Puerto Rico in November, 1972 and in Latin America on January 8, 1973.

[l] The 7th season of *Plaza Sésamo* is currently in production.

[m] In the early years of broadcast, BRT, Belgische Radio en Televisie, the Belgium Broadcaster, cooperated in the development of *Sesamstraat*, which was broadcast in The Netherlands and Belgium.

[n] In addition to Portugal, *Rua Sésamo* was developed for broadcast in the Portuguese-speaking African countries of Angola, Mozambique, Guinea, Cape Verde, and São Tomé.

[o] The 2nd season of *Ulitsa Sezam* is currently in production.

[p] This is the first *Sesame Street* international coproduction produced for radio.

[q] In Season 5 (1996), all studio segments were produced twice: once in Castilian (Barrio Sésamo) and once in Catalan (Barri Sèsam). Subsequent seasons of the program have been produced in Castilian and dubbed into Catalan for regional broadcast in Catalunya.

[r] The 7th season of *Barrio Sésamo* is currently in production.

TABLE 9.2
Chronological History of Sesame Street International Coproductions

Country of Origin	Series Title	Date First Broadcast or Produced
Brazil	*Vila Sésamo*	October 23, 1972
Mexico	*Plaza Sésamo*	November 1972[a]
Canada	*Sesame Street Canada*[b] *Sesame Park*	January 1973 October 1996
Germany	*Sesamstrasse*	January 8, 1973[c]
The Netherlands	*Sesamstraat*	January 4, 1976
France	*1, rue Sésame*	April 3, 1978
Kuwait	*Iftah Ya Simsim*	September 29, 1979
Spain	*Barrio Sésamo (Barri Sèsam)*[d]	December 24, 1979 (1996)
Sweden	*Svenska Sesam*	October 31, 1981
Israel	*Rechov Sumsum*	September 12, 1983
Philippines	*Sesame!*	December 19, 1983
Turkey	*Susam Sokagi*	October 1989
Portugal	*Rua Sésamo*	November 6, 1989
Norway	*Sesam Stasjon*	February 25, 1991
Russia	*Ulitsa Sezam*	October 22, 1996
Poland	*Ulica Sezamkowa*	October 27, 1996
China	*Zhima Jie*	February 2, 1998
Israel/Palestinian Territories	*Rechov Sumsum/ Shara'a Simsim*	April 1, 1998
Egypt	*'Alam Simsim*	Anticipated Launch Date: 2000
South Africa TV	*Takalani Sesame*	Anticipated Launch Date: July 2000
South Africa Radio	*Takalani Sesame*	Anticipated Launch Date: October 2000

[a] *Plaza Sésamo* was first broadcast in Puerto Rico in November 1972 and in Latin America on January 8, 1973. Since April 3, 1995, it has also aired in the United States

[b] *Sesame Park* is the Canadian coproduction currently in production and broadcast in Canada. *Sesame Street Canada* was the U.S. version of *Sesame Street*, broadcast in Canada, which featured some Canadian segments.

[c] The first *Sesamstrasse* show incorporated newly produced German animation and live action segments into the U.S. version of the series, which was dubbed into German. Five years later, in 1978, *Sesamstrasse* included studio segments (featuring German puppets) and Germany became a 50-50 coproducer.

[d] In Season 5 (1996), all studio segments for Spain's coproduction were produced twice: once in Castilian (*Barrio Sésamo*) and once in Catalan (*Barri Sèsam*). Subsequent seasons of the program have been produced in Castilian and dubbed into Catalan for regional broadcast in Catalunya.

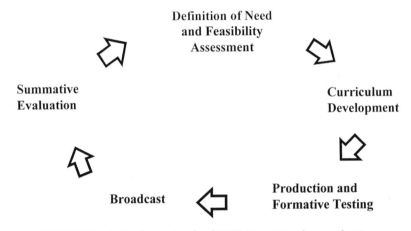

FIG. 9.1 The basic elements of a CTW International coproduction.

ners, the process of developing an educational plan begins. The local production team convenes a group of educational specialists representing a range of fields, such as child development, child language, cultural studies, sociology, gender studies, art, music, environmental studies, mathematics, literacy, and other fields relevant to children's lives. The experts meet with the production team in a formal meeting known as the "curriculum seminar" where they discuss the educational priorities for the children of their countries (cf. Lesser & Schneider, chap. 2, this volume).

Around the world, curriculum seminar discussions have resulted in determining a range of educational priorities for our coproductions. Although the ensuing educational plans or curricula contain elements in common (e.g., sections on numeracy, literacy, and affective skills), each has unique aspects that the educators from a particular country felt were of critical importance to children in their own counties. For example, the Chinese curriculum contains a section devoted to aesthetics that is not included in such detail in other curricula. In Israel and the Palestinian Territories, the program presents messages of mutual respect and understanding to children living in the region. Preparing children for life in their new open society is a critical element of the production in Russia. Thus, each series can provide educational messages on some of the broad curricular areas that are common to preschoolers around the globe, as well as educational content that more specifically addresses children's needs within a given cultural context.

Once the educational plan has been developed, production begins. Educational specialists remain involved in the production process by answering the team's questions about the specifics of the curriculum, providing educational resources to the team to enhance the effectiveness of segments, reviewing scripts for the integrity of the educational objectives, and offering suggestions with respect to how the educational messages can best be communicated clearly and accurately to our young audiences. The production process also usually includes formative research that is designed to provide the team with feedback on the appeal and comprehension of the segments. When possible, summative evaluation occurs after broadcast to examine the impact of the production as a whole and to provide information that can be used to improve future seasons of the program.

In bringing all of these elements together, the international coproduction model results in the creation of entertaining programs based on locally established educational goals that are met through culturally relevant means. It is a process that makes sense in an international context, because, as psychologists have noted, children learn from the cultural contexts within which they live (Rogoff, 1993). Television is an audiovisual medium and is, for this reason, an ideal learning vehicle for young children. Much of what children learn during the preschool years they learn through modeled behavior. It is far better to *show and tell* young children how to wash their hands than merely to *tell* them, and it is one step better yet if the images that are presented and the verbal message that accompanies them are ones that take place in situations and settings that are familiar and relevant to the child. The globalization of *Sesame Street* has proceeded under the assumption that the program is an ideal format for forwarding culturally specific messages because the images presented are created by and for people of a given culture.

Formative Research

To assist in the process of developing culturally relevant material, formative research is an integral aspect of the international coproduction process. Usually, formative research begins at the initiation of a coproduction project when the team defines the need for the project and assesses its feasibility. Although not technically *formative research* in the way the term is used in other contexts, the research process begins with feasibility research at the initiation of a coproduction. This initial work is essential to the coproduction projects. Curriculum development also includes formative work as content specialists provide information about the educational priorities for children in their country. Once production begins, formative research continues and has been used to assist the team with such aspects of the production as character development, set design, understanding elements of produced segments that appeal to children and testing the degree to which children comprehend a program's educational messages.

Definition of Need and Feasibility Assessment. The initial determination of feasibility and need is at the core of each of our coproduction projects, with the potential opportunity for a productive series decided jointly by the prospective coproducer and CTW. In most instances, we come to a given country after a producer, broadcaster, educational, or government entity has invited us there. Because *Sesame Street* is an educational endeavor that has broad reach within a given country, it is essential that a body of individuals from these various realms endorses the worth of the project and supports the coproduction effort.

The process of determining need and feasibility takes on many forms. Often, as was the case for our projects in South Africa (Children's Television Workshop, 1993) and Israel and the Palestinian Territories (Children's Television Workshop, 1996), it begins with visits to the country by members of the CTW International staff who interview individuals representing a range of fields of interest including producers, broadcasters, government officials, and representatives from nongovernment organizations. Such trips often result in a need for more formal research. For example in South Africa, after our initial fact-finding trip, we commissioned several research reports to help us better understand the state of media in the country and specifics about daily life (Kemp, 1994; Liddell, 1995; Usdin, 1996) and information about South African language policy (Alexander, Bloch, & Heugh, 1995; Constable, 1995; Luckett, 1995; Makoni, 1995). Similarly, in Israel and the Palestinian Territories, a series of position papers (Arafat, 1995; Levin, 1995; Mar'i, 1995; Yirmiya, 1995) served to inform the team about various ways of approaching a project that would use *Sesame Street* to present messages of mutual respect and understanding to children living in the region.

In China, another type of informal research contributed to the determination of need and feasibility. CTW commissioned a researcher to interview preschoolers and their parents to examine children's viewing habits and parental attitudes about television (Zhang, 1997). This type of interview study can be an effective way to gain information about viewership in countries where standard ratings data are not available, easily accessible, or specifically targeted to the *Sesame Street* age group. Furthermore, it can also assist in providing information about family interactions with television, something that can be important when making initial decisions about how to set up a production project.

Curriculum Development. As noted earlier, curriculum development on our international coproductions involves a multiple-step process that usually begins with the identification of a team of educational experts who represent a range of fields relevant to preschool education, just as is done in the United States (Lesser & Schneider, chap. 2, this volume). The role of these individuals is to attend a curriculum seminar that becomes a brainstorming session in which advisors talk about the educational priorities for the children of their country.

Typically, these seminars last 2 to 3 days. They begin by introducing seminar participants to the CTW production model and by viewing sample episodes of *Sesame Street* from the United States and international coproductions. In addition to large-group plenary sessions, attended by all participants, the seminars also include small-group discussions that enable the advisors and members of the production team to talk in-depth about specific topics and ways *Sesame Street* can best contribute to meeting the educational priorities for their country.

The results of the meetings are summarized in a curriculum document that becomes the educational plan for the coproduction. Each segment produced for *Sesame Street* is designed to focus on a single educational objective from the curriculum. The curricula developed for various countries differ from each other with respect to their emphasis and organization, with some emphasizing cognitive and academic goals and others focusing more on the social-affective domain. Most contain a range of goals including academic skills (numeracy and literacy), cognitive skills (such as sorting and classification), social-affective skills (such as social interactions, social institutions, family life, and traditions), and the environment (including the human-made and natural environments, and ecology).

What makes each curriculum unique sometimes has less to do with the goals themselves than with the way in which they are presented on the screen. A concrete example of this concerns a health goal: *washing hands before eating*. Variants of this goal are included in many of the coproduction curricula, yet each production team that has produced segments to present this goal has created something distinct. A segment from *Plaza Sésamo*, our program in Mexico, for example, features Mexican children washing their hands at Mexican sinks. The Russian coproduction, *Ulitsa Sezam*, has a segment that is strikingly similar in format, yet dramatically different, given the design of the Russian sinks and faucets, the physical features of the children on screen and the production elements involved, such as local music and songs, and stylistic differences in creative approach. When children watch these segments, they gain all the more from what they view because the images presented take place in contexts that are relevant to their own lives.

In addition to differences relating to context, other contrasts among curricula concern the content that is emphasized. For example, the curriculum for *Rechov Sumsum/Shara'a Simsim*, our project in Israel and the Palestinian Territories, contains five broad areas: (a) *Mutual Respect* (e.g., human diversity, mutual respect); (b) *The Child's World* (e.g., body parts, child's powers, health, reasoning and problem solving, affect); (c) *Social Units* (e.g., social groups and institutions, environment); (d) *Reading, Mathematics, and Writing* (e.g., prereading and writing, numbers, geometric forms); and (e) *Cognitive*

Organization (e.g., perceptual discrimination, relational concepts, classifying), with objective statements related to each goal area (*RS/SS* Content Team, 1997). Many of these areas, as noted before, are a part of the educational curricula for most of our productions, including the first goal area, Mutual Respect. But although mutual respect messages have been a part of *Sesame Street* through the years, the *Rechov Sumsum/Shara'a Simsim* project was the first to devote an entire section of the curriculum to this area and actively focus on it as a special priority due to the profound political tension in the region.

The curriculum for *Zhima Jie*, our project in China, provides an alternate example of a difference in curricular content. Like the *Rechov Sumsum/Shara'a Simsim* project, it contains several broad areas: a section on the *Child's World* that is focused on understanding self, *Family and Society* that contains social-oriented objectives, *Symbolic Representation* (that includes literacy and numeracy goals), and a *Cognitive Organization* section (that contains classification and perceptual goals). In addition to these more standard sections, the curriculum's fifth area focuses on *Aesthetics and Arts*. The three subsections in this area are: (a) *sensitivity to aesthetics* (which includes perception, sense of hearing, kinesthesia, language arts, and Chinese calligraphic arts), (b) *aesthetic experience* (that contains objectives in experiencing nature, perception of the human-made landscape, and arts appreciation), and (c) *artistic creativity* (that covers composition and model, music and body movement, and music composition).

In addition to the curriculum seminar, other means are used to assist each coproduction team in articulating an educational focus. In many countries, researchers conduct formal and informal investigations to provide a sense of the major issues of relevance to children of a given country. An example of informal work comes from our project in Russia, where a series of trips was taken to different regions of Russia (*Ulitsa Sezam* Research Department, 1995). In Ekaterinburg, Novosibirsk, and Cheboksary, researchers informally interviewed teachers, government officials, and representatives from educational institutions, such as libraries and museums, to gather ideas about issues of importance to the program. These meetings resulted in an accumulation of ideas for the series and informal endorsements of the project from the educational community.

Researchers pursued a more formal process in Egypt where the team commissioned a series of papers (Badawi, 1998; Ibrahim, 1998; Rouchdy, 1998; Shaalan, 1998; Younis, 1998) on five topics that had been identified as of particular relevance to the project: (a) *Health,* (b) *Girls' Education,* (c) *Language,* (d) *Family,* and (e) *Religion.* An Egyptian expert in each area served as the respective author of each of the five papers. The authors presented their papers to the production team during five topical seminars designed for this purpose. The papers then became references for the production team.

In addition to providing general academic information (including statistics and relevant facts), the topical papers and seminars assisted the team in making important and often complex production decisions. For example, language use is a critical issue in Egypt because different forms of Arabic are used in different contexts. The producers needed to determine whether the program should be developed in colloquial Arabic (the language of home and social situations) or Fusha (Arabic), the language of academia and the Quran. Since *Sesame Street* is an educational endeavor, it could be argued that the language of school was warranted. Children do not typically learn this level of Arabic until they enter school. Some of the project's educational advisors argued that *Sesame Street* could provide children with a jump start on learning the language used in academic settings, and, in doing so, best prepare children for their formal school experiences. (In fact, it was an extension of this argument that was used more than a decade earlier to determine the level of Arabic presented on *Iftah Ya Simsim*, the Kuwaiti version of *Sesame Street*, which uses a form of Arabic employed in academia.) Equally convincing were arguments pointing to the importance of presenting the program in the colloquial Arabic that is familiar to children, to enhance their enjoyment and attention to the program, and thus promote greater learning. The decision regarding the level of Arabic to use on the program was resolved during the topical seminar on language, in which an Egyptian language specialist provided a compelling argument for using the *context* of the segment produced to determine the level of language used. In the end, it was this strategy that was adopted by the team who produced segments that teach academic skills using the language of school and other segments in colloquial Arabic.

Production Research: Appeal.   Once production begins, formative research is conducted to assist the team in developing materials for the program. Some of this research relates specifically to production concerns, whereas other elements are more directly linked to educational content.

Set design provides an example of research that is directly linked to a production element. Formative studies of sets have been conducted on several projects including coproductions in Mexico (Gemark, 1993), Poland (Kirwil, 1996a), and Spain (*Barrio Sésamo/Barri Sèsam* Department of Research and Content, 1997). Such studies usually involve showing children prototype renderings of the sets and examining the elements that attract their attention. These studies often also include questions that elicit feedback about children's daily lives in an effort to enhance the set in ways that are most reflective of a child-centered orientation.

Character studies are another example of this type of research. Two examples come from opposite sides of the Atlantic Ocean. The fourth season of *Plaza Sésamo* (Mexico) included a particular focus on health, safety, and nutrition. The producers wanted to develop a character that could be used in animated segments to promote health messages. They began by proposing three possible characters: a space alien, a little eagle, and a little boy. Researchers individually interviewed a group of preschoolers, asking questions to gauge the relative appeal of the characters. Because the character ultimately selected would convey health and safety messages, the team was also interested in assessing the relative credibility of the three characters. They asked children a series of questions designed to capture the ways in which they perceived the characters in an effort to discern which character was closest to being a positive, trustworthy role model.

The research protocol used in this case was very simple. To gauge appeal, the investigators individually interviewed children, showing them pictures of the animated characters. They began by asking them to select the character they liked best and then asked them a series of more specific questions, such as the games each character likes to play. To gain insight into the credibility of the character, they read the children a series of sentences and asked them to point to the character that they thought said each one. Some of the sentences modeled safety messages, whereas others articulated mischievous concerns.

The investigators found that two of the three characters, the boy and the eagle, had equal appeal and equal credibility. The alien was the least popular and most often associated with mischievous behaviors. It was recommended that the eagle be used because the boy had been confused by some of the children with an animated character that was used in advertisements of chocolate milk that appeared during other children's programs. This resulted in the team selecting the eagle to be the signature character for the health segments.

In a different fashion, research conducted for the first season of *Ulica Sezamkowa* in Poland (Kirwil, 1996b) was used to help develop the production's two Muppet characters: a dragon and a lamb. Although the team had already determined the general characteristics of these characters, they used input from children to refine the look of the characters. They began by gauging the relative appeal of the characters. Since Polish children were already familiar with the U.S. version of *Sesame Street* (which had previously been broadcast in the country in English with a Polish voice-over), the researchers were able to gauge the ratings of the new Polish characters in relation to some of CTW's domestic characters. Children ages 3 to 6 years (who were a mixture of children who had viewed the U.S. program and nonviewers) were individually interviewed and were shown sketches of six of the U.S. domestic Muppets and two sketches of the proposed Polish puppets. Appeal was measured in various ways, including having the children point to their favorite characters, and having the children rate the characters using a 5-point scale that visually depicted faces representing varying levels of a continuum from very happy (5) to very sad (1).[1]

The results showed that the lamb had high appeal, but this was not the case for the dragon. Furthermore, in some cases, children thought the dragon was a dinosaur. In terms of the relative ratings of the Polish characters with respect to the U.S. domestic ones, it was found that the signature characters

---

[1]This type of visual measure is of particular importance to coproduction research given the age—3 to 6 years old—of our target audience and the consequent need to depend as little as possible on verbal indicators. Other coproductions have also effectively used a similar scale with only three points (happy, so-so, and sad). See Stifter and Fox (1986) for an example of the use of such measures in another research context.

of the U.S. program, Big Bird, Bert and Ernie, had the highest average ratings (4.3). The lamb and U.S.'s Elmo were only at a slightly lower level (4.2), whereas the dragon had the same rating as Cookie Monster (3.8). All received ratings above the less familiar U.S. character, the Count, whose rating was more than a point below the most popular characters and at a level of neutrality (3.2) on the 5-point scale.

In an effort to bolster the relative appeal of the dragon character, the team conducted an additional study consisting of focus group interviews with a group of slightly older children. The children were shown a black and white sketch of the dragon, asked to talk about it, and, at the end of the session, were asked to color in the sketch. Interestingly, many of the children finished the sketch using what they called "rainbow" colors. This concept of multihues, along with some of the additional verbal information that the children provided, was presented to the production team and was used in adapting the final rendition of the character. As a result, "Bazyli" now has fur that is more than one color.

Although the changes in the dragon character were the most dramatic, a few refinements in the physical appearance of the lamb were also made based on the children's suggestions. Such developments indicate the degree to which the findings of the formative studies were taken seriously by the production team. Interestingly, results of a follow-up interview with children who were asked to rate the characters after their development was complete (but prior to the initial broadcast) indicated that the dragon's rating was on par with Big Bird, Bert and Ernie (4.3), and the lamb's rating was even higher (4.6).

Production Research: Appeal and Engagement.

Often, formative research looks at the appeal of a given segment and/or children's engagement as they watch. These studies sometimes also simultaneously examine comprehension (see next section). In our project in Israel and the Palestinian Territories, for example, program segments were tested by Israeli and Palestinian research teams to examine children's overall reactions (*Shara'a Simsim* Research Team, 1997; Tidhar, Rivner, & Shachori, 1997a, 1997b, 1997c, 1997d, 1997e). One live-action segment, for example, called *Embroidery*, depicted a young Palestinian girl watching her grandmother embroider a dress. Thirty-six Palestinian children attending preschools in Ramallah and Jerusalem watched this segment; researchers documented children's behavior during viewing to assess their engagement and individually interviewed the children afterward to evaluate their comprehension. The study showed that children's attention to the piece was high (with girls tending to be more attentive than boys), they could describe the segment's general plot, and they had high recall of specific details. Such findings were particularly important as the primary goal of the project was to create authentic, positive images of Israeli and Palestinian culture. The fact that many children related the piece to a personal experience and were highly engaged as they viewed was a hopeful indicator that the broader aim was being addressed.

Similarly, a series of formative work in Russia used techniques employed in a comparable or adapted form elsewhere. Appeal was tested using a combination of an "eyes-on-screen" measure and observations of children's behavior while viewing. Eyes-on-screen is, at best, a general measure of the construct called attention. Attention research is designed to examine children's engagement with a given segment or episode, as well as their attention to specific content within a segment or episode. This type of research provides a sense of the elements of a segment or episode that attract children, as well as those that do not hold their interest. Although a method used by other television researchers (see Flagg, 1990 for a detailed review of attention measures; cf. Fisch & Bernstein, chap. 3, this volume; Levin & Anderson, 1976; Palmer & Fisch, chap. 1, this volume), it is, recognizably, far from perfect. Many children monitor a television program even without looking at the screen. Conversely, children who maintain a direct focus on the screen sometimes understand a minimal amount about what they have viewed. Nevertheless, eyes-on-screen measurement can provide general insight into variation in attention that can be useful to the production team if used in conjunction with other measures.

Historically, researchers have conducted eyes-on-screen studies in a variety of different ways. Our international coproducers have essentially used variations of two different approaches. One approach, known as the *interval method*, involves recording whether a child is directly watching the television (that is, whether his or her eyes are focused on the monitor) at prescribed points throughout the segment. Researchers observe children watching a segment and, at predetermined intervals, note whether or not their eyes are on the screen. The average number of children whose eyes are directed at the screen at a given moment is calculated and graphed, creating a visual linkage of varying attention levels and the content of what the children viewed.

An alternate and somewhat more subjective method is known as the *global method*. This method involves making a qualitative judgment about the attention levels of the children viewing. Researchers observe children watching and rate each child's attention to a given segment or part of a segment, determining whether the child was *highly attentive* (i.e., "the child's eyes are usually directed toward screen. He or she may occasionally glance away, but is, for the most part, engaged in watching and looking directly at the screen"), *moderately attentive* (i.e., "the child's eyes may sometimes be diverted, but return to the screen for extended periods"), and *minimally attentive* (i.e., "the child's eyes are frequently diverted from the screen. They may be drawn back to viewing periodically, but usually for only brief moments.").

As with all measures of eyes-on-screen, before the global measure is used in a study, researchers coding the behaviors work to obtain high interrater reliability. This is done using standard reliability methods that involve multiple coders rating the behavior of the same children and checking for agreement among raters.

Research on *Ulitsa Sezam* (Russia) provides an example of how attention levels are graphically presented using the interval eyes-on-screen method (*Ulitsa Sezam* Russian Department of Research and Content, 1996). Fig. 9.2 presents data from a study of a single segment and indicates the percentage of children whose eyes were focused on the screen at 10-second time periods. Note that for the segment, attention levels range from 42% to 100%, with an average rate of 81% across all intervals. Using such graphs, teams can note the points in segments or episodes that attracted children's attention and can catalogue patterns that emerge. In this particular example, attention level is varied across the roughly 3 minutes that are depicted, although the attention rate for the segment as a whole is moderately high. Graphs, such as the one presented, have greatest value when viewed in the context of data from other segments. In comparing and contrasting trends from attention studies of multiple segments, researchers gain the most complete knowledge of elements that attract children's attention, and understanding these trends assists the production team in creating the most attractive and engaging segments.

Because eyes-on-screen is such a gross measure, it is essential that eyes-on-screen data are collected in conjunction with data about children's behavioral response to what they are viewing. Capturing a sense of children's actions and verbalizations as they watch is a helpful indicator of engagement. Such was the case in the formative work done in Russia that was designed to test children's engagement with the program. In order to record the viewing behavior of each child, researchers used one coding sheet per segment and noted whether or not a given behavior (e.g., labels objects, labels letters, counts, smiles, laughs, moves to music, dances, sings, etc.) was ever present while the child viewed that segment. This information was then presented in conjunction with the eyes-on-screen data.

An interesting anecdote regarding the first formative studies conducted for the Russian coproduction is worth noting, as it illustrates the importance of adapting methodology to account for cultural differences. Initial tests of children's eyes-on-screen yielded consistently high attention rates (in fact, close to 100%) with little variation in the behavioral measures. Researchers in Moscow were concerned that this did not accurately reflect the fluctuations that one might expect to see in preschoolers' viewing. They suspected that children might have been making a concerted effort to behave properly (i.e., watching the screen attentively and quietly) in front of adults with whom they were not familiar. The Russian research team re-examined their methodology and made a significant modification. Instead of remaining in the classroom with the children to document eyes-on-screen and behaviors (as was done during studies of *Sesame Street* in the U.S.), they set up a video camera to tape children as they viewed without adults present. When attention and behavior were coded later from the tape, children's interactions fluctuated to a greater extent and reflected a seemingly more natural engagement with the television.

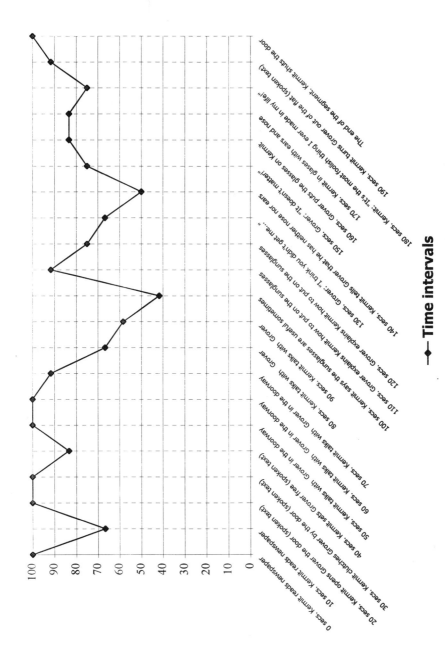

FIG. 9.2. Four-year-olds' attention level (%) during the segment "Sunglasses Salesman" in *Ulitsa Sezam*.

Production Research: Comprehension.   The format of comprehension studies generally begins with children watching episodes or segments. Viewing is followed by individual interviews in which children are asked questions about what they saw. Interviewers often begin with a broad question such as, "Can you tell me about what you just watched?," and then proceed with more narrowly-focused questions. Props and photographic stills of images that had been shown on the screen are generally employed as prompts to ensure that the children and the researchers are referring to the same parts of the shows. Production teams use the results of such testing to refine individual segments in post-production and to gain information of more general value to the production of future segments. Although the scope of each formative study is too small to provide conclusive evidence of any specific effects, the information gained collectively from studies throughout the world contributes to a larger body of research on *Sesame Street*. This has served to catalog elements that attract and engage young viewers and offered insight into the effective presentation of educational content.

For example, a study in Mexico examined the use of a song to model an environmental message about cleaning up trash (Gemark, 1994). Results illustrated that the song did a good job of attracting children's attention and reinforcing educational points that had been presented verbally prior to the song, but was less successful at conveying content that had been presented only in the song. Researchers recommended that songs be used to engage children and emphasize educational content, but should not be depended on as lone carriers of curricular messages. Such findings parallel those of a study conducted in the United States (Lorch & Anderson, 1979) that led to similar conclusions about the benefits of music to engage children, rather than communicate educational content.

In addition to the standard view-interview design described above, pre- and posttest formats are sometimes used to measure gains in children's comprehension of a given educational message. Research conducted for *Zhima Jie* (China) provides an example. The series includes 30-second bumpers that are each designed to teach a specific science goal. Researchers tested children's comprehension of several of these segments, including one designed to demonstrate relative buoyancy of different objects (*Zhima Jie* Research Team, 1998). The segment features three signature character puppets, Omni (a humorous professor) and Beacon and Watt (two "light bulbs"). In the segment, the characters demonstrate to several child-participants the floating properties of three objects: a key, a pencil, and an egg. The children on the screen are first asked to guess if a given object will float or sink, and then they watch a demonstration of each object's buoyancy.

To study viewers' understanding of these segments, researchers set up a demonstration modeled after the one presented in the segment. Prior to viewing the segment, children were presented with a clear bowl of water and the three objects (a key, a pencil, and an egg) and asked if each would float or sink. Children then viewed the segment and afterward were again asked about the floating properties of the various objects. As indicated by Fig. 9.3, the differ-

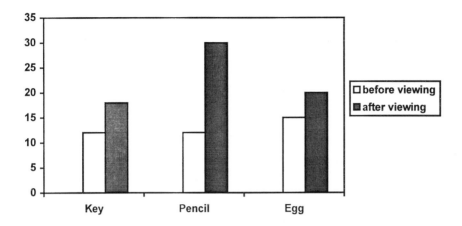

FIG. 9.3. Change in number of children correctly answering questions about floating.

ence in children's understanding before and after viewing the segment was striking. Many of the children who had misconceptions about the floating properties of the items prior to viewing were able to answer the questions correctly after viewing.

It is important to note, however, an inherent limitation in the study design. It is likely that participation in the study, itself, predisposed children to perform better on the postviewing test. Since researchers had not established a comparison group of children who had not viewed, they could not definitely attribute learning to viewing. This uncertainty brings forth an important aspect of formative research. Although researchers endeavor to set up situations that follow rigorous standards of social science research practices, in formative research, it is necessary to balance multiple constraints that do not come into play in other research situations. Time is a major factor in the inevitable puzzle of developing the best research methodology to meet the needs of the production schedule. If researchers do not deliver the results of the study within a time frame that serves the production, then their work cannot help inform the production process; conversely, if study designs lead to false conclusions, an equal disservice has been performed. Often, it is a question of how the data are interpreted and how we communicate the results to the production team that ultimately determines our success in balancing these concerns (see Fisch & Bernstein, chap. 3, this volume).

In the case of the Chinese study, the purpose was to see the degree to which children could or could not demonstrate a more refined understanding of the basic science principles conveyed in the segments. In essence, the team used the formative research to gain a broad notion of the effect of the segment.

Summative Evaluation

In addition to formative work, a number of summative evaluations have broadened our understanding of the value of *Sesame Street* across cultures. At the heart of these are studies that look at the educational effectiveness of the programs. Although these studies are the primary focus of this section, a few studies have looked at the reach of the broadcast and/or have examined the general appeal of the program. A detailed presentation of these types of market surveys is beyond the scope of this chapter, but the studies are worthy of some mention because they provide information that historically has been used by broadcasters, funders, and others to make decisions about the sustainability of some coproduction projects.

Market Research.   A study conducted in The Netherlands (Kohnstam & Cammaer, 1976) provides a useful example of research that has focused on general appeal and broadcast reach. Using audience ratings, interviews of parents and teachers, and observations of children's attention, researchers sought to determine the degree to which the first season (20 episodes) of *Sesamstraat* successfully reached its Dutch and Belgian audiences. Researchers found that more than 50% of all children between the ages of 3 to 6 years in both countries had had some access to the program. Additionally, the program was one of the most frequently mentioned when parents were asked to name their 3- to 6-year-old's three favorite programs. The study also found that kindergarten teachers were aware of the series and regarded it as useful, although some of the Dutch teachers surveyed felt that the pace of the program was too fast.

As others have noted (Palmer, Lesser, & Theroux, 1978), one important element of the *Sesamstraat* study is that it highlighted both the strengths and weaknesses of the program and in so doing, provided information that assisted the production team in improving future seasons of the series. Some of the recommendations that resulted from the report focused on the pace of the program, the quality of some of the characters' voices, the relationship between the stated objectives and the educational goals presented on the series, the appropriateness of the series for its target audience, and the broadcast schedule.

Other, more recent studies have also looked at market-oriented information. For example, a study jointly commissioned by Nestlé (Russia) and CTW (Analytics-Russia, 1998) was carried out during the summer of 1998. This research was conducted with parents and teachers, and explored viewing patterns of and attitudes toward *Ulitsa Sezam*. Interviews (1,320 in total) were completed in 11 regions of Russia across eight time zones.

The study demonstrated that awareness of *Ulitsa Sezam* among parents and teachers was quite high, with over 80% of the individuals sampled demonstrating knowledge of the program. In addition, when parents spontaneously mentioned the television shows their children watch, *Ulitsa Sezam* had the second highest rating among programs. Finally, the overwhelming majority of *Ulitsa Sezam* viewers reported liking the series. Both parents and teachers appreciated its educational value, and thought the show was interesting, entertaining, and beneficial for their children.

Similarly, a study of our new project in Israel and the Palestinian territories (Cohen & Francis, 1999) illustrated that the *Rechov Sumsum/Shara'a Simsim* program has wide reach in the region. A survey of 600 parents of children under the age of 8 years examined the viewership of the series and looked specifically at three groups of respondents: Israeli Jews, Palestinian-Israelis (that is, Palestinians with Israeli citizenship), and Palestinians living in the Palestinian Territories. The study suggested that the program is perceived as entertaining and appealing and most parents recognized the program's social mission of presenting messages of mutual respect and understanding to children living in the region.

Educational Impact.   Other summative evaluations have been more directed toward children's learning from the series. Many of these have focused on basic academic skills and, in particular, on literacy and numeracy. One of the earliest studies that examined educational impact was also one of the most comprehensive. Researchers in Mexico conducted a controlled experimental study of children's learning from *Plaza Sésamo* (Diaz-Guerrero & Holtzman, 1974). A sample of 221 3-, 4- and 5-year-olds were randomly assigned to either an experimental group who viewed the program regularly for 6 months, or a control group who viewed alternate children's programming. Researchers evaluated children's pre- and postviewing performance on a battery of tests representing various skills in the *Plaza Sésamo* curriculum. Children who had viewed the program regularly performed better than their nonviewing peers on tests of general knowledge (such as knowledge of parts of the body, numbers, letters, and word skills). The researchers also noted differences in performance on cognitive tests (such as classification and relational skills) and oral comprehension. Gains differed with respect to age, with 4-year-olds benefiting most from watching and 3-year-olds, the least.

An additional large-scale summative evaluation of *Plaza Sésamo* was conducted in 1974 (Diaz-Guerrero, Reyes-Lagunes, Witzke, & Holtzman, 1976) with 1,118 4- and 5-year-olds living in rural and urban environments. This research did not replicate the findings of the earlier summative evaluation. Results showed that children living in rural areas did not demonstrate significant gains in cognitive development from viewing *Plaza Sésamo*; only 4-year-old children, living in urban areas, who viewed the program for 12 months, showed slight gains on a General Knowledge posttest. It is important to note, however, that there were methodological difficulties with this latter study in that the control group of nonviewers had, in fact, been exposed to *Plaza Sésamo*. This, and other shortcomings associated with the design of the study, may be responsible for the disparity between the findings.

Interestingly, years later, a study of *Susam Sokagi* (Sahin, 1990), the Turkish adaptation of *Sesame Street*, noted effects that were similar to those of the initial Mexican study. The researcher evaluated the pre- and postbroadcast performance on a range of curricular skills of 1,166 children between the ages of 3 and 6 years. He found that when comparing same-age peers before and after exposure to the broadcast, children who watched the program performed better on a range of curricular skills (including literacy and numeracy), even when factors such as maturation and mother's education were taken into consideration.

A smaller-scale study was used to evaluate *Rua Sésamo*, the Portuguese adaptation of *Sesame Street* (Brederode-Santos, 1993). The researcher devised a multicomponent study that brought together a compendium of information including ratings data, surveys of parents and teachers, and pre-post viewing data from a small quasi-experimental study of 36 children from a Lisbon kindergarten. The study indicated that the reach of the program was extensive, with as much as 95% of the sample of the target population (3- to 7-year-olds) having some exposure to the program. Regarding parents' perspectives, the researcher noted that a majority of the parents studied considered the program educational and felt that the children were learning from viewing the series. An analysis of the study of children's learning revealed trends similar to those noted in other summative evaluations, with greatest gains in language and numeracy skills.

Findings in the numeracy and literacy areas also have surfaced in a fairly recent analysis in Mexico (UNICEF, 1996). The researchers studied 3- to 6-year-olds from low-income families in Mexico City (382 children) and Oaxaca (396 children). In both cities, participants were randomly assigned to a high-exposure group who regularly viewed *Plaza Sésamo* in their school classrooms for a 3-month period, or a low-exposure group who watched cartoons. Comparisons of the relationship between exposure and performance on a battery of curriculum-based tests indicated findings in the areas of symbolic representation (letter recognition, numeric skills) and geometric shapes. There was also some evidence of gains in the areas of ecology, nutrition, and hygiene in the Mexico City group.

The study is a reminder of a concern that complicated the earlier study of *Plaza Sésamo* (Diaz-Guerrero et al., 1976) and an aspect of general summative research design that must be accommodated by researchers (Mielke, chap. 5, this volume). Although there was an attempt to create experimental and control groups at the time of the 1996 study, the broadcast reach of *Plaza Sésamo* was so great that it was not possible to know the degree of incidental exposure children had had to the program. Researchers believed that it was likely that children in the control group had at least minimal exposure to the program outside of the school setting, where the testing took place. To contend with this difficulty, researchers used an admittedly imperfect proxy measure of exposure. They included in their analysis a variable that looked at children's familiarity with the *Plaza Sésamo* characters, reasoning that children who demonstrated familiarity with the characters were likely to have had exposure to the program. Thus, the study became an investigation of the association between level of exposure and performance on various curricular tasks, rather than a simple comparison of differences in performance of a control and experimental group.

In contrast, a study in Russia provided a unique opportunity to address this issue of exposure systematically. The program in Russia was initially broadcast in only some regions of the country. Researchers elected to evaluate the impact of the program in a geographical area where the series was not being broadcast, something that enabled the researchers to compare the performance of children who had viewed videotapes of each of the 65 episodes to the performance of children who had no access to the series and were shown animated Russian fairytales instead. Preliminary analysis of an experimental study of preschool children conducted in Irkutsk, Siberia indicates that after 6 months of viewing *Ulitsa Sezam*, viewers developed basic numeracy and literacy skills at a faster rate than their nonviewing peers. They also made gains in some of the social domains tested, including awareness of children with disabilities (*Ulitsa Sezam* Department of Research and Content, 1998).

Two elements of this study are particularly worthy of note. The first concerns the way in which children's performance level was determined in many of the areas tested. The research battery included questions designed to test a broad range of performance areas. For many of the questions in the social-affective domain, rather than just looking at whether a child's answer was correct or incorrect, the researchers designed questions to solicit information about the degree of a child's understanding of a given concept. For example, many children could state aspects of a given notion that were relevant, although not fully differentiated. Instead of coding these responses as incorrect, partial credit was assigned with higher scores linked to responses that included more fully differentiated information. Each child's responses were evaluated using a multilevel coding scheme that followed the general pattern described in Table 9.3. Using a continuous rather than dichotomous scale, enabled the researchers to gain a more refined understanding of children's knowledge.

The statistical technique that was employed in this study is also worth mentioning. To compare differences in the learning of the children who had watched *Ulitsa Sezam* and those who had not, the researchers used growth modeling, an innovative analytic technique especially designed for developmental data (Bryk & Raudenbush, 1992; Willett, 1988; Willett & Ayoub, 1991). The methodology is well-suited to studies that aim to assess systematic differences in development over time because it accounts for missing values less idiosyncratically than traditional repeated measure methods and provides a more reliable measure of growth (Willett, 1989). In addition to comparing group differences in performance at prescribed points in time, growth modeling permits the researcher to examine patterns of individual growth across time.

Employing the growth modeling methodology, the researchers used a two-step process in which they estimated linear growth trajectories representing performance across the three waves of data for each child in the sample. In a subsequent analysis, the researchers compared differences in the average rate of change (slope) in performance of the viewers (the experimental group) and nonviewers (the control group) on various skills in the curricu-

TABLE 9.3
Ulitsa Sezam Summative Evaluation Coding Scheme

Level 0:	**Nonrelevant Response, Nonresponse, or a Statement of No Knowledge** *Example: "I don't know."*
Level 1:	**Unidimensional Response** Statement of *single* general trait that is relevant to the presented concept, but whose linkage to the concept is unclear. *Example: In response to the question, "What happens at school?":* *"Teachers."*
Level 2:	**Multidimensional Uncoordinated Response** Statement of *more than* one general trait that is relevant to the presented concept, but whose linkage to the concept is unclear. *Example: In response to the question, "What happens at school?":* *"Teachers and chalkboards."*
Level 3:	**Coordinated Response** Statement of more than one general trait that is relevant to the presented concept *with an indication of its linkage* to the concept. *Example: In response to the question, "What happens at school?":* *"Teachers, chalkboards. Kids go there to learn."*

lum over the course of the viewing period. The influence of age, gender, and mother's education was also examined. The researchers learned that while age was the strongest predictor of children's learning (with older children performing at higher levels than younger), children who had viewed *Ulitsa Sezam* learned some skills at a *faster rate* than their nonviewing peers. Furthermore, gender and mother's education were not linked to performance.

Conclusions From the Summative Studies. The pattern of findings from the summative evaluations around the world indicates that children gain basic skills from watching *Sesame Street* coproductions. The strongest findings, both historically and across cultures, have been noted in the literacy and numeracy areas. There are several possible explanations for this. First, across a season of a given program, these areas are the most frequently and specifically represented. Most coproductions feature in each episode at least one literacy segment (often highlighting the same letter of the alphabet in multiple segments within a given episode) and one or more numeracy segments that, in parallel to the literacy segments, focus on a particular number presented multiple times throughout an episode. Such reinforcement of literacy and numeracy messages throughout a given episode is bound to maximize learning (Mielke, chap. 5, this volume). Although social and other skills are also presented in each episode, the messages cover a

broader range of skills within the social domain and are less likely to be reinforced multiple times within a given episode.

An additional explanation concerns the way in which skill level is evaluated in the summative research. Some of the studies, for example the Turkish
study, maintain a particular focus on basic skills and do not directly test performance in the social and affective realms. Quite obviously, if an area is not
tested, there is no opportunity to note effects. Furthermore, testing an understanding of elements such as emotions and social relations poses great challenges to the researcher. It is far easier, for example, to quantify how high a
child can count than to measure children's understanding of more abstract
concepts such as love and empathy. Although the field of developmental psychology has made great strides in this area, it can be argued that our research
instruments are not as refined as those available in the literacy and numeracy
domains.

Thus, it would be erroneous to conclude that because we have not found
strong findings in the social-affective domain that *Sesame Street*
coproductions are ineffective in teaching such skills. A more likely explanation is that our measures and research designs are not sensitive and reliable
enough to detect the effects and/or that we are not studying the effects for a
long enough time to note them. Future evaluations of *Sesame Street*
coproductions may wisely focus more directly on the social-affective domain.
Such is the case, for example, in a study of the Israeli–Palestinian *Rechov
Sumsum/Shara'a Simsim*. An impact study has only just begun, but its primary focus is on Israeli and Palestinian children's social reasoning, and understanding and knowledge of the "other" group. It is our hope that the battery
of tests developed for this study (Fox, Killen, & Leavitt, 1998) will be adapted
for use by other researchers gauging the effectiveness of *Sesame Street*
coproductions, initiating a trend in our coproduction studies that will delve
further into children's learning of our social messages.

Conclusion

Taken together, the body of research conducted for the international
coproductions of *Sesame Street* illustrates the importance of the cultural specificity of our production model. Both formative and summative evaluations
across cultures have provided evidence of the educational value of a series
that, in the international arena, is not a single series, but 19 unique productions designed for children living in specific cultural contexts.

The studies provide evidence of the elements of learning that children
share across cultures, and, at the same time, highlight the importance of presenting learning opportunities that relate in the most direct way to the
child's own world. A striking element of the body of research conducted for
our *Sesame Street* coproductions is the degree to which the findings have been
similar across cultures. Children around the world appreciate the programs'
characters, gain academic skills, and learn from their social messages. Parents
and educators value their contributions to children's education and under-

stand that *Sesame Street* holds an important place in the education of many children throughout the world. For some children, *Sesame Street* is the first place where they are introduced to basic academic skills that will help prepare them for school. Furthermore, the value of its social messages has also been recognized throughout the world. The project in Israel and the Palestinian Territories, for example, has been reviewed by others as a model for the creation of television designed to teach antisectarian messages (Connolly, 1998).

From its inception, *Sesame Street* has been an experiment. It is the spirit of experimentation that has maintained the vitality of the program through the years. Of course, experiments are not as tidy and neat as this written presentation of CTW's production model might imply. Rather than moving in a tight linear progression, the progress made in our research and curriculum development has advanced in fits and starts. Yet, a remarkable aspect of what Lesser (1974, p. xi) has called this "rumpled reality" is that it has, in important ways, contributed to a larger body of general knowledge about child development. In acquiring 30 years of data on children's learning in multiple cultures, there emerges an opportunity that is perhaps unique to *Sesame Street*. The previous studies illustrate a rich array of qualitative support for the benefits of approaching child development from a vantage point that values cultural specificity. *Sesame Street* is a shared experience for children around the world, and yet, within that commonality is a value on the environmental context of children's learning and an appreciation for the differences in knowledge and understanding that are associated with that context.

The broadest message carried from this body of research is that true understanding of child development can best be achieved using measures that consider the cultural relevance of learning. In looking at patterns of findings from research across cultures, the common themes can be interpreted in two ways. First, there is value concerning their contribution to our understanding of universal developmental milestones, such as the developmental points at which children gain literacy and numeracy skills. Second, and perhaps more important, we gain information that is specific with respect to the different learning opportunities to which children are exposed. Because the stimulus (the television program) varies from culture to culture, we can study children's knowledge with respect to their individual learning environments. While we have discovered, for example, that children across the world gain literacy skills from watching the program, we also have data that show more specifically the elements of literacy they acquire from watching. At the most basic level, differences in languages prompt differences in learning: In Russia, for example, children learn Cyrillic character recognition, whereas in the United States, children learn skills in the Roman alphabet. Yet, beyond that, more details emerge.

We are at only the initial stages of reaping the benefits of the data we have collected through the years. As we continue forward, there is room to further coordinate our research across cultures and gain more integrated insight into child development by such means as linking researchers from different countries in cooperative research projects and by further encouraging symposia and other means of information sharing. But the depth of what has been accomplished thus far is a testament to the worth of future endeavors and illustrates the past, present, and potential value of *Sesame Street* across cultures.

ACKNOWLEDGMENTS

This paper is an expansion of a portion of an article entitled "The Impact of *Sesame Street* on Preschool Children: A Review and Synthesis of Thirty Years' Research," which appears in *Media Psychology* (Fisch, Truglio, & Cole, 1999). In addition, some of the ideas expressed have been presented in an unpublished paper written by Cole and Richman (1997) and presented in CTW's newsletter, *Research Roundup*.

The authors gratefully acknowledge Sholly Fisch and Rosemarie Truglio for their helpful comments on this chapter, as well as the insightful contributions of Cathy Chilco, Gregg Gettas, Gerry Lesser, Steve Miller, Joel Schneider, and Baxter Urist. Many individuals contributed to the construction of Table 9.1, and for their fact-finding or recollections of the history of the *Sesame Street* International Coproductions, we especially wish to thank Lisa Annunziata, Lewis Bernstein, Gregg Gettas, Karen King, Gerry Lesser, Peter Levelt, Joan Lufrano, Michelle Manno, Ed Palmer, Barbara Stewart, and Danielle Rockhold Teplica. In addition, we express our appreciation to Alex Brown, Ginger Brown, Frank Campagna, Bea Chow, Yvonne Hill-Ogunkoya, Robert Knezevic, Maya Krueger, Victoria Kupchinetsky, Florence Lastique, Keith Mielke, Becky Ndosi, Mai Nguyen, Barbara Nikonorow, Kerry Novick, Kaoru Oda, Tina Peel, Lori Sherman, Shelley Smith, and Cooper Wright. Finally, special thanks go to Dena Guadalupe for her consistent and supportive role in managing the administrative aspects of this project.

REFERENCES

Alexander, N., Bloch, C., & Heugh, K. (1995). *Background paper on relevant aspects of language policy in South Africa. Which language(s)?: Four papers informing language decisions in the production of Sesame Street in South Africa* (unpublished research report). New York: Children's Television Workshop.

Analytics-Russia. (1998). *Viewing patterns of and attitudes toward Ulitsa Sezam: Survey of parents and kindergarten teachers* (unpublished research report). Moscow, Russia: Author.

Arafat, C. (1995). *West Bank and Gaza Strip. Position Papers for Israeli-Palestinian Sesame Street* (unpublished research report). New York: Children's Television Workshop.

Badawi, E. M. (1998). *Sesame Street Egypt: The language issue. Sesame Street Egypt project: Topical papers on family, language, religion, child health, and girls' education* (unpublished research report). Cairo, Egypt and New York: Karma Productions & Children's Television Workshop.

Barrio Sésamo/Barri Sèsam Department of Research and Content. (1997). *Barrio Sésamo/Barri Sèsam V formative research: Executive summary.* [English summary of Spanish report] (unpublished research report). New York: CTW.

Brederode-Santos, M. E. (1993). *Learning with television: The secret of Rua Sésamo.* [English translation of Portuguese, Brederode-Santos, M. E. (1991). *Com a televisão o segredo da Rua Sésamo.* Lisboa: TV Guia Editora](unpublished research report). New York: CTW.

Bryk, A. S., & Raudenbush, S. W. (1992). *Hierarchical linear models.* Newbury Park, CA: Sage.

Children's Television Workshop. (1993). *Trip itinerary for September 18-October 1 fact-finding trip* (unpublished research report). New York: Author.

Children's Television Workshop. (1996). *Report on the development and feasibility phase of Sesame Street for Israel, the West Bank and Gaza* (unpublished research report). New York: Author.

Cohen, M., & Francis, V. (1999). *Rechov Sumsum/Shara'a Simsim quantitative report.* New York: Applied Research and Consulting.

Cole, C. F., & Richman, B. A. (January, 1997). Think tank: *Sesame Street* around the world. *Research Roundup, 7,* 4–5.

Connolly, P. (1998). *Early years anti-sectarian television: Guidelines for the development of a series of television programmes directed at anti-sectarian work with children in their early years.* Belfast: Community Relations Council.

Constable, P. (1995). *Issues informing language decisions in the production of a children's television program. Which language(s)?: Four papers informing language decisions in the production of Sesame Street in South Africa* (unpublished research report). New York: Children's Television Workshop.

Diaz-Guerrero, R., & Holtzman, W. H. (1974). Learning by televised *Plaza Sésamo* in Mexico. *Journal of Educational Psychology, 66*(5), 632–643.

Diaz-Guerrero, R., Reyes-Lagunes, I., Witzke, D. B., & Holtzman, W. H. (1976). *Plaza Sésamo* in Mexico: An evaluation. *Journal of Communication, 26*(2), 145–154.

Fisch, S., Truglio, R., & Cole, C. F. (1999). The impact of *Sesame Street* on preschool children: A review and synthesis of thirty years' research. *Media Psychology, 1,* 165–190.

Flagg, B. N. (1990). *Formative evaluation for educational technologies.* Hillsdale, NJ: Lawrence Erlbaum Associates, Publishers.

Fox, N. A., Killen, M., & Leavitt, L. (1998). *Justification coding manual: Rechov Sumsum/Shara'a Simsim* (unpublished research report). New York: Children's Television Workshop.

Gemark (1993). *Plaza Sésamo IV formative research: Set evaluation* (unpublished research report). New York: Children's Television Workshop.

Gemark (1994). *Plaza Sésamo IV later formative research: Musical segments* (unpublished research report). New York: Children's Television Workshop.

Gettas, G. J. (1990). The globalization of *Sesame Street*: A producer's perspective. *Educational Technology Research and Development, 38*(4), 55–63.

Ibrahim, S. E. (1998). *Addressing religion for Egyptian children on TV. Sesame Street Egypt project: Topical papers on family, language, religion, child health, and girls' education* (unpublished research report). Cairo, Egypt and New York: Karma Productions & Children's Television Workshop.

Kemp, A. (1994). *Radio briefing* (unpublished research report). New York: Children's Television Workshop.

Kirwil, L. (1996a). *Study on the reception of the set designed for the Polish version of Sesame Street*. [English translation of Polish, Kirwil, L. (1996). *Badanie scenografii polskiei Ulicy Sezamkowei*] (unpublished research report). New York: Children's Television Workshop.

Kirwil, L. (1996b). *Ulica Sezamkowa formative character study: Executive summary*. [English summary of Polish report] (unpublished research report). New York: Children's Television Workshop.

Kohnstam, G. A., & Cammaer, H. (1976). *Sesamstraat: Preliminary results of a variety of studies on the reception of a 20-part series* (unpublished research report). Hilversum: Netherlands Broadcasting Foundation.

Lesser, G. (1974). *Children and television: Lessons from Sesame Street*. New York: Vintage Books.

Levin, I. (1995). *Preliminary thoughts on planning a TV program for preschoolers: Enhancing tolerance between Israeli Jews, Israeli Arabs, and Palestinians. Position Papers for Israeli-Palestinian Sesame Street* (unpublished research report). New York: Children's Television Workshop.

Levin, S. R., & Anderson, D. R. (1976). The development of attention. *Journal of Communication, 26,* 126–135.

Liddell, C. (1995). *Report on media use in South Africa, with particular focus on young children* (unpublished research report). Durban, South Africa: University of Natal.

Lorch, E., & Anderson, D. (1979). *Highlights of paying attention to Sesame Street. CTW International Research Notes*. New York: Children's Television Workshop.

Luckett, K. (1995). *Educational television for South African preschoolers: The language question. Which Language(s)?: Four Papers Informing Language Decisions in the Production of Sesame Street in South Africa* (unpublished research report). New York: Children's Television Workshop.

Makoni, S. B. (1995). The medium of entertainment issue. *Which Language(s)?: Four Papers Informing Language Decisions in the Production of Sesame Street in South Africa* (unpublished research report). New York: Children's Television Workshop.

Mar'i, M. (1995). *Teaching tolerance and understanding to Israeli and Palestinian children through Sesame Street. Position papers for Israeli-Palestinian Sesame Street* (unpublished research report). New York: Children's Television Workshop.

Palmer, E. L., Lesser, G. S., & Theroux, J. (1978). International adaptations of *Sesame Street. InterMedia, 6*(6), 19–23.

Rogoff, B. (1993). Guided participation in cultural activity by toddlers and caregivers. *Monographs of the Society for Research in Child Development, 58* (8, Serial No. 236).

Rouchdy, M. S. (1998). *Girls' education in Egypt. Sesame Street Egypt Project: Topical papers on family, language, religion, child health, and girls' education* (unpublished research report). Cairo, Egypt and New York: Karma Productions & CTW.

RS/SS Content Team (1997). *Rechov Sumsum/Shara'a Simsim curriculum document* (unpublished research report). Ramallah, New York, & Tel Aviv: Al-Quds Institute for

Modern Media, Children's Television Workshop and Ministry of Education and Culture, Israeli Educational Television Research Department.

Sahin, N. (1990, September). *Preliminary report on the summative evaluation of the Turkish coproduction of Sesame Street*. Paper presented at the International Conference on Adaptations of *Sesame Street*, Amsterdam, The Netherlands.

Shaalan, M. (1998). *The family in Egypt. Sesame Street Egypt Project: Topical Papers on Family, Language, Religion, Child Health, and Girls' Education* (unpublished research report). Cairo, Egypt and New York: Karma Productions & CTW.

Shara'a Simsim Research Team. (1997). *Formative research on six segments: "Embroidery," "Fishing," "The Magic Box," "Day of Cooperation," "Common Language," "The Bicycle"* (unpublished research report). Ramallah: Al-Quds Institute for Modern Media.

Stifter, C. A., & Fox, N. A. (1986). Preschool children's ability to identify emotions. *Journal of Non-Verbal Behavior, 10,* 255–266.

Tidhar, C., Rivner, M., & Shachori, N. (1997a). *An evaluation of Arabic language segments: 1. "The Camera," 2. Kareem's Box"* (unpublished research report). Tel Aviv, Israel: Ministry of Education and Culture, Israeli Educational Television Research Department.

Tidhar, C., Rivner, M., & Shachori, N. (1997b). *An evaluation of the segment "The Train" in the Rehov Sumsum series* (unpublished research report). Tel Aviv, Israel: Ministry of Education and Culture, Israeli Educational Television Research Department.

Tidhar, C., Rivner, M., & Shachori, N. (1997c). *An evaluation of the viewer's attentiveness while watching exclusively Arabic language segments: 1. "Bert and Ernie," 2. "Apple, Orange, Pear"* (unpublished research report). Tel Aviv, Israel: Ministry of Education and Culture, Israeli Educational Television Research Department.

Tidhar, C., Rivner, M., & Shachori, N. (1997d). *An evaluation of the viewer's attentiveness while watching segments in both Arabic and Hebrew: 1. "The Bicycle," 2. "The Umbrella"* (unpublished research report). Tel Aviv, Israel: Ministry of Education and Culture, Israeli Educational Television Research Department.

Tidhar, C., Rivner, M., & Shachori, N. (1997e). *An evaluation of the viewer's attentiveness while watching segments in both Arabic and in Hebrew: 1. "Two," 2. "Kareem Counting," 3. "Humus Falafel," 4. "The Neighborhood Song"* (unpublished research report). Tel Aviv, Israel: Ministry of Education and Culture, Israeli Educational Television Research Department.

Ulitsa Sezam Department of Research and Content. (1998, November). *Preliminary report of summative findings*. Report presented to the Children's Television Workshop.

Ulitsa Sezam Research Department. (Spring, 1995). *Regional trip reports: Ekaterinburg, Novosibirsk, Cheboksary* (unpublished research report). Moscow, Russia: Author.

Ulitsa Sezam Russian Department of Research and Content. (1996). *The research on the Show 21* (unpublished research report). Moscow, Russia: Author.

UNICEF (1996). *Executive summary: Summary assessment of Plaza Sésamo IV – Mexico*. [English translation of Spanish, UNICEF. (1996). *Sumario ejecutivo: Evaluacion sumativa Plaza Sésamo IV - Mexico*] (unpublished research report). Mexico City, Mexico: Author.

Usdin, S. (1996). *Report on early childhood development, radio and outreach in South Africa.* (unpublished research report). New York: Children's Television Workshop.

Willett, J. B. (1988). Questions and answers in the measurement of change. In E.Z. Rothkopf (Ed.), *Review of research in education* (Vol. 15). Washington, DC: American Educational Research Association.

Willett, J. B. (1989). Some results on reliability for the measurement of change: Implication for the design of studies of individual growth. *Educational and Psychological Measurement, 49,* 587–602.

Willett, J. B., & Ayoub C. (1991). Using growth modeling to investigate systematic differences in growth: An example of change in the functioning of families at risk of maladaptive parenting, child abuse, and neglect. *Journal of Clinical Psychology, 59,* 38–47.

Yirmiya, N. (1995). *Sesame Street position paper. Position papers for Israeli-Palestinian Sesame Street* (unpublished research report). New York: Children's Television Workshop.

Younis, A. S. (1998). *Egyptian child health and nutrition. Sesame Street Egypt Project: Topical papers on family, language, religion, child health, and girls' education* (unpublished research report). Cairo, Egypt and New York: Karma Productions & CTW.

Zhang, Y. (1997). *Children and television in Beijing, China: Results from a pilot interview study of preschoolers and their parents* (unpublished research report). New York: Children's Television Workshop.

Zhima Jie Research Team (1998). *What children like and learn from Omni, Beacon and Watt: Results of testing Zhima Jie's "GE" science segments* (unpublished research report). Shanghai, China and New York: Shanghai TV and Children's Television Workshop.

10 The Role of *Sesame Street*-Based Materials in Child-Care Settings

William Yotive
Shalom M. Fisch
Children's Television Workshop

When *Sesame Street* was first created, the cornerstone of its mission was to reach low-income and minority children. Its aim was to level the playing field so that poor, inner-city children would enter school with the knowledge and skills they needed to succeed in school. As noted elsewhere (Fisch, 1998), the birth of *Sesame Street* occurred at a moment when philanthropy was very supportive of efforts to enrich the educational experiences of preschool children. Television was an appealing medium to funders because of its potential to reach large numbers of children at relatively little cost per child.

The Children's Television Workshop (CTW) recognized that extraordinary promotional efforts would be needed in order to make low-income and minority families aware of the show. As Evelyn Davis, CTW's first Vice President of Community Relations, pointed out, the educational stations that broadcast *Sesame Street* were "not generally watched by minority communities. The programming on those stations [was] not always relevant to their needs but geared to the suburban, white, middle-class communities if the program was to reach the target community—the inner-city child and the poor white child—a special effort was going to have to be made ... [because] traditional methods of promotion and advertising do not necessarily reach these communities" (quoted in Land, 1972, p. 152).

Thus, shortly after CTW was established, a new division (which later became known as Community Education Services, or CES) was created to make presentations to church groups, at parent–teacher meetings, and at other community events to let families in inner-city and rural neighborhoods know that *Sesame Street* was a special show that their children should watch. Once the popularity of *Sesame Street* was firmly established, community outreach projects no longer needed to focus exclusively on building viewership. Eventually, outreach projects became associated less with promotional events and more with the development of educational materials that used the characters' popularity to convey important educational messages to young children and the adults who care for them.

Over time, the child-care community has become the core constituency of the CES projects. This partnership has emerged as a result of fundamental changes in the work force. When *Sesame Street* was first created, children spent most of their time at home. Over the last 30 years, however, an increasing number of women have entered the work force, creating a significant growth in the number of young children who receive child care outside of the home. In 1995, approximately 13 million children under the age of 6 years old were cared for outside of their homes and close to one third of these children were cared for in family child-care settings (West, Wright, & Hausken, 1995). As a result of this fundamental change, CES recognized the importance of developing ties with the child-care community in order to reach children who were spending increasing amounts of time outside the home. In addition, the child-care community offers a well established channel for reaching the adults (both parents and child-care providers) who care for them; materials can be directed specifically at providers and/or given to providers to distribute to parents in turn.

The outreach projects produced by CES fall into two basic categories. First, there are projects that, across a broad range of subject areas, use the *Sesame Street* television series as an educational tool in child-care settings. This type of project is epitomized by the *Sesame Street* Preschool Education Program (PEP), which helps child-care providers use television as an educational resource and develop instructional strategies that nurture a love of learning. The *Sesame Street* PEP projects treat the child-care setting as an entity in its own right and provide materials and training that support the professional development of providers who work in these settings.

The second group of projects deals with health and safety issues. Responding to a broad variety of issues, demographic trends, and potential dangers that impact on young children's well-being, these projects are centered around the development of materials to support good practices among children and the adults who care for them. To date, the materials have addressed topics such as protecting oneself in life-threatening emergencies (e.g., fires or natural hazards), preventing lead poisoning, the importance of immunization, and what to do when a child with asthma starts to have difficulty breathing. In all instances, the child-care community has served as the distribution channel through which these materials are delivered to underserved populations. In many cases, parallel sets of materials have been produced in English and Spanish to better meet the needs of Latino children.

Together, these two classes of projects help meet the increasing demand among child-care providers for quality educational materials and training designed to help improve the quality of care that children receive in these settings.

USING TELEVISION AS AN EDUCATIONAL TOOL

Over the course of the 1970s, the CES outreach model developed into programs that encouraged child-care providers to use *Sesame Street* effectively, both as an educational tool in and of itself and as a springboard for hands-on extension activities that could carry learning beyond the viewing experience. Because the target providers typically worked in low-income areas and had little resources available, this entailed efforts as basic as (in many cases) helping child-care providers secure television sets, typically by encouraging private donations of used televisions. *Sesame Street* viewing centers were established in settings as diverse as Head Start and day-care centers, libraries, storefronts, community centers, public housing projects, church basements, and private homes—essentially, any setting that would provide access to the children who needed support. Supplemental materials were created in English and Spanish to describe the content of specific episodes of *Sesame Street* and suggest activities to reinforce and extend their educational goals. Training programs served to introduce providers to the materials and furnished support for their ongoing activities. A CES Field Services department, consisting of eight regional offices spread across the United States, allowed these efforts to cover 32 states (CTW, 1971, 1975, 1979).

In some cases, the attempt to reach children in need led to efforts in unexpected settings. Outreach efforts in migrant camps allowed providers to incorporate *Sesame Street* materials into their curricula while the children's parents worked as migrant laborers in nearby fields. *Sesame Street* centers (including television sets, toys, child-sized furniture, and video-playback machines) were established in Federal prisons to provide facilities in which young children could engage in songs, games, and other educational activities while their parents visited relatives who were incarcerated. Beyond the benefits for the children involved, an additional benefit of the prison program was that because CES specialists trained inmates to run these centers, many of these inmates subsequently went on to enroll in extension courses related to the work of the centers (CTW, 1984).

Sesame Street PEP

Together, these varied efforts laid the groundwork for what would evolve, in the early 1980s, into *Sesame Street* PEP. Like its predecessors, *Sesame Street* PEP is a multimedia project that combines television viewing with books and hands-on activities in an attempt to extend the mission of *Sesame Street* and enhance the quality of preschool child care. More specifically, the major elements of *Sesame Street* PEP include: (a) active viewing of the *Sesame Street* television series, (b) active reading of children's books that relate back to something the children have watched on television, and (c) developmentally appropriate activities that are related to the television programs that the children have watched and/or the books they have read. For example, the *Sesame Street* PEP materials reinforce and extend the educational messages about diversity in various *Sesame Street* segments (see Truglio, Lovelace, Segui & Scheiner, chap. 4, this volume) through a list of more than 20 recommended children's books, plus extension activities in which children can explore multicultural music, foods from different cultures, and equivalent words in different languages.

The use of *Sesame Street* PEP materials is supported by a training component for providers that offers them opportunities to practice and discuss the key elements of the program with other professionals. In addition, "View and Do" newsletters are distributed to participating providers on a regular basis to alert the providers to the educational content of upcoming episodes of *Sesame Street* and allow them the opportunity to plan related activities in advance.

Research on *Sesame Street* PEP (and other child-care materials) differs from research conducted in support of the *Sesame Street* television series, in that it focuses not only on children, but also on the providers who care for them. To date, a limited number of studies have examined the effectiveness of *Sesame Street* PEP. Although none of these studies have evaluated its impact with proper experimental controls (and so do not provide conclusive evidence of impact), the data suggest that the *Sesame Street* PEP model has had a beneficial impact on day-care providers and the children in their care. For example, in an early evaluation (Mindel & Dangel, 1990), providers' self-confidence as teachers increased. Engagement in *Sesame Street* PEP encouraged them to think of themselves as professionals, thereby increasing their pride, sense of purpose, and job satisfaction. In addition, providers reported that *Sesame Street* PEP helped improve children's social behavior and enthusiasm for learning, as well as verbal and emergent literacy skills.

In a later pilot summative study (RMC Research Corporation, 1993), a number of outcomes suggested that *Sesame Street* PEP could also improve providers' instructional skills, particularly those related to joint reading of children's books. Some of these findings have been replicated in another evaluation conducted for the public broadcasting station in San Francisco, KQED (Acord & Romontio, 1995). For example, significant changes were found in the ways child-care providers and parents approached the joint reading of children's books after attending a *Sesame Street* PEP workshop. Participants increased the amount of time spent reading to children, utilized storytelling techniques to make books come alive, and chose books that were developmentally appropriate.

Interestingly, the data also suggest that the impact of the *Sesame Street* PEP program (in its original manifestation) may vary depending on whether it is used in child-care programs based in day-care centers or homes. In the pilot summative study mentioned above, center-based and home-based providers who had attended the *Sesame Street* PEP training were compared to another group of center-based and home-based providers who had not participated in the training. The overall quality of day-care centers that had participated in the *Sesame Street* PEP training was found to be slightly higher than the comparison group of centers that had not participated in the *Sesame Street* PEP training. However, the difference between *Sesame Street* PEP and non-*Sesame*

Street PEP family child-care homes was far greater. This suggests that *Sesame Street* PEP may have a greater impact on home-based care, where training for providers is less common, and where children are often poorer and in greater need of educational resources and providers.

Although center-based and home-based care both play an important role in helping to prepare young children for school, they are not equally accessible to low-income families. A 1989 report of the National Child-Care Staffing Study (Whitebook, Howes, & Phillips, 1989) found that a much lower proportion of low-income children are enrolled in formal center-based programs, and far more low-income families send their children to family child-care homes. Many of these homes are unlicensed and unregulated. In addition, family child-care providers typically earn very low wages (NAEYC, 1985), which contributes to a high turnover and lack of commitment. Given this state of affairs, it is not surprising that a more comprehensive study examining the quality of care that is provided in family child-care homes reported that 56% of the homes in their sample offered only adequate/custodial care (i.e., neither "growth enhancing or growth harming"), 35% provided inadequate care, and fewer than 10% of the homes provided care that was considered to enhance the growth of children (Galinsky, Howes, Kontos, & Shinn, 1994).

Because family child care is more highly concentrated in low-income and working class neighborhoods, any attempt to improve the quality of care in these settings would help advance CTW's mission. This opportunity presented itself when a noticeable percentage of the participants (roughly one third) who attended the *Sesame Street* PEP training turned out to be independent family child-care providers. Although the original *Sesame Street* PEP materials were designed for center-based programs, CTW staff made efforts to modify the *Sesame Street* PEP training whenever family child-care providers were present to make the training more relevant to their needs. In 1995, CES received funding to develop a new version of *Sesame Street* PEP (referred to as *Building on Sesame Street*) for family child-care programs.

Building on *Sesame Street* Family Child-Care Project

In preparing for the *Building on Sesame Street* family child-care project, focus groups were held with family child-care providers who had attended the *Sesame Street* PEP workshops in different regions of the country. The data from these discussions made it clear that, although the existing *Sesame Street* PEP training was of value to family child-care providers, there were still several areas where the training could be better tailored to their needs. First, one of the main differences between home-based care and center-based care is the way children are grouped. Typically, children who attend center-based programs are placed in homogeneous groups by age. In contrast, in family child-care programs, it is not unusual for providers to care for infants, toddlers, preschoolers, and school-age children in the same program. Thus, family child-care providers felt that, to be more responsive to the realities of their programs, they needed additional information about managing mixed age groupings (e.g., how to modify activities so that they are appropriate for both older and younger children). Second, many providers felt that, because of the relatively informal natures of their programs, they needed simpler materials that required little advance planning. Third, they wanted more activity ideas.

The data collected from these discussions were used to guide the development of new materials in English and Spanish for family child-care providers. A prototype of these materials included: (a) a video (that introduces providers to the basic components of the project), (b) a caregiver guide (that summarizes the most important content in writing), (c) activity cards (that are designed to help providers choose activities that would develop children's skills in a variety of learning areas), and (d) family cards (that were designed to be copied and given to parents). In addition, materials were also developed for trainers who work directly with providers. The trainers' materials included a trainer's manual for conducting 14 hours of training spread out over four sessions: 1 all-day overview of the project and 3 half-day follow-up sessions. The training component was specifically designed to address issues that family child-care providers may face (e.g., how to manage mixed-age groups).

As a result of a partnership between CTW and Camp Fire Boys and Girls, a pilot test of the newly developed materials was conducted in five Camp Fire sites in 1998 (Yotive, Rincon, & Birnbaum, 1998a). One of the main goals of the pilot study was to determine whether the materials met providers' needs. A secondary goal was to identify potential areas of impact in preparation for an evaluation to be conducted during the second year of the project.

Data from the pilot test showed that, overall, providers were very satisfied with what they learned during the training sessions and found the materials very appealing (with 96% rating them excellent or good). Many of them reported that the materials helped them to plan better, to communicate more effectively with their children, and to teach with a better curriculum in mind.

The activity cards were the most highly rated components of the providers' materials. All of the providers rated the cards as excellent and felt that the activities were a useful tool for introducing new ideas, helped them to organize and structure the day, were easy to prepare, and did not require extra materials that could not be found in the home. Moreover, several providers felt that the cards allowed them to do activities spontaneously if they could not plan a lesson in advance.

Although formative research helped to confirm that the *Building on Sesame Street* materials were successful in meeting providers' needs, the research also helped to identify issues that needed to be addressed before the materials were finalized. For example, most of the providers felt that the Family Cards were a good idea, but few had actually used them with their parents and families. Because of chronic difficulties in communicating with parents and getting them involved in programs, many providers felt that parents would not read the cards and, therefore, did not send any information home. As a result of this finding, more time was allotted in the training to discuss ways to get parents more involved. Moreover, the family cards were replaced with a colorful brochure about *Sesame Street* with ideas for simple activities that parents could do with their child.

After the training was completed, we interviewed providers to find out if they were implementing the ideas that had been discussed during the training and that were summarized in the materials. The data indicated that a high percentage of providers reported that they were implementing many of the key ideas that were discussed. In-home observations conducted in two of the sites supported these claims. Some of the providers who had participated in the training reinforced the educational content of television shows more often. A few made hands-on activities more interactive and complex, a few began to plan activities around themes and topics, and some asked more open-ended questions while reading books to children. Most increased the degree to which they linked books to television shows they had viewed and activities they had done with the children.

The results from the pilot test were used to guide final revisions in the materials. Once the materials were completed, a more formal evaluation was conducted using an experimental design (Program Research Department, 1999). This study provided, for the first time, definitive evidence regarding the extent to which these materials have a beneficial impact on the quality of care that children receive in family child care.

Data were gathered from 27 family child-care providers (17 English-speaking and 10 Spanish-speaking). The treatment group comprised 18 providers who attended four *Building on Sesame Street* training workshops. The control group included 9 providers who attended a different training workshop that was unrelated to any of the content covered in the *Building on Sesame Street* materials. The providers participating in this evaluation were recruited from 3 of the 14 sites that participated in the *Building on Sesame Street* project nationwide during the second year of this project. The research sites that were chosen offered geographic and ethnic diversity in our sample, and access to both English- and Spanish-speaking providers.

Data showed that the *Building on Sesame Street* project helped family child-care providers give children a stronger educational experience as a result of the training and materials that they received. The *Building on Sesame Street* training and materials had a significant impact in each of the three main areas of interest: active viewing of educational television series, the use of developmentally appropriate hands-on activities, and reading related children's books. Some of the chief findings of the study were:

- After training, providers who participated in the *Building on Sesame* Street project used significantly more coviewing techniques (e.g., responding to children's questions during viewing, reinforcing the educational content during viewing) than control group providers while viewing television programs with children. Treatment providers also reinforced the content of the programs more often after viewing. Some of the largest increases in the use of coviewing techniques occurred among Spanish-speaking provides in the treatment group.

- Although the treatment providers did not show increases in the overall percentage of activities that they planned in advance, their planning became more sophisticated as a result of linking more of the activities to shows they watched and books they read.
- Both English- and Spanish-speaking providers read more books to children, on average, after receiving the *Building on Sesame Street* training. Although they used roughly the same number of reading techniques before and after training, some improvements were noted in the use of individual techniques among the English- and Spanish-speaking providers after training (e.g., holding the book so that all children could see, changing one's voice to reflect different characters and feelings).
- After training, providers showed a significant increase in the degree to which they linked television shows, activities, and books. This increase was strongest for the Spanish-speaking providers.

It is interesting to note that providers who had shown a higher level of quality in these areas (i.e., viewing educational television programs, doing activities, and reading books) prior to training also showed greater change in their practices as a result of participating in the *Building on Sesame Street* program. This finding points to an important issue in considering the effects of materials and training designed for child care, as opposed to the impact of educational television programs alone. In general, the presentation of content in an educational television program is fairly consistent across the thousands or millions of children viewing (although, naturally, various distractions will occur in individual homes). However, because child-care providers are integral to the effective use of television programs, books, and hands-on activities in child-care settings, variations in the expertise and motivation of individual providers can result in very different experiences for children and, thus, different levels of impact.

HEALTH AND SAFETY OUTREACH PROJECTS

Within 10 years of the premiere of *Sesame Street*, safety messages started to appear in the television series. Initially, these messages focused on fire safety at the request of the U.S. Fire Administration of the Federal Emergency Management Agency (FEMA). Extensive research was conducted to identify the messages that would be appropriate for young children to learn. Careful thought had to be given to the content of these messages since misunderstandings could occur if a child was viewing alone. To support these efforts, CES created a kit to help fire safety educators, parents, and child-care providers teach young children good fire safety practices. Thus, a new type of outreach effort was born (Davis, Friedman, & Martin, 1990).

Materials in the health and safety area have addressed a broad range of topics, including lead poisoning, natural hazards such as hurricanes and earthquakes, asthma, and visits to the doctor, as well as subsequent revisions of the original fire safety materials. In recent years, most of these materials have been created in the form of multiple media kits that include, not only activity guides and other print materials for child-care providers, but also specially-produced videos and/or audiotapes that use *Sesame Street* characters to convey key messages about the relevant topics. In many cases, the kits also include parallel versions of the materials in both English and Spanish.

In contrast to *Sesame Street* PEP, these health and safety projects are not designed to have an impact on the quality of child care per se. Instead, they are created to meet the need for high-quality materials that impact on specific aspects of preschoolers' health and well-being—areas for which materials are often not available for this population.

Formative research is used throughout the development of the materials to inform the creation of the various components in each kit. This formative research can be grouped into three phases: (a) *needs assessments* that gauge the need for information before materials are developed, (b) *formative studies* that guide the development process, and (c) *use tests* evaluating use and/or impact once the materials have been completed.

Case Study: *Sesame Street A Is for Asthma*

A concrete example of this process is provided by the recent *Sesame Street A Is for Asthma* project, which arose in response to the need to educate preschool children, their families, and child-care providers about asthma. The *Sesame Street A Is for Asthma* kit consisted of a video, caregiver guide, and poster, and was distributed to child-care and health care settings. Because there is a disproportionately high incidence of this chronic illness in Latino and African-American communities, these materials were produced in both English and Spanish.

Formative research informed the development of the materials at all stages, and was conducted with English-speaking and Spanish-speaking children and adults. Before the materials were developed, CTW researchers interviewed parents of children with asthma and child-care providers who had taught children with asthma (Yotive, Cappella, & Rincon, 1997a). This was done to find out which aspects of this chronic illness were commonly understood or misunderstood as well as which aspects they felt they needed to understand better (e.g., what position should a child be in when they are having difficulty breathing, should they drink water, etc.). In addition, we interviewed children with asthma (Yotive, Cappella, & Rincon, 1997b) in order to hear the words and phrases they used to describe their illness; for example, when children with asthma were interviewed at a pediatric clinic, most children explained that they come to the clinic because they are sick and need to get their medicine. Only a couple of children mentioned the word "asthma." This information helped the project team make decisions about which educational messages to include in the video and print materials and how to say them.

The second step (conducted prior to studio production of the *Sesame Street A Is for Asthma* video) involved creating a "rough draft" of the video, using a series of still drawings to illustrate visuals, which were then matched to a rough version of the audio track. This gave us the opportunity to assess children's comprehension of key educational messages and then to make revisions based on the data that were collected (Yotive, Cappella, & Rincon, 1997c).

The third step involved giving the video and print materials to child-care providers to review, observing them as they did activities that were suggested in the caregiver guide, and then interviewing them about the guide and the activities. At the same time, researchers also interviewed children to assess the appeal and comprehension of the materials (Yotive, Rincon, & Birnbaum, 1998b).

The final step involved recontacting child-care providers, health professionals, and librarians who had received these materials to find out how they had been used (Yotive, McCann Brown, Sullivan, & Ragasa, 1999) and conducting a pretest–posttest study to assess what children learned from the materials (ARC, 1999). The results from the pretest–posttest study indicated that children made significant gains in their awareness of asthma as a condition or illness that impacts on one's ability to breathe, how to respond when a child is having difficulty breathing, and in their knowledge of some environmental triggers.

Reach and Impact

In addition to the evaluation of *Sesame Street A is for Asthma* project, use tests on other *Sesame Street*-based health and safety materials have also pointed to their potential reach and impact. From the standpoint of reach, for example, a national telephone survey on *Sesame Street* lead poisoning materials found that, within only a few months of having received the materials, the 200 participants in the survey had already used the materials with more than 25,000 children. Moreover, approximately three fourths of the participants who had already used the materials hands-on with children used it more than once (Fisch, McCann Brown, & Cohen, 1996; cf. Fisch et al., 1997).

These studies have also shown, in general, that children comprehend the educational messages presented. However, because so much of the presentation of these messages is not standardized, but mediated by individual providers, it is not surprising that comprehension is affected by various aspects of the providers' presentation. For example, research on the most recent edition of the *Sesame Street* fire safety materials found that comprehension of their fire safety messages was greatly impacted by three factors: (a) the number of messages presented in a single session (with comprehension enhanced when providers or fire safety educators focused on only a small number of messages at a time), (b) repetition and reinforcement, and (c) the degree to which the presentation of the messages was made interactive (Einzig, Cappella, & Michaelis, 1996). When used well by skilled providers, the materials were an effective vehicle for conveying fire safety information.

Because some of these projects speak directly to issues that affect children's physical safety, comprehension of messages in this area have unusually strong implications for children's well-being. It is particularly gratifying, for example, that there are at least two documented cases of families whose lives were saved because of their children's exposure to *Sesame Street* materials (Davis et al., 1990).

Finally, data from use tests in this area have also pointed to the importance of creating versions of materials in Spanish as well as English. For example, the telephone survey on *Sesame Street* lead poisoning materials found that both the English- and Spanish-language materials were well received by their users. However, the two parallel sets of materials were well received for different reasons. Reasons for the perceived value of the English-language materials centered on the clear presentation of the messages, the importance of the subject matter, and the inclusion of the *Sesame Street* characters. By contrast, the appeal of the Spanish-language materials typically stemmed from the feeling that they met the needs of the participants' communities; for example, a lead educator in Yonkers, NY commented, "I'm not fluent in Spanish but I always make an effort to get Spanish materials. Very few [suppliers] offer it" (Fisch, McCann Brown, & Cohen, 1996; cf. Fisch et al., 1997b). So few Spanish-language outreach materials are currently available to help providers deal with these important topics that it makes the existing ones all the more valuable.

ADDED VALUE OF *SESAME STREET*-BASED OUTREACH

The various *Sesame Street*-based outreach projects represent a unique partnership between CTW and child-care providers in contributing to the lives and development of young children. As such, these projects enrich the ongoing efforts of both CTW and the providers who work with children on a daily basis.

Value for Child-Care Providers

From the perspective of child-care providers, the use of *Sesame Street*-based materials carry several broad benefits. First, these projects supply providers with effective educational materials—in both English and Spanish—whose foundation lies in the input of prominent experts in the relevant subject areas, formative research data, and a proven, 30-year track record in developing age-appropriate materials of this kind. Moreover, these materials are typically offered at little or no cost, an important consideration for child-care providers who often must work with severely limited resources.

Second, the familiarity and appeal of the *Sesame Street* characters and materials used in these projects supply providers with a fun, attractive context in which to conduct educational activities. This appeal plays a crucial role in engaging children's attention, and can contribute to their motivation and enthusiasm in engaging in follow-up extension activities.

Third, the materials provide an important starting point for child-care providers to explore issues that might be difficult for them to on their own. Topics such as fire safety and natural hazards must be approached carefully with young children, so that discussions of these subjects do not inadvertently cause fear or anxiety and interfere with children's ability to absorb the necessary educational messages. *Sesame Street*'s ability to deal with such topics in a nonthreatening way gives providers the first step and models language and approaches that providers can also adopt.

Finally, in addition to print or audiovisual materials, many of these projects incorporate training components to benefit providers themselves. The training (particularly training for *Sesame Street* PEP) not only pertains to effective use of the specific project materials, but is also intended to help enhance the quality of their child care more generally.

Value for *Sesame Street*

From the standpoint of *Sesame Street*, one of the primary benefits of CTW's partnership with child-care providers is the opportunity it presents for reinforcing and extending the series' educational content. As discussed elsewhere in this volume, numerous studies have demonstrated that, even without the benefit of adult input, regular exposure to the *Sesame Street* television series can produce significant positive effects among viewers (Huston et al., chap. 8, this volume; Mielke, chap. 5, this volume; Wright, Huston, Scantlin, & Kotler, chap. 6, this volume; Zill, chap. 7, this volume). Although children can and do learn from *Sesame Street* on their own, however, several studies have shown that learning can be enhanced via parental commentary during coviewing with their children (Reiser, Tessmer, & Phelps, 1984; Reiser, Williamson, & Suzuki, 1988). The outreach materials developed by CES have taken this principle one step further by emphasizing the importance of reinforcing educational content during activities and daily routines; thus, *Sesame Street* television programs and videos become just one component of the learning process that involves interactions between children and the adults who care for them as well.

Related to this point is a second benefit—namely, the opportunity for individualized instruction. Because it is based in mass media, the broadcast presentation of the *Sesame Street* television series is necessarily identical for every child who watches it. Yet, the follow-up discussions, book reading, and hands-on activities involved in *Sesame Street* PEP and other outreach activities pose opportunities for providers to expand and tailor the educational content of *Sesame Street* to fit the specific needs of the children with whom they work.

Third, a targeted distribution system often allows the distribution of outreach materials to focus on the children who need them most. In general, distribution is typically concentrated in low-income and minority neighborhoods. However, in some cases, distribution is focused even more precisely for projects that serve more specific needs; for example, many copies of the *Sesame Street* fire safety materials were earmarked for child-care providers in what is known as the "Burn Belt," a region of the United States in which there is a high incidence of fires. Similarly, efforts were made to distribute the *Sesame Street A is for Asthma* kits to regions of the country where the incidence of asthma is high.

Finally, outreach materials provide opportunities to create videos, audiotapes, and print materials that are linguistically and culturally relevant to different ethnic groups. Almost all of the outreach materials currently created by CES are made available in both English and Spanish, because the Latino population is among the largest and fastest-growing in the United States; in 1990, the government estimated that there were approximately 17 million Spanish speakers in this country, and roughly one half of them did not speak English well or at all (OBLEMA, 1992).

Making materials linguistically accessible to non-English speaking adults and children is more difficult than it may appear. Outside of CTW, bilingual materials are typically created first in English and then translated into Spanish. Yet, although verbatim translations from one language to another are common, they are not always the best approach, because verbatim translations may lack the cultural relevance that can affect interest and appeal. As Betancourt (1997, p. 6) pointed out, imagine a set of materials "describing the need for a well-balanced diet that is nutritional and incorporates a wide range of healthy foods such as fruit, vegetables, grains, etc. If the materials that are translated [into Spanish] refer only to those foods typical of the healthy American diet but do not reference familiar foods of the Latino community, then the relevance of the information and its impact is greatly reduced."

For this reason, current *Sesame Street* outreach projects more often employ an alternate approach called *versioning*. This process results in the creation, not of Spanish-language translations of preexisting English-language materials, but of parallel sets of materials that convey equivalent content and key messages in ways that are culturally and linguistically relevant to Latino children, parents, and child-care providers. A vital component of this process is gathering information from the start about the cultural practices and beliefs of the primary ethnic groups that will be receiving the outreach materials. Information is gathered through a combination of consultation with experts and formative research conducted in both English and Spanish.

For example, efforts in support of some of the health and safety projects revealed that many Latino (and African-American) parents use home remedies to treat their children's illnesses. This posed serious issues for projects related to both asthma (because of potentially fatal side effects if these remedies are used at the same time as other prescribed medicine) and lead poisoning (because some of these home remedies contain lead). This knowledge led to the inclusion of issues regarding home remedies in the materials produced for both of these projects—important points that would have been missed if not for a concerted effort to learn about cultural differences relevant to these topics.

Making sure that materials are both accessible and culturally relevant is an outgrowth of *Sesame Street*'s focus on teaching children about diversity. This integral component of the series is widely recognized as something that makes it different from other children's programs (CTW, 1999); when a random sample of adults was asked what television program "teaches children the most about learning to get along with people of different races, cultures, and abilities," *Sesame Street* was named most often. It has been a key curriculum goal since 1971 (Season 3), and is critical to the ongoing educational objectives of *Sesame Street* and CTW as a whole.

CONCLUSION

Although CES has also developed outreach projects that support other television shows created by CTW, *Sesame Street* continues to be the mainspring of its activities. Its objectives with regard to the show, however, have changed considerably. Whereas its original goal was to increase awareness of the show's existence, today it builds on the public's widespread familiarity with *Sesame Street* characters by using them to convey information in areas that are of great importance to children's lives.

When *Sesame Street* was first created, very little was known about whether television could be an effective educational tool. Thirty years later, there is convincing data that it has enriched children's cognitive and social development in significant ways. The outreach projects developed by CES since the late 1960s attest to the importance of supplementing the power of television with human interactions that nurture their love of learning and reinforce the educational messages that they may be exposed to through this revolutionary medium.

ACKNOWLEDGMENTS

We gratefully acknowledge the contributions of several members of the Community Education Services staff at CTW—Digna Sanchez, Joanne Livesey, Jeanette Betancourt, and Donna Chandler—for their help in supplying information and reviewing an earlier draft of this chapter. Archival information on early CTW outreach efforts was located and supplied by Susan McCann Brown.

REFERENCES

Acord, K., & Romontio, N. (1995). *An evaluation of Sesame Street PEP trainings and program utilization by Bay area child-care providers, 1994–1995: A final report submitted to the California Department of Education, Child Development Division.* San Francisco: KQED Center for Education and Lifelong Learning.

Applied Research & Consulting. (1999). *Sesame Street A is for asthma impact study*. New York: Children's Television Workshop.

Betancourt, J. (1997, March). Translating and versioning: What is the difference and what difference does it make? In S. M. Fisch (Chair), *Translating and versioning: Issues in creating media-based materials in English and Spanish*. Symposium presented at the annual meeting of the American Educational Association, Chicago, IL.

Children's Television Workshop. (1971). *Sesame Street and the community*. New York: Author.

Children's Television Workshop. (1975). *CTW review, 1973–1975*. New York: Author.

Children's Television Workshop. (1979). *1979 corporate review*. New York: Author.

Children's Television Workshop. (1984). *Children's Television Workshop corporate profile: 1984*. New York: Author.

Children's Television Workshop, Education and Research Department. (1999). *Research findings for the diversity seminar* (unpublished research report). New York: Children's Television Workshop.

Davis, E. P., Friedman, G. I., & Martin, L. (1990). Community education and child-care programs. *Educational Technology Research and Development, 38*(4), 45–53.

Einzig, R., Cappella, E., & Michaelis, B. (1996). *Sesame Street Fire Safety Station: Third edition fire safety materials, Phase II research report* (unpublished research report). New York: Children's Television Workshop.

Fisch, S. M. (1998). The Children's Television Workshop: The experiment continues. In R. G. Noll, & M. E. Price (Eds.), *A communications cornucopia: Markle Foundation essays on information policy* (pp. 297–337). Washington, DC: Brookings Institution Press.

Fisch, S., McCann Brown, S., & Cohen, D. (1996). *Sesame Street Lead Away! lead poisoning prevention kit telephone survey* (unpublished research report). New York: Children's Television Workshop.

Fisch, S. M., Williams, M. E., Cappella, E., Einzig, R. K., Richman, B. A., McCann Brown, S. K., & Cohen, D. I. (1997, May). Taking *Sesame Street* beyond its curriculum: Elmo and Oscar combat lead poisoning. In S. M. Fisch (Chair), *Extending the power of Sesame Street: Other media, other goals, other cultures*. Symposium presented at the annual meeting of the International Communication Association, Montreal, Canada.

Fisch, S. M., Williams, M. E., Cappella, E., Richman, B., Einzig, R. K., Michaelis, B., McCann Brown, S. K., & Cohen, D. I. (1997, April). *Sesame Street* Lead Away!: A review of research on English- and Spanish-language outreach materials. In S. M. Fisch (Chair), *Translating and versioning: Issues in creating media-based materials in English and Spanish*. Symposium presented at the annual meeting of the American Educational Research Association, Chicago, IL.

Galinsky, E., Howes, C., Kontos, S., & Shinn, M. (1994). *The study of children in family child care and relative care*. New York: Families and Work Institute.

Land, H. W. (1972). *The Children's Television Workshop: How and why it works*. New York: Nassau Board of Cooperative Educational Services.

Mindel, C. H., & Dangel, R. F. (1990). *The Sesame Street PEP project: Final research report*. Arlington, TX: The University of Texas at Arlington.

National Association for the Education of Young Children. (1985). *In whose hands? A demographic fact sheet on child-care providers*. Washington, DC: Author.

Office of Bilingual and Minority Language Affairs. (1992). *The condition of bilingual education in the nation*. Washington, DC: OBLEMA, Department of Education.

Program Research Department. (1999). *Building on Sesame Street project: Second year impact study* (unpublished research report). New York: Children's Television Workshop.

Reiser, R. A., Tessmer, M. A., & Phelps, P. C. (1984). Adult–child interaction in children's learning from *Sesame Street*. *Educational Communication and Technology Journal, 32,* 217–223.

Reiser, R. A., Williamson, N., & Suzuki, K. (1988). Using *Sesame Street*. *Educational Communication and Technology Journal, 36,* 15–21.

RMC Research Corporation. (1993). *Pilot summative report: Sesame Street Preschool Educational Project Initiative*. Portland, OR: Author.

West, J., Wright, D., & Hausken, E. G. (1995). *Child care and early education program participation of infants, toddlers, and preschoolers*. Washington, DC: U.S. Department of Education, Office of Educational Research and Improvement. (NCES No. 95–824)

Whitebook, M., Howes, C., & Phillips, D. (1989) *Who cares? Child-care teachers and the quality of care in America: The national child-care staffing study*. Oakland, CA: Child-Care Employee Project.

Yotive, W., Cappella, E., & Rincon, C. (1997a). *Parent and caregiver focus groups for Sesame Street A Is for Asthma preschool awareness project* (unpublished research report). New York: Children's Television Workshop.

Yotive, W., Cappella, E., & Rincon, C. (1997b). *What preschool children who have asthma know about their illness* (unpublished research report). New York: Children's Television Workshop.

Yotive, W., Cappella, E., & Rincon, C. (1997c). *Board-a-matic study: Sesame Street A Is for Asthma preschool awareness project* (unpublished research report). New York: Children's Television Workshop.

Yotive, W., McCann Brown, S., Sullivan, C., & Ragasa, D. (1999). *Use of the Sesame Street A is for Asthma kit among teachers, child-care providers, health care professionals, trainers, and librarians* (unpublished research report). New York: Children's Television Workshop.

Yotive, W., Rincon, C., & Birnbaum, A. (1998a). *First year formative study: Building on Sesame Street family child-care project* (unpublished research report). New York: Children's Television Workshop.

Yotive, W., Rincon, C., & Birnbaum, A. (1998b). *Print and video study: Sesame Street A Is for Asthma preschool awareness project* (unpublished research report). New York: Children's Television Workshop.

11 Carrying *Sesame Street* Into Print: *Sesame Street Magazine*, *Sesame Street Parents*, and *Sesame Street* Books

Renée Cherow-O'Leary
Rutgers University

In 1970, a department of "nonbroadcast" materials was organized at Children's Television Workshop (CTW) to explore the role that books, toys, recordings, and magazines might play in the extension of the message and the educational mission of the newly established television program, *Sesame Street*. This department supported the earliest vision of Joan Ganz Cooney, founder of CTW, to create a "multiple media institution." One and one half years of preparation had gone into the development of nonbroadcast materials with steps similar to those taken by research for the television show. This included: a feasibility study to determine whether such a department was viable; seminars with a subcommittee of the CTW advisory board plus new advisors for this purpose; the establishment of educational goals for nonbroadcast materials; testing various approaches to the development of these materials; determining staff requirements; and finally, going into production. Thirty years later, the print materials produced by CTW have been an enduring part of the legacy of *Sesame Street*. Print media include three magazines—*Sesame Street Magazine* (for young children of *Sesame Street* viewing age), *Sesame Street Parents* (aimed at English-speaking parents), and *Padres de Sesame Street* (for Spanish-speaking parents)—as well as a range of books for children. All of these publications have derived from the curriculum goals of the television program and have utilized the characters, style, tone, and some of the features of the program.

Consistent with the CTW Model (Truglio & Fisch, Introduction, this volume), formative research is an integral component in the creation and revision of all print media. The demands of print on the young child and the time-stressed adult have created special research needs. Originally, the same research department responsible for the *Sesame Street* television show was also responsible for print media research. In 1975, The Magazine Research Department was formed to serve the growing research needs of the Magazine Group. This department continued as a self-contained unit until 1995. Shortly thereafter, the responsibilities for research for *Sesame Street Magazine* were integrated back into the scope of work for the *Sesame Street* Research Department. This allows for better integration of the show curriculum and formative research across media. (Simultaneously, other CTW research teams working across media projects for school-age children conduct the research for CTW's school-age magazines, *Kid City* and *Contact Kids*.) The collaboration between the producers of print materials and researchers has created print media with their own unique characteristics. These are discussed in this chapter.

A MAGAZINE FOR NONREADERS: *SESAME STREET MAGAZINE*

When *Sesame Street* was created for television, the potential audience for the series was seen to be all preschool children, but particularly those who might not receive instruction at home in the preliminary skills of early literacy. Such knowledge as learning the letters of the alphabet, auditory distinctions and letter sounds, blending letter sounds into words, and the sequencing of ideas were integral to the curriculum on which the show was based (Lesser & Schneider, chap. 2, this volume). Soon after the inception of the show, it was decided that a children's magazine be produced to reinforce these curriculum goals and to be a catalyst and natural vehicle for early literacy. Thus, the first issue of the magazine debuted with a cover date of October, 1970. In 1971, a corporate sponsor provided a grant for distribution of *Sesame Street Magazine* to parents in disadvantaged areas. Soon after, the magazine began to be published regularly and later became available for parents of preschoolers to purchase via newsstands and subscriptions.

From the start, *Sesame Street Magazine* had the paradoxical mission of being a magazine for nonreaders. The goal was to create interest in reading on the part of the child and to engage parents in reading the magazine to their children. This dual-pronged approach still holds true today. The child, building familiarity with the magazine, begins to develop an understanding of the conventions of print, such as matching picture and text, labeling key words, captioning, sequencing, and learning words by sound as well as sight. It cannot be assumed that these conventions will be learned by the child alone, although the magazine creates many visual cues that can assist the child. Yet, the magazine is created for 2- to 6-year-old children and through that period, a child generally moves from inability to read at all to the ability to recognize all the conventions of print if not yet read the words.

Observing these distinct stages of learning to read was part of the research agenda for *Sesame Street Magazine*, and knowing how children understood the information offered to them was an important guide to positioning text and picture in ways that would reinforce the intended message. The goal, however, was not overtly didactic. The magazine alone would not teach the child how to read. It would begin a process, ideally with input from a parental figure, to help children recognize the joy of reading. That joy was at the heart of the literacy approach developed by the editors, writers, and illustrators whose teamwork went into the creation of the magazine.

Although the magazine uses the essentials of literacy as the core of its approach, it also incorporates the other curriculum goals of the show, such as: identifying and labeling numbers; enumeration; labeling body parts; auditory discrimination of rhyme and rhythm; relational concepts of size, position, and distance; classification of objects; reasoning and problem solving (e.g., understanding inference and causality, evaluating explanations and solutions); and others. The magazine represents the social environment of the child by creating stories about cooperation, rules of behavior, and differences in points of view, and of personalities. The magazine also follows the curriculum goals from the television show concerning physical phenomena and the natural environment.

Each issue of the magazine has an overarching theme that lends additional coherence to its content. A sample of themes from a range of magazines dated 1985–1998 included topics such as: "Inside and Outside with Bert and Ernie," "I Am Some Body" (body and self-esteem), "Join the Team" (sports and cooperation), "Play It Safe" (safety tips), "Back to School," "On the Road," "Friends and Family," "Welcome to My Room," "Costumes and Disguises," "Sunny Days" (weather), and "Tickle Me! Elmo" and "Friends Get Silly" (humor and games). The theme is often, but not always, related to the curriculum focus of the concurrent season of the television show (see Lesser & Schneider, chap. 2, this volume) and is always tailored to suit the developmental level of preschool children.

These themes are actualized within each issue through a wide range of features. These include: alphabet activities, coloring pages, a calendar, contests, cut-out activities, mazes, music for sing-alongs, picture comparisons, posters, short stories about the *Sesame Street* characters, animal recognition activities and stories, counting activities, matching games, poems, hidden picture puzzles, holiday activities, and readers' artwork and writing, as well as jokes, riddles, and "silly" pages. New ideas continue to be added as the magazine evolves.

The intersection of the diversity of activities, the multi-faceted themes, and the challenges of early literacy acquisition has fed into a research agenda for the children's magazine that measures appeal, comprehension, and use across the age range from 2 to 6 years old. This research process is tied to the exigencies of the publication deadlines and magazine production in a unique mix.

RESEARCH PROCESS FOR *SESAME STREET MAGAZINE* FOR CHILDREN

Formative research conducted in support of *Sesame Street Magazine* involved investigating four basic areas: the editorial content for appeal and comprehension, the structure and format of the magazine (including layout, presentation of art, flow of material, and organization of the magazine), literacy skills in early childhood, and subscriber information. Together, these complementary streams of information help the CTW Magazine Group better understand the readers and the demographics of the audience.

Formative Research on Editorial Content

Much of the formative research concerning *Sesame Street Magazine* has focused on the content of individual stories or features. Some of this research has assessed the appeal and comprehensibility of specific features; over time, this cumulative body of research has pointed to topics that are consistently appealing and relevant to preschool children. Other studies have held implications for means by which comprehension can be maximized, such as methods for grouping objects on a page to facilitate counting or the use of a small perforated line with a small picture of scissors as an icon to signal a cut-out activity. Still others have led to conclusions regarding ways to make puzzles and activities as challenging as possible for preschoolers without making them too difficult for the children to solve, such as the optimal number of choice points in a maze. In these ways, research on the editorial content of *Sesame Street Magazine* has simultaneously informed revisions to the specific material tested and guidelines for the creation of future materials (e.g., Brenner & Freck, 1979; CTW Magazine Research Department, 1992, 1993; Kirk & Bernstein, 1975; Kozak, 1971; cf. CTW Program Research School-Age Team, 1998).

As in the case of the *Sesame Street* television series (Fisch & Bernstein, chap. 3, this volume), formative research on the editorial content of *Sesame Street Magazine* must fit the constraints of the magazine's production schedule. *Sesame Street Magazine* is prepared by a cadre of writers and illustrators, some of whom are drawn from the in-house editorial and art staff, but many of whom work on a freelance basis. Because the work comes from many different sources, the research process begins when all the materials are assembled into a "packet" that represents an entire upcoming issue, for review by editorial and research staff. The researchers read each packet with an eye toward developmental appropriateness and anything that might cause confusion or misinterpretation among preschool children. When sections of the packet raise issues that require feedback from children, testing is arranged.

Because of the complexities of magazine production, especially before some of the computerized editorial processes now in common use, lead time for production of an issue of the magazine is typically 4 to 6 months in advance of distribution. This means that research is conducted well in advance of publication and must be run fairly quickly, if the data are to inform any revisions to text or art. For several years, the Magazine Research Department facilitated the testing process by establishing a network in the New York metropolitan area that included public and private nursery schools and a variety of kindergarten classes that could be visited on short notice.

Over a period of years, this network was invaluable in conducting research for *Sesame Street Magazine*. However, some research issues are uniquely relevant to children who already read *Sesame Street Magazine* on a regular basis, and can be investigated only with children who are already familiar with the magazine. Because subscribers to *Sesame Street Magazine* are spread across the United States, a considerable investment of time and money would be required to involve them in this type of ongoing research. Instead, the Magazine Research Department decided to "create" a base of regular readers of *Sesame Street Magazine* by selecting several schools and preschools to become "subscriber schools." In these, the children received the magazine every month at school and the teachers either read the magazine with them or they kept it among other books and periodicals so the children could read it when they wished. The principals of the subscriber schools were contacted, as were the parents of the children, to be sure that everyone agreed to their participation in research. The subscriber schools proved to be effective vehicles for research with children who were already familiar with the specifics of *Sesame Street Magazine* and the conventions of print. This gave researchers better insight into the subscriber community at large during testing.

Research on Format and Structure

In contrast to research on editorial content, formative research on format and structure focuses, not on individual stories or features, but on the overall look, feel, and organization of the magazine. Naturally, many of the relevant issues in this area relate to the target audience of preschool children. In addition, however, because it is expected that many parents will read the magazine with their children (and, indeed, many do), some issues are related to parents' own use of the magazine with their children.

Some research in this area has focused on developing ways to identify the age level of individual features in the magazine or the types of activities they contain. Much of this information has been conveyed in the Table of Contents to provide a simple reference for parents who read the magazine with their children. The Table of Contents has been revised many times through the years to give parents a clear overview of the scope of the magazine, the theme of each issue, and ways to use the magazine for maximum educational effect. In the early years of the magazine, there was an educational description under each article or activity. Then, there was a letter from the editor of the magazine in each issue. Most recently, icons have been used to provide visual indicators of the level and nature of various features; for example, an illustration of Big Bird's friend Little Bird indicates that a story or game is intended for the youngest readers. The development of each of these means was accompanied by formative research that helped to implement it effectively (e.g., Song, 1992).

Another means by which parents have been supported in using the magazine is through the use of educational tips presented on the same pages as the articles or activities themselves. In its early years, various pages of *Sesame Street Magazine* included a structural component called "Extra." This consisted of boxes on given pages that were geared toward parents, rather than children; the "Extra" boxes were intended to help parents extend the activity by giving suggestions of other ways to approach the topic. Although these were helpful, they also cluttered the pages, and it was later decided that information meant for parents should be included in a separate, accompanying publication for parents, rather than intruding into the publication for the child (CTW Magazine Research Department, 1985). (More about the development of the parents' magazine is presented later in this chapter.)

Today, the magazine uses a dual approach. Included alongside the relevant feature in *Sesame Street Magazine* are brief suggestions for extension activities that can be performed on the spot; these are signaled by an icon of Little Bird. For example, a recent issue on parts of the body included a coloring activity in which Big Bird was shown making hand shadows, and was accompanied by a suggestion for parents to make hand shadows with their children. More extensive suggestions for hands-on extension activities related to parts of the body (e.g., finger painting, movement games), along with explanations of their educational value, were reserved for the accompanying issue of the parents' magazine and were signaled by icons of other Muppets.

Other format issues are related to the visual design of the magazine. For example, in 1992, specialists in magazine redesign were consulted to give the magazine an updated look. This meant that the art director, editors, and research director had to incorporate new approaches to text and graphics presentation. However, revisions to the design of the magazine took into account, not only the aesthetic sensibilities of those involved, but also characteristics of its readership. In particular, the redesign followed a 1990 readership survey that showed that the average reader of *Sesame Street Magazine* was younger than in earlier surveys. There was greater readership from the 2- to 3-year-old age group than from the 4- to 5-year-old group that had been the accepted norm for several years prior (CTW Magazine Research Department, 1990). Thus, the magazine had to adapt the redesign not only for a fresh look but to respond to the younger audience that needed a simpler and clearer presentation in word and art.

Finally, research on the format of *Sesame Street Magazine* has included studies to inform the development of new monthly features for the magazine, such as: the calendar included in each issue (with activities connected to the theme of the issue) or the inclusion of children's letters and artwork (and optimal ways to represent their contributions in the magazine). Each element was researched in classrooms, mail surveys, and in telephone research with a group of parent-subscribers who volunteered each year to be available for more immediate feedback on issues of concern to research.

Early Literacy

One of the biggest educational issues that confronts the editors of the children's magazine is how to create an appealing issue that will serve 2- to 6-year-old children, given their varying understanding of print. Apart from the annual curriculum seminars that are organized by the researchers who support the *Sesame Street* television series (and which are attended by representatives of *Sesame Street Magazine*), the children's and parents' magazines are informed by their own advisory boards as well. Ongoing consultation with these advisors informs *Sesame Street Magazine*'s approach to print, in an attempt to build comprehension and appeal. For many years, the Magazine Research Department also organized annual meetings with these advisors and guest editors for the children's magazine, which provided further opportunities to discuss issues with key researchers in early literacy. Presently, advisors are consulted on a monthly basis to review the content of each issue.

The Magazine Research Department also developed a circulating file of "Research Briefs" that were culled, on a monthly basis, from scholarly journals and a range of popular and trade publications. These informed the *Sesame Street Magazine* staff about current research in literacy. These materials were supplemented by attendance at professional meetings, such as the National Association for the Education of Young Children, the International Reading Association, the Educational Press Association, and the American Educational Research Association. Currently, although the process has grown less formal over the years, researchers and magazine staff members continue to attend conferences to stay up-to-date on the latest theory, practice, and empirical findings regarding literacy.

Subscriber Information and Market Research

As mentioned earlier, demographic research is an essential component of magazine viability. It is essential to know who the readership is and how it changes over time, what their preferences are, and which features have made an impact on them. This is especially true in a subscriber magazine, because if there are families who do not renew the magazine, the Magazine Group circulation department needs research data to understand these market trends. To aid in this effort, the Magazine Research Department conducted several "Subscriber Surveys," sent to a sample of subscribers nationwide; each survey was developed by in-house CTW researchers and managed by an outside research firm dealing in large mail surveys. When each survey was completed (generally a 6- to 8-week process), the results were presented to every division of the Magazine group and the data were fed back into the editorial content and marketing of the magazine.

Such research has become particularly important over time and will continue to be a part of the overall research agenda for the magazine. In the early years of *Sesame Street Magazine*, there were few competitive publications. However, recent years have seen an explosion of television programming and publications for young children. This has made it incumbent on the magazine staff to keep abreast of the competition. Children's magazines (and now, Web sites and other new media for children) must be seen as part of the world of choices to which the child and the parent have access. Every 4 years, there is a new audience for *Sesame Street Magazine* because, eventually, children outgrow the publication. The challenge is to foresee trends and stay fresh.

SESAME STREET PARENTS:
THE EVOLUTION OF A CONCEPT

In 1981, Nina Link, then publisher of the CTW Magazine Group, decided to develop the *Sesame Street Parents' Newsletter*. In the premiere issue, she described the way in which CTW's ongoing research with children had been extended to parents, to provide the basis for a tool to offer parents insight into the child rearing process and to make parenting a little easier:

> I want to share with you some of the excitement and enthusiasm generated by the *Sesame Street Parents' Newsletter* ... It is a natural extension of the innovative work we have done for the past decade in both television and print ... Now ... we have the opportunity to share with you some of the information we have discovered ... Our network of people in the preschool field is already established and research is being conducted every day. We have reached out to speak to parents on a one-to-one basis in much the same way we have interacted with children ... Our goal is to bring you timely, useful information that will help you in the increasingly difficult role of being a parent ... (Link, 1981, p.1)

Research formed the primary base for the magazine and the assumption that parents should benefit from what CTW was learning about children, about literacy, and about parenting. The first issue included articles on the theme of "TV and Fear." Topics of articles included "What's real and what's imaginary?," "Why are there Muppet monsters on the *Sesame Street* television program?," and "How much do parents need to worry that television will unduly frighten their child?" Ideas from parents (called "Tricks of the Trade") were included, as was a Parents' Forum to discuss the important issue of discipline. Finally, a Reader's Poll on bedtime experiences was included to serve as the basis of an article in a subsequent issue. Thus, the heart of the newsletter—and the subsequent *Sesame Street Parents Magazine*—was born of input and feedback from parents themselves, as well as solid connections to the educational dimensions of the *Sesame Street* television program and magazine.

Research for Parents, Research With Parents

The decision to publish a separate newsletter for parents was the basis of many new research questions in the Magazine Group. First, how directly should the parent materials connect to the children's magazine? How didactic should the features be? What should be the balance between information strictly for parents and that related to children? What format should be adopted?

Format.   When the newsletter was first published, it had a rough-hewn feel to it. Although it was full of professional information, the look of the publication was casual. It was printed on a heavy, beige newsprint paper with colored ink. There were no photos or complex graphics. Shortly thereafter, the newsletter was stapled into the children's magazine, at first in the middle and then in the back. However, this format was not satisfactory for parent or child because research showed that children and parents had different needs for their magazines. They did not want to tear the parent material out of the magazine or to restrict their children's use of the magazine while reading the parent material; instead, they wanted the parent material to be kept in a pristine state so they could read it at their leisure (CTW Magazine Research Department, 1985).

Based in part on these findings, the parents' magazine was separated permanently. It began to be printed on a glossier paper. The cover showed color photos of parents and children and the articles employed a wide variety of attractive graphics. Although the magazine was separate, it was shrink-wrapped with the children's magazine in a sealed plastic bag for mailing to the subscriber. This packaging itself made a statement: the children's magazine and the parents' magazine were separate but inseparable. Parents and children are inextricably connected, and this joined approach continues to this day.

Advertising.   The economics of publishing gave rise to another key decision that affected research and raised new questions. In the mid-1980s, it was decided that, to become self-supporting and competitive with other established parenting magazines, the *Sesame Street Parents Guide* (its name at the time) would have to contain advertising.

The decision to include advertising necessitated the creation of guidelines for that advertising. First and foremost, in light of concerns about advertising directed at preschool children, it was decided that advertising would be included only in the parents' magazine, and not in the children's magazine. Even within the parents' magazine, however, stringent guidelines for advertising were developed, including the decision to turn down ads for highly sugary, salty, or fatty foods commonly marketed to children. There were also guidelines for safety in toys and in other products advertised.

The presence of advertising meant that the magazine suddenly needed, not only academic research, but research that would convince advertisers about the consumer preferences of the readership. As with the children's magazine, several types of research activities have come to support the parents' magazine simultaneously (although the list has been slightly different): research on editorial content, research on structure and format, and market research.

Research on Editorial Content

Researchers support the editorial content both by supplying resources for parenting information and conducting formative testing as needed. For many years, one of the most prominent ways in which a solid base of valid and up-to-date parenting information was provided was through yearly advisory board meetings. Where curriculum seminars and advisory board meetings conducted in support of the *Sesame Street* television series and children's magazine have focused on issues directly relevant to children, meetings of the advisory board for the parents' magazine focused instead on issues related to parenting. In these meetings, experts gave suggestions for making the magazine even more responsive to parents, and guest consultants offered their specialized insights into the editorial process. Over time, due in part to these meetings, the magazine staff itself became more conversant with the relevant issues, and the process was able to be streamlined as the questions to be addressed became increasingly specific. Thus, these formal advisory board meetings no longer occur annually; instead, the advisory board is consulted on a monthly basis to review the magazine prior to publication and individual advisors are contacted as needed to speak to specific issues as they arise.

In addition to review by the advisory board, researchers (first from the Magazine Research Department and now from the *Sesame Street* Research Department) review the content of each upcoming issue, provide topic links to upcoming *Sesame Street* episodes, and gather relevant information on particular topics as needed.

Parallel to research on *Sesame Street Magazine*, formative research on *Sesame Street Parents* assesses parents' reactions to the material in the magazine on a timely basis. To meet this need, just as research on the children's magazine entailed the creation of networks of preschools for testing purposes, the Magazine Research Department organized a Parents Research Network. In the first issue of the late Summer/early Fall, a coupon in the parents' magazine would request names and contact information of parents who were willing to be contacted—generally by telephone but sometimes by mail—to respond to editorial questions. Hundreds of parents replied from across the United States, giving their responses a regional flavor that was important to the magazine. Today, this group of parents is referred to as the Parent Advisory Board and it includes over 600 readers. This panel informs editors on a wide variety of parenting issues and the *Sesame Street* Research Department manages this research.

At times, issues arise that need to be addressed in greater depth in a face-to-face context. In these instances, researchers conduct focus groups with parents around the country. These sessions provide candid responses on a wide variety of new ideas for the magazine.

Research as Editorial Content.   In some cases, research data have not only informed, but actually become part of the editorial content of the parents' magazine itself. A series of polls, featured in the magazine, have been created jointly by editors and researchers. These polls have received thousands of replies on various topics and the data have formed the basis of articles and commentary in subsequent issues of the magazine (e.g., Cherow-O'Leary, 1991). Examples of some topics covered are: "Raising Kids in a Changing World" (which asked how today's parents were raising their children compared to how they had been raised) and a "Mom and Dad Report" (which asked mothers and fathers how they feel about being a parent, work, and marriage). One poll, which garnered an Educational Press Association award for the magazine, appeared in the magazine prior to the 1992 presidential election. This poll asked many questions about what the term *family values*, an issue much in the news at the time, meant to the readers of the magazine. The results of the poll became the basis of an article by an established Washington reporter who could put many of the issues that were raised in the larger political context of how proposed bills (such as the Family Leave Act) might affect families.

Another example of research data as editorial content is the annual feature article on "toy testing" that appears in the parents' magazine prior to each Christmas shopping season. Originally, an in-house researcher would work closely with the editors to bring parents and children to CTW over a weekend, when the families had the leisure to spend time at the CTW offices. Once there, the parents and children were observed as they tried out a wide variety of toys. Data from these sessions fed into recommendations about favorite toys for various age groups, sex differences in use, safety factors, educational value for children, and parent reactions to the toys.

The annual toy test continues today, although the procedure has been simplified somewhat. With the assistance of an outside research firm, batches of toys are sent to parents around the country, and parents living in New York City are asked to attend a focus groups at CTW to discuss their children's experiences with the toys.

The polls and toy tests serve as unique examples of formative research, in that the primary audience for these data is not only the staff of the magazine, but also the readers themselves. The toy tests have provided research that parents can use to take action of their own, and feedback from parents suggests that they have.

Research on Format and Structure

By and large, the format issue that has most concerned the editors of the magazine is providing easy access to features for busy parents; the magazine has to be informative, yet easy to read on a tight schedule. Through the years, input from parents on a wide variety of approaches has helped the magazine evolve to a more bulleted format, with the art director playing a strong role in creating welcoming and appealing graphics. Many photos, white space, bright color, and easily identifiable monthly departments have helped to create an inviting structure for the magazine.

One key aspect of connecting the parents' magazine to the children's magazine has been to identify features in the parents' magazine that link directly to the content of the children's magazine. As discussed earlier, this was accomplished originally through "Extra" boxes inserted in relevant places in the children's magazine. However, these boxes proved intrusive, so the information was moved to the parents' magazine, where it appeared in a monthly column (written by the Research Director) called "Extending This Issue." The column was loosely tied to the descriptions in the Table of Contents in the children's magazine, but it took advantage of the greater amount of space available in the parents' magazine to discuss suggested activities in greater depth than had been possible in the "Extra" boxes.

Yet, this was not the final word, either. Over the years, the magazine's approach to this column kept evolving and changing as information was obtained from readers through formative research. Currently, information relevant to the theme of the children's magazine is no longer confined to a single column, but can appear throughout the magazine. Parents are alerted to these connections through the use of visual icons (called linkups) that employ pictures of Muppets and appear beside the relevant parents' article. The linkups direct the parent, not only to connections with the children's magazine, but also to connections with the *Sesame Street* television show, Web site, or other products when appropriate.

Subscriber Information and Market Research

When the parents' magazine began to take advertising, the Magazine Research Department needed to supply a new kind of information beyond editorial feedback. The Subscriber Survey began to incorporate not only questions intended to inform the development of editorial content but also consumer data such as: the types of products subscribers purchased regularly, whether they intended to move in the next 6 months, the types of vehicles they drove, and the number of older and younger children in their families.

Each survey was developed by in-house CTW researchers but was conducted by mail through outside firms that specialized in this type of research. The scope of the surveys meant that each one took several months to field and analyze. Currently, primary responsibility for managing this research has shifted to an outside research firm, Media Mark Research. The publisher, advertising director, circulation director, and others on the business side of *Sesame Street Parents* use these data to make decisions about marketing. The editors, as always, use pertinent information to evaluate the effectiveness and impact of the publication and inform subsequent changes.

Online Resources

With the advent of e-mail and Web sites, a new dimension has been added to the research process supporting *Sesame Street Parents*. Because of the immediacy of the feedback that is possible through these media, the new philosophy of the magazine is to consider itself a voice of the parent in much the same way two parents might sit sharing information on a park bench. This "park bench philosophy" assumes that the magazine can have a more personal focus than ever before. This means including readers' input and opinions, not only through letters to the editor (as the magazine has always done), but also through quotes from children and parents that are sent online. Polls are conducted weekly through the *Sesame Street* Web site (with a much faster turnaround than the magazine's monthly schedule and long lead time used to allow). These polls typically draw at least 500 to 600 responses each week, and the data help shape article ideas in the magazine.

E-mail also provides an efficient means by which members of the Parents' Research Network can send feedback on *Sesame Street Parents* and contribute parenting experiences and ideas to be included in the magazine's "Parent-to-Parent" column. Online parent discussion groups (also included within the CTW Web site) provide additional contexts in which parents can communicate with each other and with specialists who write for the magazine.

By adding electronic resources to the mix, research for *Sesame Street Parents* has become more interdisciplinary, as online polls and discussions play increasingly large roles in the creation of the magazine. Modern communication technology enables research that is speedier and more systematic than prior efforts. As more readers go online, this will be an ever more important part of the research effort.

SESAME STREET BOOKS:
PERMANENT AND PORTABLE

In addition to *Sesame Street Magazine*, the series has also been carried into print through a successful series of *Sesame Street* books. As early as the Fall of 1971, the Western Publishing Company (publishers of Golden Books for children) sold between 6 and 7 million copies of its series of books based on *Sesame Street*, the greatest volume in its history until that time. Today, there are over 600 books, on a host of topics, available in the *Sesame Street* library.

Applying Television Research to Print

Traditionally, formative research studies have not been conducted as part of the creation of individual books. However, *Sesame Street* books have been infused with the curricular activities and formative research conducted for the *Sesame Street* television series. Ideas for books are reviewed by the research team for the *Sesame Street* television series, with an eye toward appeal, the presentation of curriculum, age-appropriateness, and the suitable use of the Muppet characters.

One key resource in the development of these books, since their inception, has been the annual *Sesame Street* curriculum seminars. As Lesser and Schneider (chap. 2, this volume) have discussed, these introduce the curriculum focus for each season of *Sesame Street* by bringing experts to CTW to delve deeply into ways to translate complex curricula into entertaining and informative shows for young children. For example, an extraordinary 4-year curriculum covered the sensitive issues of race relations (Truglio, Lovelace, Seguí, & Scheiner, chap. 4, this volume). Each year was devoted to the study of a different group: African Americans, Latinos, Asian-Americans, and American Indians. Educators and leaders from these different communities discussed research on ways to promote cross-cultural understanding and friendship among young children. These thoughtful discussions (along with accompanying formative research studies) were the basis of not only the production of television segments but also a series of books called *We're Different, We're the Same*. Humans and Muppets of all colors interact in these books and make the curriculum come alive.

Some books have been developed as even more direct extensions of themes originating on the television programs. Some of the more memorable projects include a book based on the *Sesame Street* episode that dealt with the death of Mr. Hooper, a beloved, elderly character on the show. When he died, the cast and producers had to make some explanation and chose to discuss the meaning of death on the show (Truglio et al., chap. 4, this volume). The book editors also chose to deal with this sensitive topic. Working with the *Sesame Street* television research staff, writers and editors drew on the same educational content information and formative data that informed its treatment on television. The result was a book entitled *I'll Miss You, Mr. Hooper* that reinforced and supported the key ideas introduced on the program.

Another difficult issue that the television show introduced was the adoption of a baby, Miles, by regular show characters, Susan and Gordon. Defining this new kind of family was delicate, and the research team added their comments and suggestions from their testing of the television scripts into the book production process.

The sensitive addressing of the social subjects and difficult human emotions incorporated into the books utilize research extensively. But from the early days of *Sesame Street* to the present day, equal attention has been given to the treatment of key academic concepts, such as letters and numbers, to avoid confusion wherever possible. Labeling is key, so that children know which word refers to which picture, and ambiguity has to be minimized. For example, if Oscar the Grouch were depicted as a king, children might be more likely to label the picture as "Oscar" than as "King." Thus, it is unlikely that such an illustration would be used to illustrate the letter *K* in a *Sesame Street* alphabet book.

Books for Nonreaders

As in the case of *Sesame Street Magazine*, it is critical to remember that the books need to tell a story to nonreaders. As a result, the art in the books is extremely important; it must be sufficiently stimulating to allow preliterate children "reading" alone to invent a story that they can tell to themselves. In addition, the books (like the magazines) build on parent–child interaction. When adults read to children and use the books to promote learning and bonding through play and conversation, the books become the vehicles for dialogue, laughter, learning, and surprise that the editors, writers, and illustrators intend them to be.

To achieve this end, CTW books have always had the parent in mind as a "shadow" audience, in much the same way that the television series employs humor for both children and parents. The goal of the books is to provide an experience that is funny, charming, and keeps children's attention. At the same time, for parents who often are asked to read the same book over and over, there needs to be an appealing "zaniness" that maintains the parents' own enthusiasm.

Standards for Appropriateness

Consistent with the philosophy of the *Sesame Street* television program, the books have strict standards for what can and cannot be shown. Care is taken to avoid content that might frighten or be dangerous for young readers. Thus, when a Muppet version of *Hansel and Gretel* was published, no child was put in the oven as in the classic story. A firehouse can be depicted in *Sesame Street* books, but not flames. Even lit candles on a birthday cake cannot be shown!

These restrictions pose a challenge for authors and illustrators. It is essential for them to learn the *Sesame Street* "code" as part of any publishing program engaged in by CTW. This code encompasses a broad scope of considerations, ranging from the way the Muppets are drawn to adherence to curriculum goals.

Because of this atypical approach to book production, it is fair to ask why publishers would accede to these demands. What the publisher gets is the appeal of *Sesame Street* and its characters, as well as the benefit of a significant body of research, which is a highly valuable asset in itself. In the end, the very standards of *Sesame Street* materials are a guarantee of quality.

New Directions for *Sesame Street* Books

As the book publishing program has progressed throughout the years, new materials have been developed with a broader mandate than the original one. This broadening includes both new topics and new formats for upcoming books.

The future of book publishing at CTW is tied, as always, to the ever-expanding and challenging curriculum developed for the television show. For example, a current series of 40-page "start-to-read" books uses a carefully chosen beginning reading vocabulary to focus on emotions and social development, in keeping with *Sesame Street*'s curriculum focus on social development in recent years (Lesser & Schneider, chap. 2, this volume).

At the same time, there is a new sense of flexibility and experimentation in the creation of books that reflects the innovation taking place at the Workshop. Novel formats include interactive books that flip in different directions and a book called *Tattoo Tales* that allows children to put stickers on their own bodies. (This book carries the warning that the book must be used with adult supervision.)

Most recently, it has become acceptable for a book to require multitasking, rather than focusing on only one skill at a time. For example, a question in a traditional *Sesame Street* book might ask readers how many elephants are on a page (i.e., a counting task). In a new book, this question might accompany a page that includes more than one kind of animal, such as two elephants and two kangaroos, thus combining counting with a classification task (i.e., differentiating the kangaroos from the elephants). This more complex task is part of the experimentation in a recent book, *The Count Counts Scary Things*, in which there are up to 100 items to count in 10 groups of 10! This new approach, based on research and experience, accepts that children today are highly oriented to a visual culture and that more risks can be taken with the material than in the past.

Even as the domestic line of *Sesame Street* books expands, international coproductions of the *Sesame Street* television series (Cole, Richman, & McCann Brown, chap. 9, this volume) have led some international publishers to purchase the rights to specific *Sesame Street* books for use in their own countries. In some cases, CTW book editors help these publishers choose the existing books that are best suited to their own countries, and these books are translated into the native tongue of the relevant country. In other cases, new books are created independently for use in the publishers' countries.

Although the line of *Sesame Street* books continues to experiment with format and content in an increasing number of countries, there is also enormous respect for what has worked well in the past. *Another Monster at the End of This Book*, a recently published and well-received sequel to one of the early *Sesame Street* best sellers, *The Monster at the End of This Book*, is proof that books endure and provide learning and pleasure to generations of children. They will remain a critical part of a continuum of materials that enhance the mission of *Sesame Street*.

THE FUTURE OF CTW PRINT RESEARCH

The books and magazines that Joan Ganz Cooney, founder of the Children's Television Workshop, envisioned 30 years ago are now truly part of a multimedia approach to the delivery of educational information. The growth of online resources is changing the face of data gathering and creating the opportunity for new publishing vehicles. Material from *Sesame Street Parents* is available on the CTW Web site, and CTW produces an e-mail newsletter for parents that is sent to more than 35,000 subscribers each week.

Print research is also taking this path. As increasing numbers of families are connected to the Internet, online family focus groups will become more common and more letters to the editor will be received in this way. Immediate access to families on a national level will allow more research to be conducted on ways to address changes in families and family dynamics, new *literacies* that children are acquiring, and new areas of curriculum development.

Whatever means are used, however, the most important thing to remember is that the magazines and books must serve contemporary parents and children. Past successes do not necessarily mean that the magazines continue to meet current needs, so research must be ongoing. In 1998, during some focus groups, a phrase emerged that has stuck as part of the evolving magazine for parents. The phrase is "down-on-the-floor moms and dads," referring to parents who routinely get down on the floor to engage deeply in activities with their children. Connecting with these "down-on-the-floor" parents, who want to create a rich childhood for their kids and who seek out rich information resources, is a key function of print research at CTW. Identifying who the reader is and what the reader needs to know will be perpetual research questions in the new millennium.

ACKNOWLEDGMENTS

The author thanks the following members of the staff of the Children's Television Workshop whose expertise in producing print creates the magazines and the books: Anna Jane Hays, former Vice President, Books; Rebecca Herman, Editor of *Sesame Street Magazine*; Susan Lapinski, Editor of *Sesame Street Parents*; Ira Wolfman, Vice President and Editorial Director, Magazines; and Nina Link, former Group President, Publishing and New Media.

REFERENCES

Brenner, A., & Freck, M. (1979). *Sesame Street Magazine skills research* (unpublished research report). New York: Children's Television Workshop.

Cherow-O'Leary, R. (1991). *Parents' Guide reader poll: "Raising Kids in a Changing World"* (unpublished research report). New York: Children's Television Workshop.

CTW Magazine Research Department. (1985). *SSM focus group testing with parents* (unpublished research report). New York: Children's Television Workshop.

CTW Magazine Research Department. (1990). *Sesame Street Magazine and Sesame Street Parent's Guide subscriber survey* (unpublished research report). New York: Children's Television Workshop.

CTW Magazine Research Department. (1992). *Prepublication testing of "Connect the Dots Cake" and "Two-Way Pictures"* (unpublished research report). New York: Children's Television Workshop.

CTW Magazine Research Department. (1993). *Sesame Street game study* (unpublished research report). New York: Children's Television Workshop.

CTW Program Research School-Age Team. (1998). *Magazine research: What we've learned* (unpublished research report). New York: Children's Television Workshop.

Kirk, G., & Bernstein, L. (1975, March). *Sesame Street Magazine research report* (unpublished research report). New York: Children's Television Workshop.

Kozak, N. (1971). *"Counting Trees"* (unpublished research report). New York: Children's Television Workshop.

Link, N. (1981, March). *Sesame Street Parents' Newsletter, 1*(1).

Song, C. (1992). *Sesame Street Magazine redesign phone survey* (unpublished research report). New York: Children's Television Workshop.

12 Interactive Technologies Research at Children's Television Workshop

Glenda L. Revelle
University of Maryland Institute for Advanced Computer Studies

Lisa Medoff
Children's Television Workshop

Erik F. Strommen
Microsoft Corporation

About 10 years after the original *Sesame Street* experiment began, Children's Television Workshop (CTW) decided to push the experiment into the exciting and adventure-filled (but sometimes treacherous) waters of new technologies. In 1979, CTW began planning its theme-park, Sesame Place, and one of the features of the park was a Computer Gallery. CTW formed a small in-house team that developed approximately 55 computer programs for the Gallery, and this team has evolved over the years into what is today the Interactive Technologies division of CTW.

Today the Interactive group has a full-time staff of approximately 35, with additional freelance staff on a project-specific basis. The expertise of the Interactive group covers a wide range of disciplines, including interactive design, curriculum development, script writing, art and animation, sound design, computer programming, production management, research, and marketing. In the mid-1990s, CTW added a second team to create interactive materials to be used online.

CTW's interactive product line currently offers almost two dozen *Sesame Street* titles, in formats ranging from CD-ROM to Sony Playstation, Nintendo 64, and Color Gameboy (Table 12.1), plus Internet-based activities. These *Sesame Street* interactive products are designed for children ages 2 to 6

TABLE 12.1
Sesame Street **Interactive Product Line, 1999**

Title	Format	Publisher
Sesame Street Baby and Me	CD-ROM	The Learning Co.
Sesame Street Toddlers Deluxe:		
Numbers and Letters	CD-ROM	The Learning Co.
Art Workshop	CD-ROM	The Learning Co.
Elmo's Preschool Deluxe:		
Elmo's Preschool	CD-ROM	The Learning Co.
Search & Learn Adventures	CD-ROM	The Learning Co.
Get Set for Kindergarten:		
Get Set to Learn	CD-ROM	The Learning Co.
Let's Make a Word	CD-ROM	The Learning Co.
Reading is Fun, Toddler:		
The Three Grouchketeers	CD-ROM	The Learning Co.
Grover's Travels	CD-ROM	The Learning Co.
Elmo's Reading, Preschool and Kindergarten:		
Get Set to Read	CD-ROM	The Learning Co.
Elmo Through the Looking Glass	CD-ROM	The Learning Co.
Sesame Street Music Maker	CD-ROM	The Learning Co.
Elmo in Grouchland	CD-ROM	The Learning Co.
Create and Draw in Elmo's World	CD-ROM	The Learning Co.
Elmo's Letter Adventure	Sony Playstation	NewKidCo
Elmo's Number Journey	Sony Playstation	NewKidCo
Elmo in Grouchland	Sony Playstation	NewKidCo
Elmo's Letter Adventure	Nintendo 64	NewKidCo
Elmo's Number Journey	Nintendo 64	NewKidCo
Elmo's ABC's	Color Gameboy	NewKidCo
Elmo's 123's	Color Gameboy	NewKidCo
Elmo in Grouchland	Color Gameboy	NewKidCo

years old and are based on the characters and curriculum goals of the *Sesame Street* television show. They cover a very diverse set of content areas, ranging from traditional academic skills to creativity and social skills.

The role of research in the development of interactive products through the years has previously been described by Leona Schauble (1990), the Interactive group's first Research Director, and by Erik Strommen and Glenda Revelle (1990), each of whom has also served as Research Director for the group. To summarize briefly, research in Interactive Technologies at CTW has always served the goal of informing the product development process; that is, to help ensure the creation of the most usable, comprehensible, enjoyable, and educational interactive products possible.

These goals are in many ways similar to the goals of *Sesame Street*'s television research (cf., Fisch, 1998). However, as Schauble (1990) pointed out, there are some key differences between television and interactive media that put an even heavier burden on interactive research. The most important distinction in this regard is the fact that television programming is linear whereas computer software is interactive. If a child fails to understand a particular television segment, the program keeps going and in most cases the child simply begins understanding the show again at a later point. When using computer software, however, the child's understanding and engagement is critical at every point in the experience. If the child doesn't understand what to do next or loses interest at any point, the interaction stops.

Because computer software is under the user's control, the user must understand what to do and how to do it if the experience is even to continue, let alone progress. In addition, computer software usage requires (whereas television viewing does not) that the child is physically and cognitively able to execute the required responses, an area of research commonly known as *usability research*. Thus, the role of research in the software development process is crucial, not only to ensure that children in the target age group understand what to do and how to do it, but even more fundamentally, to confirm that the software's demands are not beyond the developing child's capabilities.

Researchers inform the interactive product development process in a variety of different ways. These include: (a) reviewing relevant academic theory or research literature, (b) conducting basic research to address general issues related to children's use of computers, (c) participating as a member of the interactive design team, (d) conducting formative research to address product-specific concerns during each product's development cycle, and (e) reviewing summative research regarding the effects of various kinds of computer experiences on children's learning. We discuss each of these research functions in turn.

REVIEWING RESEARCH LITERATURE

Academic research on user-computer interaction is a relatively young field, with reports of pioneering work having only started to become widely available in the mid-1980s (e.g., Card, Moran, & Newell, 1983; Norman & Draper, 1986; Nickerson, 1986), and almost all of this early work was focused on adults. The earliest research on children's computer use was generally focused on the issues involved in integrating the computer into the classroom environment (e.g., Shade, Nida, Lipinski, & Watson, 1986), although such studies did occasionally yield incidental information about the nature of children's computer interactions. There have been a handful of studies reported over the years that have focused specifically on young children's computer interactions (e.g., Grover, 1986; Silvern, Williamson, & Countermine, 1988; Liu, 1996; Jones & Liu, 1997), but these typically have been very small-scale exploratory studies. Nevertheless, the research team at CTW works to keep abreast of whatever relevant research has been reported, and updates the development team whenever useful, generalizable information is found.

There has been a growing body of research relating to children's ability to use a variety of computer input devices, including the mouse, keyboard, touch screen, and so on (e.g., Char, 1990; Crook, 1992; King & Alloway, 1993; Lane & Ziviani, 1997). It is in this context that CTW's Interactive group has done most of its own basic research, as discussed in the next section.

CONDUCTING BASIC RESEARCH

Computer interfaces, the system of hardware and software used to access and interact with a computer, have changed radically during the lifespan of CTW Interactive. In the late 1970s, users had to indicate their program choices by typing the number on the keyboard associated with an item they selected from a text menu. After several years, during which a variety of interfaces for making onscreen selections were developed (e.g., use of arrow keys on the keyboard, a joystick or a trackball to move a cursor on a graphical display), the computer industry adopted the now-universal "point and click" graphical user-interface model, using the now-standard mouse as the input device to control the interactions. As each of the alternatives that predated the mouse was introduced, there was meager if any research to guide our implementation or adaptation of such technologies to an interface for young children. Thus, interface use by young children became the primary focus of our basic research program in Interactive Technologies at CTW.

In our first study (Revelle, Strommen, & Offerman, 1990), we examined the performance of 3- and 4-year-old children using six different input devices to move a cursor on the screen: keyboard arrow keys, a touch screen, a light pen, a joystick, a trackball, and a mouse. The results indicated that the light pen and touch screen were easiest for children to use, followed by the mouse and trackball. The arrow keys and joystick proved to be the most difficult devices for young children to control. Unfortunately, light pens and touch screens were not then—and still are not—readily available to young children using computers in their homes, so we focused our subsequent efforts on the devices most widely available in homes and schools: the joystick, the trackball, and especially the mouse.

Having examined the relative ease of children's initial use of these devices, we subsequently looked at the effects of practice on children's ability to use these three computer input devices (Revelle & Strommen, 1990). In this study, we tested 3-year-olds with either a joystick, a trackball, or a mouse once each day for 5 days and measured their accuracy and speed in moving the cursor and selecting onscreen objects.

For all three devices, children became significantly faster at making object selections over the course of the five sessions. However, children using the trackball and the mouse were faster than those using the joystick, both initially and after practice. More interesting, children using the mouse made more errors on Day 1 than children using the other two devices, but by Day 5 mouse errors had decreased into the same range as the trackball and were lower than those for the joystick. A qualitative analysis of the mouse errors of these first-time users, and an examination of what accounted for improvement over the 5-day period, enabled us to create a parent-directed section of "Mouse Tips" in our software products, designed to equip parents to help their young children learn how to use the mouse.

Continuing this line of research, we conducted a much more thorough examination of young children's ability to move a cursor and select target objects on-screen using either a joystick, a trackball, or a mouse (Strommen, Revelle, Medoff, & Razavi, 1996). In this study we not only examined general measures such as task completion time and errors, but also analyzed the elements of effective input device use. Component measures included the time to first contact with the "hotspot" (i.e., the target object that users need to click on), number of contacts with the hotspot before it was selected (which is a measure of "overshooting," a situation in which the user moves the cursor over the target hotspot and beyond, unable stop the cursor in time), amount of time cursor was "out-of-bounds" (i.e., stuck against the borders of the screen or moving away from target areas), and so on.

Children's performance with joysticks was found to be fast but error-prone, whereas trackball and mouse use was both slower and more accurate. In comparing trackball and mouse performance, it became clear that the trackball was the ideal input device for young children first learning to use a "point and click" interface. From the very first day of use, children were able to use the trackball with the most precision and control of any of the devices. Those using the trackball engaged in the least "overshooting" and the least time with the cursor "out-of-bounds." Although children using the joystick and the mouse did improve on these measures over the 5-day learning period, the relative rank of the three devices on these control measures did not change, leaving the trackball as the best device for young children overall.

There are a number of reasons why the trackball is the easiest input device for very young, novice users to control. First, with the mouse and the trackball there is a much more direct relationship between the physical movement of the user's hand and the way the cursor moves on the screen than there is with the joystick. With the mouse and trackball, as the child moves his or her hand up, down, left, or right the cursor moves in the same direction, in increments that are proportional to the amount of hand movement.

In addition, when the child's hand stops moving, the cursor stops as well. In contrast, when using a joystick, the user must *stop* moving his/her hand

and hold the joystick stationary in one position to keep the cursor moving in that direction, and then *move* the joystick to a different position to make the cursor stop.

The superiority of the trackball over the mouse can be accounted for in large part by one crucial design difference between the two devices: the trackball housing is stationary, and the trackball and buttons are fixed separately within this housing. This makes moving the cursor (rolling the ball) a distinct action from hotspot selection (pressing the button). In contrast, the entire mouse must be moved, which causes children to experience difficulty keeping the mouse in the proper *orientation* with relation to their bodies and the screen. They tend to point the mouse in different directions as if driving a toy car around the desk, rather than keeping it in a "straight-ahead" orientation under their hands. In addition, when children want to move the cursor all the way across the screen, for example, their natural tendency is to simply keep the mouse in contact with the mouse pad or desk top, moving it continuously in one direction until it falls off the edge of the desk, or runs into the computer. The idea of moving the mouse in one direction, picking it up, repositioning it back in the other direction, and then moving some more is not at all intuitive to children and must be learned. Furthermore, children have trouble keeping the mouse still while pressing its button to register a response, and often move the cursor off the target hotspot unintentionally while trying to click to select it. This problem is, in part, due to the size of the mouse in relation to the size of the average preschooler's hand. The typical mouse is much too large to fit comfortably under a preschooler's hand, making it extremely difficult to reach the buttons without lifting the hand and inadvertently moving the entire unit.

The results of this research were used to inform the development of a new input device for children, created by CTW's Interactive group and Philips Electronics. A specialized trackball called the "Roller Controller" was marketed by Philips as a children's input device for their CD-I system, an interactive entertainment unit that was designed to be used with a television set. Research helped the design team learn that the "Roller Controller" needed to be larger than a traditional computer trackball, and housed in a bigger base, for two reasons: (a) to enable children to use large motor movements rather than fine motor precision to control it, and (b) because it would be used on the floor or a lap rather than on a stable desktop. In addition, the research suggested that several specific features, including handles and rubber strips on the bottom, would be needed to help children keep the device stable and oriented properly (Strommen, 1992).

THE ROLE OF RESEARCH IN PRODUCT DESIGN

The development process for interactive products involves a heavily team-oriented, interdisciplinary approach. During the earliest stages of the process (concept development and design), the researcher serves as an integral member of the design team, with the primary role of serving as an advocate of the child's point of view. A good researcher has a solid understanding of the general level of cognitive development and specific skills children in each age range are likely to bring to an interactive task, and contributes this knowledge to the design process. As potential concepts and ideas are discussed throughout the brainstorming process, the researcher provides feedback on likely appeal, developmental appropriateness, usability concerns, and so on.

The researcher's role is especially central to developing the curriculum goals for the product and structuring multiple levels of difficulty for the product's activities. It is our goal, as often as possible, to provide added challenge in the more advanced levels of an activity by increasing the level of the cognitive skills necessary to solve the problem, rather than simply increasing the demands on manual dexterity, eye–hand coordination, or other psychomotor skills. The challenges presented to the child are automatically increased or decreased in difficulty based on the child's performance.

For example, a recent activity focusing on size relationships was structured to present four levels of difficulty. In the first level, children are asked to select either the longer or shorter of two objects, with a big discrepancy in size between the two objects. If the child succeeds three times in a row at this task, he or she is moved to the second level, in which the child must choose the longest or shortest of three, with smaller size discrepancies among the objects in the set. If the child keeps succeeding, the third level then presents four objects, still requiring selection of the longest or shortest, but with relationally-worded instructions, as in "Find the sock that's shorter than the brown one." Finally, if successful at Level 3, the child is moved to Level 4, which requires the most difficult relational understanding of all (e.g., "Find the car that's longer than the green one, but shorter than the yellow one," still from a group of four objects). If at any point in this progression the child makes occasional errors, the level remains the same rather than advancing. If the child makes consistent errors, the task difficulty is decreased back to the previous level. Researchers play a primary role on the design team in structuring levels of task difficulty and determining rules for evaluating a child's performance and adjusting the task accordingly.

The researcher is also instrumental in developing hint structures to be employed when a child makes an error. Rather than simply informing the child that an answer is wrong, we create a series of hints to help "scaffold" the child into succeeding with the problem. (See Wood, Bruner, & Ross, 1976, and Vygotsky, 1978 for the theory behind scaffolding as an educational strategy; see Jackson, Krajcik, & Soloway, 1998 for an excellent example of scaffolding theory applied to educational software for older children.) These hints take the form of multiple levels of further information that can be revealed to the child to help bring the problem to a level that the child is capable of solving. For example, if Big Bird asks the child to find a triangle and the child selects something other than a triangle, Big Bird's first hint might be, "Find a triangle—it has three sides." If the child still has trouble, the next hint could be "Find a triangle—it's shaped like a piece of pizza," and so on. Based on their knowledge of child development and on formative testing with children (which is described in the next section), researchers help the design team structure these successive hints in such a way that the child is given only as much support as he or she needs to succeed.

Finally, researchers play a crucial role in determining the wording of instructions and feedback dialogue, in order to help the design team communicate as effectively as possible with children in the target age range (see Strommen, 1991, for a summary of the issues and some general guidelines for using speech in preschool software). The team typically starts by creating placeholder dialogue for all the characters in the product. Then, based on feedback from formative testing sessions (as described in the next section), revisions are made to instructional and feedback dialogue before it is actually recorded for the final product.

CONDUCTING FORMATIVE RESEARCH

Research on CD-ROM and Videogames

During the design phase of each product's development, the researcher begins to develop a formative research plan for the project. Formative research involves testing different versions of a product with children during the product's development cycle. There are usually several stages of formative research.

Research may begin by testing either competitive products that are already on the market or existing products that share specific features with the one being planned. For example, if the researcher or design team has concerns about the use of certain features with the target age group (e.g., pull-down menus, scrolling backgrounds), products that have those capabilities can be tested with children to determine whether they can understand and use such features. In this way, the early formative research provides a context for developing the product, based on what has already been seen to be successful (or unsuccessful) with children in the target age range.

Another common early step is "paper testing" of certain concepts with the target age group before any software prototypes have even been created. For example, when creating an activity in which children were asked to identify and respond to Elmo's emotions, the research team showed children paper sketches of Elmo expressing a variety of emotions (Strommen & Medoff, 1995). The goal of this research was to determine which features (e.g., body posture, mouth shape, eyebrow positioning, etc.) children were most responsive to in interpreting emotion as conveyed by Elmo, so that the computer animators could be directed as to the most effective ways to convey Elmo's emotions to young children in the final product.

Once production of the game is underway, the production team creates a series of product prototypes that implement various product features in an unfinished but usable form, analogous to creating a rough draft of a document. Researchers then take the software prototypes out and observe children using them. This kind of testing typically takes place in a preschool or day-care setting, and children are taken out of the classroom one at a time to use the product with the researcher. Researchers observe children playing the activities, noting the kinds of things that cause problems, anything that children ask questions about, and so on. Often these sessions are videotaped to allow further analysis later. Based on these formative research sessions, researchers evaluate appeal, usability, and comprehension, and provide feedback to the production team so that any necessary revisions and changes can be made before the product is completed.

Through the years, CTW's Interactive research team has conducted formative research on a wide range of *Sesame Street* activities in both computer software formats (e.g., Medoff, 1997a, 1997b; Strommen, 1991) and videogame formats (e.g., Medoff, 1998a; Strommen, 1993; Strommen, Razavi, & Medoff, 1992). Some of the testing involves general issues that must be addressed in almost all products. For example, most products require some research feedback to help fine-tune hotspot size and placement, to ensure that hotspots are large enough for children to successfully stop on without overshooting, yet far enough apart that children do not inadvertently click one when aiming for another (cf. Medoff, 1997b, 1998a, 1999b). In addition, instructional dialogue often requires tweaking to ensure children's optimal understanding (cf. Medoff, 1997a, 1998b, 1999a).

In other cases, formative research addresses issues that are very specific to the nature of the activities being designed in a particular product. In a recent reading product, for example, an activity was planned that was relatively sophisticated for the preschool age group, but very similar in kind to activities children are expected to complete when they reach kindergarten or first grade. To complete the task successfully, children had to choose the correct word or picture from the bottom of the screen to complete a sentence displayed in the middle of the screen, and in order to determine which of the options was correct, children needed to look at a scene displayed on the top portion of the screen. Formative research (Medoff, 1998b) was essential in helping to develop a method for effectively guiding children through the steps involved in completing this activity. For example, based on the formative data, the interface was revised so that children could click on Elmo to have him reread the sentence at any given time. In addition, revisions were made so that Elmo would direct children's attention by pointing to the relevant portions of the screen and asking questions when appropriate. To complete the sentence "The hat is on the ___," for example, Elmo would first read the sentence, ask "Where is the hat?" and point to the picture, then point at the pool of possible answers at the bottom of the screen while asking children to find the correct answer.

Research on Online Activities

In 1992, CTW explored another new frontier with the debut of its initial online venture, *Sesame Street on Prodigy*. CTW continued to experiment with online possibilities and conduct research and development work until 1998, when the "CTW Family Workshop" (*www.ctw.org* or *www.sesamestreet.com*) was launched. The Internet environment provides a means of reaching an increasing number of families directly. A 1998 survey found that 43% of U.S. households currently have online access, including 18% of children aged 2 to 12 years old for a total of 7.9 million children, and this number continues to grow (Jupiter Communications, 1998).

The CTW Family Workshop is aimed at the entire family, with material targeted specifically at preschool children, school-age children, and parents. Because this book is focused on *Sesame Street*, however, this chapter only covers the preschool section of the service, which is designed for young children and their parents to use together.

Many of the *Sesame Street* online activities are similar in kind to activities that could be delivered via CD-ROM (on-screen puzzles, interactive stories, letter and number games, etc.), but others take advantage of the unique characteristics of the Internet. It is challenging to design such activities for preschoolers, because many of the Internet's defining features (communities based on common interests, multiplayer games, news, and other time-sensitive information) are beyond the abilities or interests of such young children. CTW's Interactive designers try, whenever possible, to create "junior versions" of these kinds of interactions specifically for preschoolers.

One such example is the "*Sesame Street* Post Office," an activity in which children can send questions via e-mail to their favorite *Sesame Street* Muppets and receive responses the next day. Because preschool children typically are not capable of writing or typing, users choose a Muppet from a set of pictures and then choose questions to ask from a list tailored to that Muppet. When the Muppet responds, he or she also asks the child a question, furthering the exchange. For example, if a child's e-mail asks Ernie whether he likes bath time, Ernie responds that he *loves* bath time, and asks whether the child prefers playing with a rubber duckie, sailing a toy boat, or splashing in bubbles. Depending on the child's choice, an appropriate picture is displayed (e.g., a picture of Ernie playing with his rubber duckie in the bathtub). In this way, the activity introduces children to letter-writing and models the exchange of messages that e-mail entails.

Formative research in the online area plays much the same role as has been described for other interactive products, to ensure that activities are age-appropriate in terms of usability, curricular content, and appeal. During the early stages of development of the "*Sesame Street* Post Office," for example, researchers pointed out that preschool children have little (if any) prior experience sending e-mail—or, indeed, composing letters at all. It was recommended that the activity be made more concrete by displaying the child's message before it was sent, so that children could see how their choices led to a completed letter. Researchers also suggested beginning the mock e-mail with "Dear [Name of Muppet]" and ending it with "Your friend, [Name of child]," to introduce children subtly to the conventions of letter-writing (Fisch, Sekigahama, & Shulman, 1999).

The focus on joint use by parents and children carries implications not only for the design of the material, but for the way formative research is conducted as well. In some cases, testing is conducted with parent–child pairs, as in the case of formative research for "My Page About Me" (CTW Program Research, 1998). In this activity, children are given the opportunity to describe themselves by building their own simple Web page that can be printed out or sent to friends and family via e-mail. Testing of an early prototype of this activity, conducted with parent–child pairs, suggested several revisions that made the interface easier to use (e.g., allowing users to remove people from a representation of their family individually, rather than simply erasing the entire group). At the same time, it identified the true educational value of the activity as providing a springboard for offline communication between parents and children as children reflected on themselves and the immediate world around them.

In other cases, researchers work with children alone to establish how much the children can do on their own and determine the amount of support they are likely to need from an adult. This type of research informed the creation of "Make-a-Story," an activity enabling preschool children to create their own *Sesame Street* storybooks. Children construct their stories by selecting pictures to insert into a background illustration, and differential story text appears depending on the child's choices. For example, one story begins with Grover standing on a beach near the water. If the child places the sun in the scene, the following text will start the story: "Oh boy, it is a such a beautiful day here at the beach." If, however, the child moves clouds into the scene, the story begins with this line instead: "It is cloudy today, but I, Grover, will still have fun at the beach." Children can also produce differences in story text based on where they place objects within an illustration; for example, putting a sandwich in Grover's hand produces "All this building is making me hungry. I will eat my sandwich for a little snack," while placing it on the ground results in "That sandwich must be awfully sandy. I do not like sandy sandwiches."

While the "Make-a-Story" activity was being built, one page of a prototype story was tested with a sample of 3- and 4-year-old children (Medoff, 1998c). Data showed that the appeal of the activity was relatively high; children were fascinated by the fact that, depending on their placement of the pictures, different things would happen. Children were frustrated, however, because they couldn't place pictures wherever they liked, but only within designated regions of the illustration. In addition, formative research uncovered the fact that richly detailed background illustrations made it difficult for children to differentiate the foreground objects they had placed, and interfered with children's understanding of the results of their actions. In response to these findings, the product was modified to include simpler backgrounds, and to enable children to place objects anywhere on the backgrounds.

Finally, it is important to note that although the above examples concern the testing of early prototypes, formative research on online materials need not be limited to the prototype stage. One of the strengths of online—and one that separates it from most of the other media discussed in this book—is the fact that such research can continue to have an impact even beyond the development period. When producing educational materials in most media (e.g., television, magazines, CD-ROM), changes can be made up to a certain point in the production process, but once the materials have been delivered to the audience, they can no longer be changed easily or frequently. By contrast, the nature of online is such that even after a product has been delivered and is already being used by its audience, research can continue because change is still possible. Thanks to this additional level of flexibility, the material can continue to evolve, to become as educationally effective, appealing, and usable as possible.

REVIEWING SUMMATIVE RESEARCH

Traditionally, the educational impact of any kind of product or intervention on learners has been assessed through summative research, which examines children's knowledge or understanding of the topics addressed in the product. Summative studies usually either compare the learner's knowledge level before and after the intervention, or compare the knowledge level of children who have used the product with those who have not. Although CTW's Interactive group has not had the resources to conduct summative research when its products are finished, the research team does keep abreast of any relevant findings that are reported in the academic literature and apply them to the design of CTW's interactive products when possible.

For example, in the late 1990s, there has been mounting evidence that computer software can help young children in the process of learning to read, especially children who haven't been read to much at home (Johnston, 1997; Talley, Lancy, & Lee, 1997). There is also some evidence that using computers may help children as young as 3 years old with some aspects of learning to write, particularly spelling and story writing (Moxley, Warash, Coffman, Brinton, Concannon, 1997).

Moreover, and of even more interest from a software development point of view, Shute and Miksad (1997) found that certain features of software programs could be isolated that increased young children's general cognitive skill levels more than use of software programs without those features. Shute and Miksad's study examined the impact of using counting and word knowledge software activities on preschoolers' cognitive development. Specifically, they compared the effects of software designed to include a high degree of scaffolding (modeling, prompting, and clues where needed) with software providing minimal scaffolding. After children had used the software for a period of 8 weeks, those using the "high-scaffolding" software had significantly greater gains in both general cognitive development and verbal skills when compared to the "low-scaffolding" group. Part of the job of a researcher is to bring new information of this sort back to the Interactive development team, so that whenever possible it can be used to inform the design of the group's new products.

IMPLICATIONS OF TECHNOLOGICAL ADVANCES

Over the 20-year life of interactive work at CTW, there have been tremendous changes in the capabilities of computers that are accessible to children in their homes and in schools. Hardware and software conventions for user interfaces to computer software have changed radically in the past two decades. Developments in video display technology, processor speed, memory, storage device size, and so on have also had a big impact on the design of interactive products.

These advances have enabled us to progress, for example, from blocky, color-challenged, robotic versions of the *Sesame Street* Muppet characters to fully animated, life-like characters that are now much better able to convey the personalities children know from the television show. Improvements in audio capabilities have been even more dramatic, allowing us to advance from relying solely on primitive blips and beeps for user-feedback to having the full capabilities of CD-quality audio with which to implement instructions, feedback, and musical scores.

These technological developments have improved our ability to design high-quality educational products for preschoolers tremendously. Although good interactive design and a solid educational approach are essential to engaging children regardless of the level of production values, it is also true that more sophisticated audio and video capabilities lead to higher entertainment and engagement and, as a result, higher attention and potentially higher learning (e.g., Chen, 1997). More important, the technological advances have enabled us to do a variety of things that are critical to usability and comprehension by young children that we simply couldn't do before, such as spoken instructions rather than text instructions for prereaders, graphical menus instead of text menus, and so on.

Ironically, these huge technology advances have also increased the challenge we face in designing for this age group. The availability of audio for instructions, complex navigational possibilities, 3-D worlds, and so on have dramatically increased the educational and entertainment potential of the medium. However, the same advances have simultaneously intensified the need for research to help ensure that the increasing complexity of the interactive experience does not distract children and prevent them from understanding, using, enjoying, and learning from it.

The one thing that is certain in the world of interactive technology is that technical capabilities will always continue to evolve and develop, and there will be a continual progression toward more and more sophisticated technologies becoming available at lower and lower prices. It appears that DVDs will become widely available to consumers in the immediate future, enabling the integration of high-resolution, full screen, full-motion video into interactive products. This innovation is simply an example of the many future technological developments we can anticipate.

Although it is impossible to guess exactly what the innovations might be or when they will be made, we can be sure that there will always be new capabilities presenting new and unique design challenges for developers of interactive applications. Thus the role of research, to determine how each new capability can be most effectively utilized in educational products for children, is secure for quite some time to come.

REFERENCES

Card, S. K., Moran, T. P., & Newell, A. (1983). *The psychology of human-computer interaction*. Hillsdale, NJ: Lawrence Erlbaum Associates.

Char, C. (1990, March). *Touch, click, or jump? The relative merits of different input devices for use by young children*. Paper presented at the annual meeting of the American Educational Research Association, Boston, MA.

Chen, L. C. (1997). The effects of color and background information in motion visuals on children's memory and comprehension. In *Proceedings of selected research and development presentations, AECT '97*, (pp. 429–440). Albuquerque, NM: Association for Educational Communications and Technology.

Crook, C. (1992). Young children's skill using a mouse to control a graphical computer interface. *Computers and Education, 19*(3), 199–207.

CTW Program Research. (1998). *"My Page About Me" Prototype Test* (unpublished research report). New York: Children's Television Workshop.

Fisch, S. M. (1998). The Children's Television Workshop: The experiment continues. In R. G. Noll & M. E. Price (Eds.), *A communications cornucopia: Markle Foundation essays on information policy* (pp. 297–336). Washington, DC: The Brookings Institution Press.

Fisch, S. M., Sekigahama, L. M., & Shulman, J. S. (1999, May). *Sesame Street* and the information superhighway: Using the Internet to encourage communication and self-expression among preschool children. In S. M. Fisch (Chair), *Using mass media to encourage children's communication: Lessons from Sesame Street and Ghostwriter*. Symposium presented at the annual meeting of the International Communication Association, San Francisco, CA.

Grover, S. C. (1986). A field study of the use of cognitive-developmental principles in micro-computer design for young children. *Journal of Educational Research, 79*, 325–332.

Jackson, S. L., Krajcik, J., & Soloway, E. (1998). The design of guided learner-adaptable scaffolding in interactive learning environments. In *Proceedings of CHI'98* (pp. 187–194). New York: ACM/SIGCHI.

Johnston, C. B. (1997). Interactive storybook software: Effects on verbal development in kindergarten children. *Early Child Development and Care, 132*, 33–44.

Jones, M., & Liu, M. (1997). Introducing interactive multimedia to young children: A case study of how two-year-olds interact with technology. *Journal of Computing in Childhood Education, 8*(4), 313–343.

Jupiter Communications (1998, Fall). Presentation to Children's Television Workshop.

King, J., & Alloway, N. (1993). Young children's use of microcomputer input devices. *Computers in the Schools, 9*(4), 39–53.

Lane, A., & Ziviani, J. (1997). The suitability of the mouse for children's use: A review of the literature. *Journal of Computing in Childhood Education, 8*(2/3), 227–245.

Liu, M. (1996). An exploratory study of how pre-kindergarten children use interactive multimedia technology: Implications for multimedia software design. *Journal of Computing in Childhood Education, 7*(1/2), 71–92.

Medoff, L. (1997a). *Elmo Through the Looking Glass: Matching game formative testing* (unpublished research report). New York: Children's Television Workshop.

Medoff, L. (1997b). *Get Set to Read: Super-Grover game formative testing* (unpublished research report). New York: Children's Television Workshop.

Medoff, L. (1998a). *Elmo's Letter Adventure: Playstation formative testing, round 1* (unpublished research report). New York: Children's Television Workshop.

Medoff, L. (1998b). *Get Set to Read: Elmo's Wild Kingdom formative testing* (unpublished research report). New York: Children's Television Workshop.

Medoff, L. (1998c). *"Make-a-Story" formative study* (unpublished research report). New York: Children's Television Workshop.

Medoff, L. (1999a). *The Adventures of Elmo in Grouchland: Coal mine game formative testing* (unpublished research report).New York: Children's Television Workshop.

Medoff, L. (1999b). *Create and Draw in Elmo's World: First formative testing* (unpublished research report). New York: Children's Television Workshop.

Moxley, R. A., Warash, B., Coffman, G., Brinton, K., & Concannon, K. R. (1997). Writing development using computers in a class of three-year-olds. *Journal of Computing in Childhood Education, 8*(2/3), 133–164.

Nickerson, R. S. (1986). *Using computers: Human factors in information systems.* Cambridge, MA: MIT Press.

Norman, D. A., & Draper, S. W. (Eds.). (1986). *User-centered system design.* Hillsdale, NJ: Lawrence Erlbaum Associates.

Revelle, G. L., & Strommen, E. F. (1990). The effects of practice and input device used on young children's computer control. *Journal of Computing in Childhood Education, 2*(1), 33–41.

Revelle, G. L., Strommen, E. F., & Offerman, S. (1990). Cursor and device differences in children's computer control (unpublished research report). New York: Children's Television Workshop.

Schauble, L. (1990). Formative evaluation in the design of educational software at the Children's Television Workshop. In B. N. Flagg (Ed.), *Formative evaluation for educational technologies* (pp. 51–66). Hillsdale, NJ: Lawrence Erlbaum Associates.

Shade, D. D., Nida, R. E., Lipinski, J. M., & Watson, J. A. (1986). Micro-computers and preschoolers: Working together in a classroom setting. *Computers in the Schools, 3*(2), 53–61.

Shute, R., & Miksad, J. (1997). Computer assisted instruction and cognitive development in preschoolers. *Child Study Journal, 27*(3), 237–253.

Silvern, S. B., Williamson, P. A., & Countermine, T. M. (1988). Young children's interaction with a microcomputer. *Early Childhood Development and Care, 21,* 23–35.

Strommen, E. F. (1991). "What did he say?": Speech output in preschool software. In S. Gayle (Ed.), *Proceedings of NECC '91* (pp. 149–151). Eugene, OR: International Society for Technology in Education.

Strommen, E. F. (1992). Formative studies in the development of a new computer pointing device for young children. *Educational Technology, 32*(4), 43–51.

Strommen, E. F. (1993). Is it easier to hop or walk? Developmental issues in interface design. *Human-Computer Interaction, 8,* 337–352.

Strommen, E. F., & Medoff, L. (1995). *Elmo's Preschool: Face room formative study* (unpublished research report). New York: Children's Television Workshop.

Strommen, E. F., Razavi, S., & Medoff, L. M. (1992). This button makes you go up: Three year olds and the Nintendo controller. *Applied Ergonomics, 23,* 409–413.

Strommen, E. F., & Revelle, G. L. (1990). Research in interactive technologies at Children's Television Workshop. *Educational Technology Research and Development, 38*(4), 65–80.

Strommen, E. F., Revelle, G. L., Medoff, L., & Razavi, S. (1996). Slow and steady wins the race? Three-year-old children and pointing device use. *Behaviour and Information Technology, 15*(1), 57–64.

Talley, S., Lancy, D. F., & Lee, T. R. (1997). Children, storybooks, and computers. *Reading Horizons, 38*(2), 116–128.

Vygotsky, L. S. (1978). *Mind in society: The development of higher psychological processes.* Cambridge, MA: Harvard University Press.

Wood, D., Bruner, J., & Ross, G. (1976) The role of tutoring in problem solving. *Journal of Child Psychology & Psychiatry & Allied Disciplines, 17*(2), 89–100.

IV Conclusion

13 Why Children Learn From *Sesame Street*

Shalom M. Fisch
Rosemarie T. Truglio
Children's Television Workshop

We began this volume with the observation that, since the late 1960s, *Sesame Street* has become the most heavily researched series in the history of television. Formative research has informed the production of both the domestic U.S. version of *Sesame Street* and its many coproductions in other countries (see Cole, Richman, & McCann Brown, chap. 9, this volume; Fisch & Bernstein, chap. 3, this volume; Palmer & Fisch, chap. 1, this volume; Truglio, Lovelace, Seguí, & Scheiner, chap. 4, this volume). In addition, formative research has been instrumental in the creation of *Sesame Street*-based material for magazines, outreach, interactive technology, and many other media (Cherow-O'Leary, chap. 11, this volume; Revelle, Medoff, & Strommen, chap. 12, this volume; Yotive & Fisch, chap. 10, this volume).

At the same time, numerous summative research studies have demonstrated the educational impact of *Sesame Street* on preschool children, both in the United States and around the world. A consistent pattern of significant effects has attested to *Sesame Street*'s impact in academic areas, such as number skills, emergent literacy, and school readiness (see Cole et al., chap. 9, this volume; Mielke, chap. 5, this volume; Wright, Huston, Scantlin, & Kotler, chap. 6, this volume; Zill, chap. 7, this volume). Effects within the domain of social behavior (e.g., promoting cooperation) typically have been less strong and consistent, but significant effects have been found across several independent research studies nevertheless (see Mielke, chap. 5, this volume). Indeed, longitudinal studies have shown the educational impact of *Sesame Street* to continue over a period of years (Wright et al., chap. 5, this volume), and significant differences between the academic performance of preschool *Sesame Street* viewers and nonviewers have appeared as late as high school (Huston, Anderson, Wright, Linebarger, & Schmitt, chap. 8, this volume).

Taken together, this pattern of effects and (where measured) the long-term durability of the effects are striking. The fact that television can be effective in enhancing growth in areas as diverse as (for example) literacy, prosocial behavior, mathematics skills, race relations, and preschoolers' understanding of death is impressive. The fact that all of these effects—and more—have been produced by the same television series is truly remarkable.

Why Do Children Learn From *Sesame Street*?

Having established the fact that children benefit and learn from their exposure to *Sesame Street*, the question that follows naturally is why. Elsewhere, Fisch (2000) has proposed a model to explain some of the processing at work in children's comprehension of educational television. Here, our focus is less on children's mental processing than on the nature of the television series itself: What are the characteristics of *Sesame Street* (and its related ancillary products, such as magazines, outreach materials, and interactive materials) that contribute to its power as an educational tool?

If we examine the pattern of educational effects observed for *Sesame Street* (including significant effects emerging from summative research and smaller-scale comprehension data from formative research), alongside various features of *Sesame Street* itself, several common factors emerge as potentially playing a role in comprehension and learning. Let us consider each of these factors in turn.

A Detailed Curriculum.   One of the characteristics that distinguishes *Sesame Street* from almost every other series on television is its foundation in a comprehensive educational curriculum and the process that surrounds it (Lesser & Schneider, chap. 2, this volume). Even among educational television programs for children, most have been produced without a written curriculum, or with only a broad philosophy or small number of general goals that provide little concrete direction for production. (Notably, apart from a few programs such as *Blue's Clues*, most of the exceptions to this rule are television series that have also been produced by CTW.)

By contrast, the curriculum for *Sesame Street* provides detailed guidance on both the subject areas to be addressed in the series and the specifics of what is to be accomplished within those areas. Regularly-scheduled curriculum seminars bring noted experts to CTW each season to keep the curriculum consistent with current educational theory and practice, and to provide the production team with a greater understanding of the issues that underlie these topics. In-house content and research specialists supply additional resources (e.g., related children's books, accurate information on practices in other cultures, suggestions for science activities) as needed, and review material as it is written and produced. Because all of this information and support is available before and during production, each segment can be created specifically to address a particular goal. And because in-house specialists are available to collaborate closely with producers and writers on an ongoing basis, they can help the production staff (who typically have little, if any, formal background in education themselves) to actualize and convey educational content effectively in the segments that are produced.

Appeal. It seems almost like common sense to posit that the appeal of televised material is likely to play a role in children's comprehension of that material. Because home viewing is almost invariably voluntary, educational television programs must be appealing, or else children will simply choose not to watch them. As David Connell, the first Executive Producer for *Sesame Street*, often said, "You've got to get them into the church before you can preach to them."

Moreover, even when children have already chosen to watch a program, they often engage in multiple activities (e.g., coloring, playing with toys) at the same time as they watch television (Anderson, Field, Collins, Lorch, & Nathan, 1985). Given the presence of these competing activities, it seems reasonable to expect children to pay greater attention to a television program if they find it appealing, and for this greater attention to lead to stronger comprehension. Along similar lines, Fisch and McCann (1993) have argued for appeal as a contributing factor in older children's choice to play along while viewing participatory activities on television as well.

However, the relationship between appeal and comprehension is probably more complex than that. Although appeal does appear to contribute to comprehension, comprehensibility can contribute to attention and appeal as well. For example, Anderson, Lorch, Field, and Sanders (1981) found that English-speaking preschoolers paid greater attention to *Sesame Street* segments when the dialogue was in English than when the segments were dubbed into Greek. In this case, the greater comprehensibility of the English-language segments contributed to their attractiveness, rather than the other way around. (Admittedly, a wholesale change in language is an extreme example of the difference in comprehensibility between two versions of a segment. However, we suspect that a similar principle can be applied even within material produced in English: Children may be turned off by material that is presented at an intellectual level that they are not ready to grasp.)

Together, these data suggest that the relationship between comprehension and appeal is actually reciprocal. The appeal of televised material can help to draw children to the material and lead to greater comprehension. At the same time, the material is more likely to sustain its appeal if it is comprehensible and tailored to the developmental level of its target audience.

Explicitness and "Concreteness." A long research tradition, dating back to researchers such as Piaget and his colleagues (e.g., Inhelder & Piaget, 1958) has shown young children to think concretely and to have difficulty in tasks that require more abstract thinking. To maximize comprehension among preschool children, then, it is important that treatments of educational content on television be both explicit and as concrete as possible. If the treatment of a piece of educational content requires too much background knowledge or too elaborate a series of inferences on the part of the audience, then young children may fail to understand it properly.

For example, formative data showed that after viewing a segment in which Kermit the Frog sang the song "It's Not Easy Being Green," many preschool children failed to recognize that Kermit felt happy about being green by the end of the song (*Sesame Street* Research, 1989). By contrast, comprehension was found to be far stronger for more explicit material produced under *Sesame Street*'s race relations curriculum (see Truglio et al., chap. 4, this volume). Making the messages more explicit and concrete made them more comprehensible to young children as well.

Child-Centered and Child-Relevant Content.

Fisch (2000) has argued that children are better able to process educational content when it is presented in a narrative context that is familiar and meaningful to them than when they must first devote their attention to figuring out the context itself. In other words, to take an absurd example for the sake of illustration, children would be more likely to grasp messages about cooperation in the context of a story about playing on a see-saw than in the context of a story about a joint checking account.

To this end, *Sesame Street* has generally strived to embed educational content in contexts that are both familiar and relevant to children's lives. Familiarity and relevance are affected by both the age-appropriateness of the material (i.e., whether the context is likely to be meaningful for a 3- to 5-year-old child) and the degree to which it is culturally appropriate (i.e., whether the situation is one that is likely to be comparable to real-life situations that a child has experienced within his or her culture; cf. Newcomb & Collins, 1979). The use of such contexts can help tie new material to children's prior knowledge, thus building comprehension of the new material on a foundation of existing knowledge.

This is not to say, of course, that children should never be exposed to new contexts or situations. In fact, one of the strengths of television is that it can introduce children to new places and cultures that they would not otherwise have the opportunity to experience. For example, *Sesame Street* has taken viewers into the homes of children from other cultural and ethnic backgrounds, and even into space with positive results (as discussed by Truglio et al., chap. 4, this volume). However, such material must be particularly explicit in its descriptions and explanations, to compensate for children's lack of prior knowledge in these areas. And even here, it is helpful to draw links to children's own experiences. Thus, for example, the *Sesame Street* race relations segment "Play Date" (in which a White boy visited the home of his African-American friend) emphasized the similarities between their home experiences (e.g., playing videogames) as well as the differences (e.g., the White boy's eating collard greens for the first time). Such commonalities provided a bridge for the White boy (and White viewers at home) to relate their own experiences to those of another culture, and provided an entry for understanding and appreciating the differences.

Repetition and Reinforcement. Because of its magazine format, *Sesame Street* is well positioned to reinforce its educational messages through either repetition of the same segments across a number of episodes or the placement of several different segments that deal with the same topic (e.g., the letter *B*) within a single episode. In fact, the earliest summative research on the impact of *Sesame Street* found that the educational content areas that had received the greatest emphasis within the series also produced the greatest effects on children's learning (Ball & Bogatz, 1970).

Multiple repetition of the same segments can encourage comprehension among viewers in two main ways. First, if children have failed to grasp the segments' educational content during their first viewing, such repetition allows additional opportunities to understand the material (at a point when the material is a little more familiar). Second, if children have begun to grasp a new concept during their first viewing, a second viewing can help to reinforce mastery of the concepts presented.

Comprehension can also be aided by children's viewing several different segments that all address the same underlying educational content. In this case, the same content is presented each time, but in several different contexts. For example, the letter *B* might be presented and labeled in the context of the words *Bed*, *Bath*, and *Bird*, or the concept of cooperation might be presented in several different contexts: sharing a toy, working together to assemble a puzzle, and helping to clean a room. We would argue that over time, seeing the same content presented in multiple contexts may help to encourage generalization; because they have seen these concepts at work in several different contexts, children may become sensitized toward looking for the letter *B* in a variety of words or seeing cooperation as a strategy that can be applied in a variety of social situations (perhaps even words or situations that have not been presented in the segments viewed).

For such reinforcement to be effective, however, two considerations must be taken into account. First, viewers must recognize that the related segments do, in fact, deal with the same content. For example, because (as noted previously) many preschool children failed to recognize Kermit's pride in his skin color in the song "It's Not Easy Being Green," this segment would be unlikely to be highly effective in reinforcing other, more explicit segments about race and ethnicity, simply because many children would miss the connection.

Second, there is the question of how much reinforcement is needed to accomplish the desired purpose. This consideration plays into both the number of related segments that are included within a single episode of *Sesame Street*, and the placement of those segments within the episode. Indeed, even after 30 years of formative research on *Sesame Street*, new studies are still being conducted to address this question. For example, adjustments to the clustering of letters and numbers in *Sesame Street* are still being made to enhance children's learning even further (*Sesame Street* Research & Applied Research & Consulting, 1998; see Truglio et al., chap. 4, this volume).

Modeling and Identification.   At the same time that we consider the substance of the educational content that is conveyed and the ways in which it is conveyed, it is also important to consider *who* is conveying that information. When *Sesame Street* debuted in 1969, it was the first children's television series to feature minority characters among its regular cast. For many children of the time, it was their first opportunity to see people "like them" on television. Indeed, even Sonia Manzano, who has played the part of Maria on *Sesame Street* for approximately 25 years, still recalls being struck by the presence of non-White characters when she first saw *Sesame Street* as a college student.

Even today, when the presence of minorities is more common (although by no means prevalent; cf. Calvert, Stolkin, & Lee, 1997; Gerbner, 1993) on television, there is great value to the use of diverse characters in delivering educational content on *Sesame Street*. Indeed, this value is manifest on three levels simultaneously. First, because research has shown that children sometimes attend more to models who are similar to themselves (as in the case of Luecke-Aleksa, Anderson, Collins, & Schmitt's [1995] research on same-sex models), it seems reasonable to expect that children may attend more to—and learn more from—models who are "like them." Thus, the use of a broad range of characters to deliver educational content may help to maximize the power of that content for the children who, in many cases, need it most.

At the same time, the use of diverse models also holds value on an attitudinal level. When an African-American character is shown, for example, using scientific experimentation to discover something new, the lesson for viewers is not merely the science lesson itself. Because the activity has been driven by an African American, it also shows viewers that African Americans can be confident and successful in pursuing scientific activities. The inclusion of a diverse cast of characters in *Sesame Street* means that a broad audience of children—regardless of race, sex, ethnicity, or physical disability—can find positive role models with whom they can identify (and also sends a positive message to viewers who are not of that particular group).

Finally, on an even broader level, it is important to recognize that all of the characters on *Sesame Street* are shown as enjoying the process of learning. Viewers' exposure to role models who enjoy learning can promote a general love of learning among the viewers themselves, a concept that is consistent with the explanation that Huston et al. (chap. 8, this volume) have proposed for the long-term effects of *Sesame Street*. The inclusion of diverse characters among the *Sesame Street* cast may help to ensure that this love of learning is fostered across physical, ethnic, and cultural boundaries.

Involving Viewers and the Role of Participation.   Finally, it is important to remember that viewers do not passively receive information from television. Rather, they are actively engaged in seeking out information and constructing their own understanding of the material being viewed (e.g., Anderson & Burns, 1991). Thus, if viewers can be encouraged to rehearse, elaborate on, and work with the educational content presented, they may be more likely to recall that content later.

From its very beginnings, *Sesame Street* has attempted to encourage this sort of involvement on the part of its viewers through various means. One means that has been employed is the use of games in which viewers are invited explicitly to participate, such as the classic "One of These Things Is Not Like the Others" (or its successor, "Three of These Things Belong Together"), a matching game in which viewers are asked to decide which of four items are the same or different.[1]

A second means lies in allowing opportunities for children to supply answers before the characters on screen do. A prototypic example from the early days of *Sesame Street* came to be known as the "James Earl Jones Effect." The phenomenon was named for an early segment in which actor James Earl Jones looked directly into the camera and recited the alphabet in a deep, compelling voice. However, each letter appeared next to his head for a moment *before* he named it, allowing viewers the opportunity to not only join in, but even beat the actor to the punch.

A third, related means is the use of characters who hesitate or make mistakes that viewers can correct. When a Muppet character is counting and momentarily forgets the number that comes after six, for example, there is an implicit invitation for viewers to supply the missing number themselves. In this case, supplying the answer may be particularly satisfying because the viewer has been, not only faster, but also "smarter" than the character.

Each of these means has been employed, not only in *Sesame Street*, but also in subsequent preschool television series that place a heavier emphasis on viewer participation, such as Nickelodeon's *Blue's Clues*, Disney's *Out of the Box*, and CTW's *Big Bag* (produced for the Cartoon Network).

Naturally, because much of children's participation during *Sesame Street* is internal, occurring within the mind of the viewer, it is difficult to gauge accurately the degree to which such techniques are successful in encouraging active processing of the educational content among viewers. However, young children's participation is frequently not silent; children often display behaviors such as pointing at or talking to the screen (or to peers, in group viewing situations), all of which can be recorded by observers. Although observational data may miss any active participation that occurs only mentally, observations of children as they watch *Sesame Street* have often shown the series to elicit overt participation among viewers. For example, research on "Elmo's World" found that, while viewing, children responded with behaviors such as counting along with Elmo, imitating actions, and moving to music (*Sesame Street* Research Department, 1999). Moreover, research on the James Earl Jones segment discussed above found that on repeated viewing of the segment, children progressed among three levels of participation. First, they be-

---

[1] "One of These Things Is Not Like the Other" and "Three of These Things Belong Together" are essentially inverse versions of the same game. The name (and accompanying song) were changed because of subtle social cues embedded in the game; in light of *Sesame Street*'s emphasis on social diversity and inclusion, the *Sesame Street* team felt that it was more appropriate to foster a tendency among children to look for similarities rather than differences.

gan reciting the alphabet along with Jones. Next, they began to say the letters before he did. Finally, they began to anticipate the letters and call out letter names even before the letters appeared on screen (Lesser, 1974). Similar results were found, more recently, for a segment in which ballet dancer Angel Corella dances while each letter of the alphabet appears on screen beside him and is labeled (*Sesame Street* Research, 1998).

Ongoing Formative and Summative Research. Last, we must acknowledge the critical role that research plays in the production of *Sesame Street*. *Sesame Street* has always been characterized by a sense of bold experimentation in finding new ways to entertain children and deliver educational content simultaneously. As numerous examples throughout this volume have shown, empirical research has been an integral part of this continual experimentation, by suggesting directions for new approaches, providing an objective gauge of their strengths and weaknesses, and informing revisions that have helped to maximize their effectiveness. Indeed, in many ways, it is difficult to imagine how the process of experimentation would operate without the ability to receive feedback from children. Thus, research has served to bring the voice of the target audience into the production process and has allowed the production team to know what works and what does not ... *before* material is put on the air.

The CTW Model. Together, these points underscore the power of the CTW Model that has been discussed in various places throughout this volume (e.g., Truglio & Fisch, Introduction, this volume). The close, ongoing process of collaboration among producers, researchers, and educational content specialists described by the Model allows all three of these disparate perspectives to be represented and integrated in the production of *Sesame Street*. The producers' involvement ensures that the product will be "good television." Content specialists ensure that the product will be educationally strong. And researchers ensure that it will be comprehensible and appealing to children. The resulting television series thus becomes something stronger than any one of these groups could have created on its own.

The Role of Parents and Caregivers

For all its educational value, the power of *Sesame Street* is still limited by its nature as a form of mass media. One of the greatest strengths of broadcast television is its tremendous reach to literally millions of children. However, at the same time, the medium does not lend itself to individualized instruction that can be tailored to the needs of a specific, single viewer. For this reason, the educational power of *Sesame Street* can be made even greater if the program is used as a springboard for discussion or activities conducted by a parent or caregiver. Such interactions can reinforce the lessons learned in the series and extend them beyond the material presented on *Sesame Street*.

From its inception, *Sesame Street* has been designed to encourage coviewing by parents and children together. The humor in the series has always been written at two levels—the child's level and the adult level simultaneously—to attract parents and invite them to watch *Sesame Street* with their children. Both can enjoy the series together; for example, parents can appreciate Cookie Monster's role as "Alistair Cookie" in "Monsterpiece Theater" as a parody of *Masterpiece Theater*'s Alistair Cooke, while their children enjoy the same segment simply because it is funny.

The presence of adults alongside their children provides the opportunity for richer learning to occur. Several studies have shown that young children's learning from *Sesame Street* can be enhanced by parental coviewing and commentary (Reiser, Tessmer, & Phelps, 1984; Reiser, Williamson, & Suzuki, 1988; Salomon, 1977). Effective interactions among parents and children can help to direct children's attention to important information in *Sesame Street*, explain and reinforce concepts that children may have not grasped completely, and encourage them to think more elaborately and deeply about the educational content in the series.

As increasing numbers of preschool children spend sizable amounts of time in child care, the potential role that child-care providers can play in this regard has grown as well. Outreach projects such as the *Sesame Street* Preschool Education Program (PEP) help to train providers to use television effectively as an educational tool, and other projects adopt similar approaches to address specific topics such as fire safety or asthma awareness (Yotive & Fisch, chap. 10, this volume). Such projects often use *Sesame Street* broadcasts and/or videotapes, not only to convey educational concepts and messages in and of themselves, but also as springboards for group activities that carry the educational content forward in concrete, hands-on ways (e.g., reading related books, practicing the correct way to exit a building during a fire).

From the standpoint of parents and caregivers, *Sesame Street* thus becomes a powerful tool that can be helpful in their ongoing efforts to educate children. Conversely, from the standpoint of *Sesame Street*, parents and other caregivers provide a means by which to deliver the kinds of personalized instruction that are difficult, if not impossible, to deliver via broadcast television.

Extending Into Other Media

Many of the educational strengths that we have discussed with regard to *Sesame Street* as a television series are also present in the *Sesame Street*-based materials that have been created in other media. The use of the *Sesame Street* characters, and their connection to a familiar and appealing television series, provide a foundation on which can be built equally appealing print materials, interactive products, educational toys, and so on. The same use of explicit educational content, child-centered situations, and diverse role models that is used to good effect in the television series is also built into *Sesame Street*-based materials across other media as well.

At the same time, each medium holds its own particular strengths and its own unique opportunities for conveying educational content. For example, whereas the *Sesame Street* television series has employed formats that are designed to promote viewer participation, *Sesame Street*-based CD-ROM games and online activities can go further, offering children feedback that is genuinely contingent on their own responses (something that cannot be done via broadcast television). The widespread use of *Sesame Street* home videos provides new opportunities for reinforcement of educational messages, as children engage in multiple viewings of the same material at their own convenience (not to mention the parallel possibilities for repeated use that have been available for many years through children's reading and rereading *Sesame Street* books and magazines).

Similarly, although opportunities for joint learning experiences between adults and children are supported in the television series, they are almost necessary in using some of these other media. Preliterate children cannot read stories in *Sesame Street Magazine* or instructions for activities on the Web site by themselves. Although young children can (and do) enjoy looking at these materials on their own, they cannot use the material to its fullest potential without involvement by an adult or older child. Indeed, research has shown these media to be effective in promoting joint experiences of this sort; for example, one survey of 2000 subscribers to the magazine found that, on average, parents and children spent between 1 and 1.7 hours reading each issue of *Sesame Street Magazine* together (CTW Magazine Research Department, 1993). This figure represents, not only time spent with the magazine itself, but also time that children and parents spent together sharing meaningful, literacy-based experiences.

The Future

As the previous examples demonstrate, each new medium presents new opportunities for reaching children and new strengths for learning. As a result, it may not be surprising that, as new technologies evolve, CTW continues to experiment with ways to extend the power of *Sesame Street* into these new media as well. Recently, for example, CTW joined with Web TV to develop and test an experimental prototype of an enhanced version of *Sesame Street* that would allow viewers to play interactive games through their televisions while watching *Sesame Street* on television. A second example emerged as the growing reach of cable and satellite television led CTW and Nickelodeon into a partnership to create a new channel called Noggin. Noggin debuted in early 1999 and brought older episodes of *Sesame Street* from the CTW library (as well as past CTW television series, such as *The Electric Company, Ghostwriter,* and *Square One TV*) to children too young to have seen them before.

But what of the ongoing *Sesame Street* television series itself? It, too, continues to evolve and to grow. In considering the data from summative studies of the impact of the *Sesame Street* television series, it is striking to note the consistency of effects that have been found over a period of decades; the same types of effects found among children in the early 1970s (Mielke, chap. 5, this volume) have continued to be found among a new generation of children in the 1990s (Huston et al., chap. 8, this volume; Wright et al., chap. 6, this volume; Zill, chap. 7, this volume).

The reason for this consistency likely stems from the fact that, as the chapters in the first section of this volume have shown, *Sesame Street* has not remained static over the years. The first season of *Sesame Street* was referred to as the "first experimental season," and it is noteworthy that the current season is referred to as the "30th experimental season." Production techniques and formats are constantly updated to reflect children's viewing preferences and the current state of the art. Curriculum goals are continually revisited and revised to reflect current thinking on best practices in education. Formative research is used on an ongoing basis to help ensure that material is appealing and comprehensible to its target audience.

All of these factors have come together to form an underlying foundation that has allowed *Sesame Street* to remain timely and educate children since the late 1960s. Rather than lapse into a rote, predictable formula, the creators of *Sesame Street* have remained conscious of changes in children's lives and environments, and alert to advances in our understanding of the ways in which children learn and grow. With that knowledge has come a constant evolution of formats and approaches through which material is implemented in the series.

Yet, although formats and approaches may be subject to change, one thing that has remained constant is *Sesame Street*'s passionate commitment to transforming media to serve the best interests of children. At a time when there is great public concern over potential negative effects of media such as television or the Internet, *Sesame Street* has harnessed these very media and applied them to positive, educational ends instead. By addressing children on their own level, by employing appealing characters and authentic depictions of children's own worlds, and by continually demonstrating the fun of learning, *Sesame Street* strives to help all preschool children reach their greatest potential. This singularity of purpose, coupled with an ongoing refinement and adaptation of the means by which it is achieved, has carried *Sesame Street* through the past 30 years. We fully expect that this same spirit of dedication and innovation will continue to carry the power of *Sesame Street* on into the next millennium.

REFERENCES

Anderson, D. R., & Burns, J. (1991). Paying attention to television. In J. Bryant, & D. Zillmann (Eds.), *Responding to the screen: Reception and reaction processes* (pp. 3–25). Hillsdale, NJ: Lawrence Erlbaum Associates.

Anderson, D. R., Lorch, E. P., Field, D. E., & Sanders, J. (1981). The effects of TV program comprehensibility on preschool children's visual attention to television. *Child Development, 52,* 151–157.

Anderson, D. R., Field, D. E., Collins, P. A., Lorch, E. P., & Nathan, J. G. (1985). Estimates of young children's time with television: A methodological comparison of parent reports with time-lapse video home observations. *Child Development, 56,* 1345–1357.

Ball, S., & Bogatz, G. A. (1970). *The first year of Sesame Street: An evaluation.* Princeton, NJ: Educational Testing Service.

Calvert, S. L., Stolkin, A., & Lee, J. (1997, April). *Gender and ethnic portrayals in Saturday morning television programs.* Poster session presented at the biennial meeting of the Society for Research in Child Development, Washington, DC.

CTW Magazine Research Department (1993). *Sesame Street readership survey* (unpublished research report). New York: Children's Television Workshop.

Fisch, S. M. (2000). A capacity model of children's comprehension of educational content on television. *Media Psychology, 2,* 63–91.

Fisch, S. M., & McCann, S. K. (1993). Making broadcast television participative: Eliciting mathematical behavior through *Square One TV. Educational Technology Research and Development, 41*(3), 103–109.

Gerbner, G. (1993). *Women and minorities on television: A study in casting and fate* (report to the Screen Actors Guild and the American Federation of Radio and Television Artists). Philadelphia, PA: Annenberg School of Communication.

Inhelder, B., & Piaget, J. (1958). *The growth of logical thinking: From childhood to adolescence.* New York: Basic Books.

Lesser, G. S. (1974). *Children and television: Lessons from Sesame Street.* New York: Vintage Books/Random House.

Luecke-Aleksa, D., Anderson, D. R., Collins, P. A., & Schmitt, K. (1995). Gender constancy and television viewing. *Developmental Psychology, 31,* 773–780.

Newcomb, A. F., & Collins, W. A. (1979). Children's comprehension of family role portrayals in televised dramas: Effects of socioeconomic status, ethnicity, and age. *Developmental Psychology, 15,* 417–423.

Reiser, R. A., Tessmer, M. A., & Phelps, P. C. (1984). Adult–child interaction in children's learning from *Sesame Street. Educational Communication and Technology Journal, 32,* 217–223.

Reiser, R. A., Williamson, N., & Suzuki, K. (1988). Using *Sesame Street* to facilitate children's recognition of letters and numbers. *Educational Communication and Technology Journal, 36,* 15–21.

Salomon, G. (1977). Effects of encouraging Israeli mothers to co-observe *Sesame Street* with their five-year-olds. *Child Development, 48,* 1146–1151.

Sesame Street Research. (1989). *Race relations study #1: "Kermit, Cookie, and the Chocolate Princess"* (unpublished research report). New York: Children's Television Workshop.

Sesame Street Research. (1998). *Assessing the appeal, engagement, and comprehension of Show #3786, "Alan Is Introduced"* (unpublished research report). New York: Children's Television Workshop.

Sesame Street Research. (1999). *Elmo's World research update* (unpublished research report). New York: Children's Television Workshop.

Sesame Street Research & Applied Research & Consulting. (1998). *Sesame Street letters and numbers cluster study* (unpublished research report). New York: Children's Television Workshop.

Afterword

It is hard to believe now that there was once a time when introducing research into the process of making television was a novel, even strange idea. So deeply ingrained has research become in the culture of the Workshop, that it is unimaginable to think of creating useful and effective products without it.

Research is even more important today than it was 30 years ago because it is called on to navigate multiple media across multiple continents and cultures. *Sesame Street* began as a domestic television show, and like the meaning of the word *media*, has grown to include much more—books and magazines, video and film, audiocassettes and CDs, CD-ROMs, online interactivity, licensed products, and more. All are informed by research, often *first-of-its-kind* research, that puts the needs and learning styles of children first.

So, too, does research ensure *Sesame Street*'s efficacy around the world. Over the years, *Sesame Street* has been seen (heard, read, interacted with) in almost 150 countries. And 19 international coproductions with local partners have served local needs as determined by local experts—all kept on track by research.

Back at home, the folklore of the Workshop includes a number of close-call anecdotes about how research has identified programs that won't work; research that spared our audiences from subjects or actions signaling unintentional, or even worse—wrong—messages. I remember, for example, that after careful study, we shelved a *Sesame Street* program about divorce, determining that no matter how sensitively we addressed it, too many children would still feel frightened—a decision taken *after* the segments were produced. So, too, has research guided us at the opposite end of the production spectrum, lending direction and sensitivity before scripts are written, as well as during script review and production in a continuing vigilance to serve the best interests and highest possibilities for children.

Because many of the anecdotes are about what saved us and our audiences from what would not work, it is easy to lose sight of the more powerful facts—how much research has helped us determine what *does* work and what *will* engage the attention and built-in learning drives of children.

For us, research is quite simply a pragmatic necessity, a crucial key to continuing success. For that, we have the individuals who have contributed to this collection and their many colleagues to thank. Not only have they been instrumental to *Sesame Street*'s success, they have informed, and in a number of cases, invented, the field at large. Together, their knowledge, intellect, and experience have lifted the quality of children's media in this country and around the world.

There are enormous changes today, for better or worse, in the variety of programming aimed at children and in the new technologies kids use. What seems clear is that, without necessarily being able to specify which of these technologies will dominate the future, mass media—whatever its configuration—will continue to play a powerful and ever growing role in the lives of children. This places even greater importance on finding constructive ways of using media to help children succeed in life and consequently, relying even more on research as an essential tool.

Looking ahead to the next 30 years and the "second edition" of this volume, my sense is that although the world will have certainly changed, our focus on using media to help children learn—and on research's role in keeping us fixed on that focus—will remain steadfast.

—*David V. B. Britt*
Children's Television Workshop

About the Authors

Daniel R. Anderson is Professor of Psychology at the University of Massachusetts at Amherst. He has investigated children's television viewing since the early 1970s and has published numerous papers related to *Sesame Street*.

Lewis Bernstein is currently Vice President of Special Projects and the Executive Director of the *Sesame English* project, a broadcast-based, multimedia project that will teach English to young children and their families around the world, at Children's Television Workshop. Dr. Bernstein was the Director of Research for *Sesame Street* for nearly a decade. He recently served as Project Director and Executive Producer for *Rechov Sumsum/Shara'a Simsim*, the Israeli/Palestinian coproduction of *Sesame Street*.

David V. B. Britt joined Children's Television Workshop in 1971, and has served as its President and Chief Executive Officer since 1990. Britt leads the organization's focus in serving the educational needs of children and families while capturing the opportunities opening up in new technologies and around the world.

Susan K. McCann Brown is Assistant Director of Research for International Research at Children's Television Workshop, where she helps oversee research and educational content for the *Sesame Street* international coproductions. A member of the CTW research team since 1988, she has also conducted research for *Sesame Street* outreach projects, as well as many of the television programs and magazines produced by CTW.

Renée Cherow-O'Leary is President of Education for 21st Century, a New York-based research and consulting firm. She is also Visiting Professor of Communications at Rutgers University, Newark campus. From 1989 through 1995, she was Director of Research in the Publishing/Schools Group at Children's Television Workshop.

Charlotte F. Cole, Vice President for International Research at Children's Television Workshop, oversees the research and curriculum development for all of CTW's international coproductions. Prior to joining CTW, Dr. Cole worked as a Senior Researcher at Joslin Diabetes Center in Boston, served as a consultant to the Harvard Institute for International Development, and was an instructor at Saint Mary-of-the Woods College in Terre Haute, Indiana.

Joan Ganz Cooney is cofounder of Children's Television Workshop and the originator of *Sesame Street.* She served as CTW's President and Chief Executive Officer until 1990, and is currently Chairman of the Executive Committee of CTW's Board.

Shalom M. Fisch is Vice President for Program Research at Children's Television Workshop, where he oversees research and educational content for a broad variety of projects across media. Since joining CTW in 1986, he has been Director of Research for numerous *Sesame Street* home videos, outreach projects, and online activities, as well as many non-*Sesame Street* media projects. In addition, he served as interim Director of Research for the *Sesame Street* television series in Season 28.

Aletha C. Huston is the Priscilla Pond Flawn Regents Professor of Child Development at the University of Texas at Austin and codirector with John C. Wright of the Center for Research on the Influence of Television on Children (CRITC) at the University of Texas. She was formerly a professor at the University of Kansas. She is the lead author of *Big World, Small Screen: The Role of Television in American Society.*

Jennifer Kotler is a Post-Doctoral Fellow in the Department of Psychology at Georgetown University. While a graduate student in Child Development at the University of Texas at Austin, she was a research assistant for the Early Window Project, a 3-year longitudinal study examining the effects of *Sesame Street* on children's school readiness. She is particularly interested in the ways parents affect children's experience with television.

Gerald S. Lesser is Professor Emeritus at Harvard University, where he served as Bigelow Professor of Education and Developmental Psychology since 1963. He joined Children's Television Workshop in 1968 when it was formed, and continued as Chairman of its Board of Advisors until 1996. In that capacity, he participated actively in setting the Workshop's educational goals, and in planning research, production, and community efforts to achieve these goals. He now contributes to the educational and research activities associated with CTW's development of its international coproductions, and is writing a history of CTW's international coproductions from 1972 to the present.

Deborah L. Linebarger is an Assistant Research Professor in the Schiefelbusch Institute for Life Span Studies at the University of Kansas, where she conducts research on language and literacy outcomes related to early television viewing and child-care experiences. In graduate school, she worked with Aletha Huston, John Wright, and Daniel Anderson investigating the long-term outcomes associated with early television viewing, including viewing of *Sesame Street*.

Valeria O. Lovelace is President and founder of Media Transformations, an educational research company dedicated to the creation of educational projects for children. Previously, she was Assistant Vice President of Research for *Sesame Street* from Season 14 to Season 28.

Lisa Medoff is the Director of Research for the Interactive Technologies Division of Children's Television Workshop. She holds a masters degree in Education from Brooklyn College, and has worked in the area of Interactive Technologies since the early 1990s.

Keith W. Mielke, while a faculty member at Indiana University in 1972, was awarded a Spencer Foundation fellowship to examine the formative research methods used at CTW with *Sesame Street* and *The Electric Company*. Between joining the CTW staff in 1977 and retiring in 1995, he served in a variety of research and administrative roles, including serving for more than 10 years as Vice President of Research for all of CTW's television programming.

Edward L. Palmer was the first Director of Research for *Sesame Street* and first Vice President of Research for Children's Television Workshop. Outside CTW, he served as president of World Media Partners, and taught at several universities, including Harvard University and the Annenberg School of Communications. A child advocate, writer, and media consultant for more than 30 years, he applied his talents to a broad range of media projects worldwide, toward purposes ranging from promoting literacy in the Arab region to easing tensions in Burundi. Palmer passed away in August, 1999.

Glenda L. Revelle is a Research Scientist at the University of Maryland and Educational Advisor to the Interactive group at Children's Television Workshop. She holds a PhD. in Child Development from the University of Michigan, where her research program focused on cognitive development in infants and preschool children.

Beth A. Richman is Director of Content for *Sesame English*, a multi-media project designed to teach English as a Foreign Language, at Children's Television Workshop. Previously, she served as Assistant Director for International Research, helping to oversee the research and educational content development for *Sesame Street* internationally.

Ronda Scantlin, a graduate student in Child Development at the University of Texas at Austin, is a research assistant for the Early Window Project, a 3-year longitudinal study examining the effects of *Sesame Street* on children's school readiness. Her research focuses on children's use of interactive media.

Joel Schneider is Vice President for Education and Research at CTW, leading the division responsible for the educational wherewithal of all products and services of CTW, including those related to *Sesame Street*.

Susan Scheiner is in the process of completing her PhD in Developmental Psychology at Teachers College, Columbia University. She joined Children's Television Workshop in Season 19 as a *Sesame Street* intern, and left in Season 29 as the Assistant Director of *Sesame Street* Research.

Kelly L. Schmitt is a Research Fellow for the Annenberg Public Policy Center at the University of Pennsylvania where she conducts research on the quantity and quality of children's educational programming.

Ivelisse Seguí is currently the Assistant Director for *Sesame Street* Research and has supervised various *Sesame Street* projects since joining the company in Season 20 as the Latino Curriculum Coordinator. She received her PhD in Developmental Psychology from the Graduate Center, City University of New York.

Erik F. Strommen received his doctorate in Developmental Psychology from Rutgers University, and was a college lecturer prior to joining Children's Television Workshop as Research Director for the Interactive Technologies Division in 1988. Since 1996, he has been supervising the design and development of interactive learning toys and software for Microsoft Corporation.

Rosemarie T. Truglio is Vice President for *Sesame Street* Research at Children's Television Workshop, where she has overseen research and curriculum activities for *Sesame Street* since Season 29. Previously, she was an assistant professor at Teachers College, Columbia University.

John C. Wright, is Director of CRITC, The Center for Research on the Influences of Television on Children at the University of Texas at Austin. A developmental psychologist, he has studied the development of children's attention to and comprehension of television from an experimental perspective. CRITC's research has been supported by more than $4 million in grants. Its studies of the long-term positive effects of watching informational and educational television on children's school readiness a few years later, and on academic achievement in high school more than 10 years later have established the long-term academic benefits of watching educational programs like *Sesame Street* in the preschool years.

William Yotive is Director of Research in the Program Research Department of Children's Television Workshop. He has been Research Director for several *Sesame Street*-based outreach projects, including the *Building on Sesame Street* family child-care project, *Sesame Street A is for Asthma*, and *Sesame Street Beginnings: The Road From Language to Literacy*.

Nicholas Zill is the Director of the Child and Family Study Area and a Vice President at Westat, a survey research firm in Rockville, MD. In 1994, he used data from the National Household Education Survey, a study that Westat conducts for the U.S. Department of Education, to examine the effects of *Sesame Street* viewing on children's school readiness. Dr. Zill is currently directing a 5-year national study of the performance of the Head Start program, and serving as Senior Technical Adviser to the Department of Education's Early Childhood Longitudinal Study.

Author Index

Subject Index